the Normals

ADAM GLASS

DENNIS CALERO

VOLUME

1

"SAME AS IT EVER WAS"

ADRIANO AUGUSTO

COREY BREEN

AFTERSHOCK

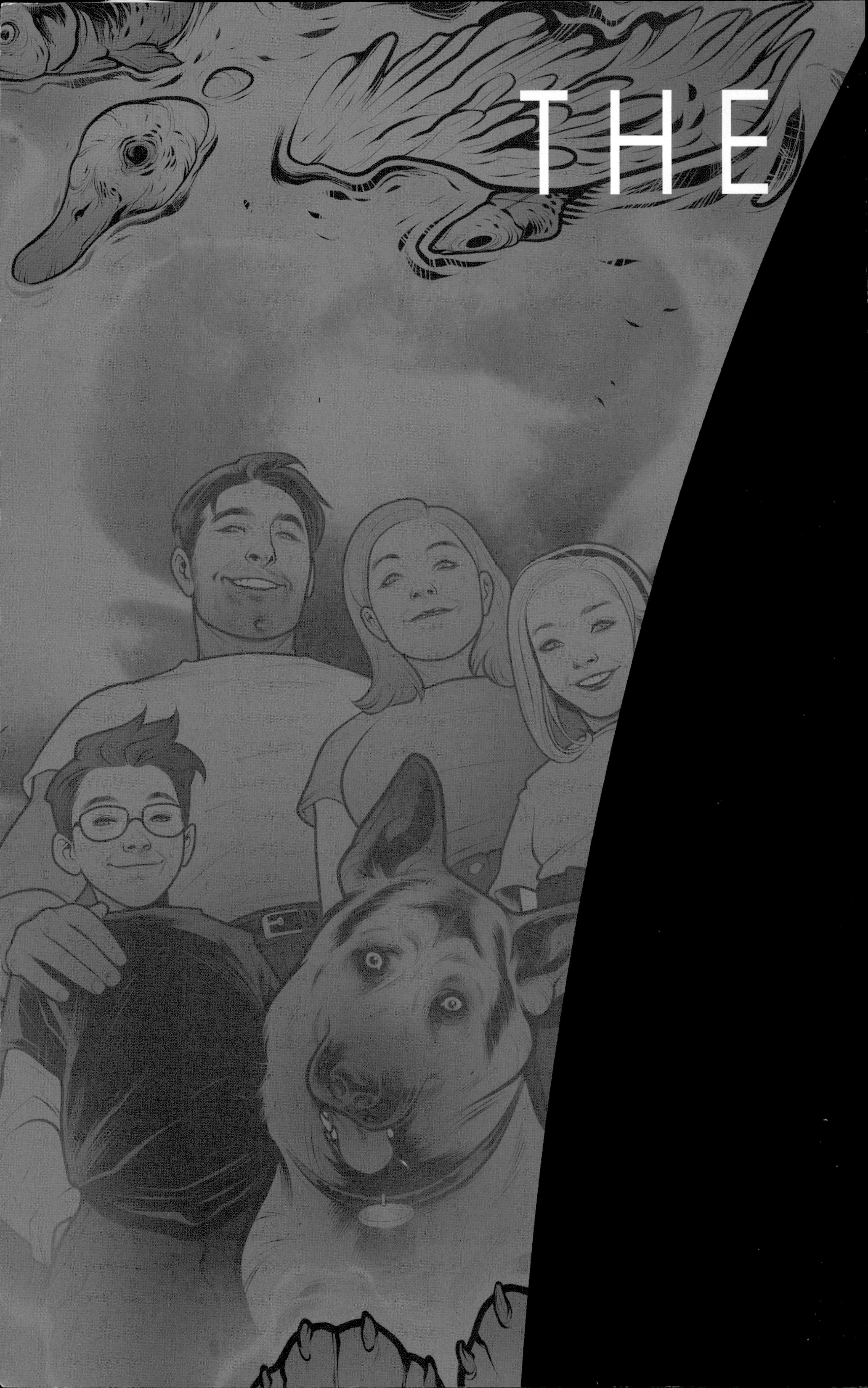
THE

NORMALS™

VOLUME 1

"SAME AS IT EVER WAS"

ADAM GLASS creator & writer

DENNIS CALERO artist

ADRIANO AUGUSTO colorist

COREY BREEN letterer

JUAN DOE front cover & original covers

DENNIS CALERO issue #2 original cover

ELIZABETH TORQUE variant cover

JOHN J. HILL logo designer

COREY BREEN book designer

MIKE MARTS editor

AFTERSHOCK™

MIKE MARTS - Editor-in-Chief • JOE PRUETT - Publisher/CCO • LEE KRAMER - President • JON KRAMER - Chief Executive Officer
STEVE ROTTERDAM - SVP, Sales & Marketing • LISA Y. WU - Retailer/Fan Relations Manager
CHRISTINA HARRINGTON - Managing Editor • JAY BEHLING - Chief Financial Officer • JAWAD QURESHI - SVP, Investor Relations
AARON MARION - Publicist • CHRIS LA TORRE & KIM PAGNOTTA - Sales Associates • LISA MOODY - Finance
CHARLES PRITCHETT - Comics Production • COREY BREEN - Collections Production • TEDDY LEO - Editorial Assistant
STEPHANIE CASEBIER & SARAH PRUETT - Publishing Assistants

AfterShock Logo Design by COMICRAFT
Publicity: contact AARON MARION (aaron@publichausagency.com) & RYAN CROY (ryan@publichausagency.com) at PUBLICHAUS
Special thanks to: IRA KURGAN, STEPHAN NILSON, JULIE PIFHER

THE NORMALS VOL.1: SAME AS IT EVER WAS Published by AfterShock Comics, LLC, 15300 Ventura Boulevard Suite 507, Sherman Oaks, CA 91403. Originally published as The Normals #1-6. PRINTED IN KOREA.
First Printing: September 2018. 10 9 8 7 6 5 4 3 2 1

AFTERSHOCKCOMICS.COM Follow us on social media

I N T R O D U C T I O N

Writers tend to write about what they aspire to or what they fear the most. For me, this story was a way of trying to deal with the dread my wife, Mia, and I have been feeling about our daughter, Josephine, leaving for college in a year. Our son, Aidan, is not that far behind her.

When your life is so invested in being a parent for nearly twenty years, you find yourself suddenly asking...what's next? I know that we'll always be a family, but it will never really be the same again. It will never be just the four of us against the world: playing, traveling and learning, loving, and laughing together in such close proximity to one another on a daily basis anymore. While nothing lasts forever, these memories Mia and I have with our children will be cherished forever.

So, like any writer, that "fear" manifested itself into a sci-fi story about a family man who discovers that everything he ever believed to be true was not real, including himself. And what would that man do and how far he would go to keep his family together?

I spent many sleepless nights thinking and writing this, and now I share my nightmare with you.

the Normals™

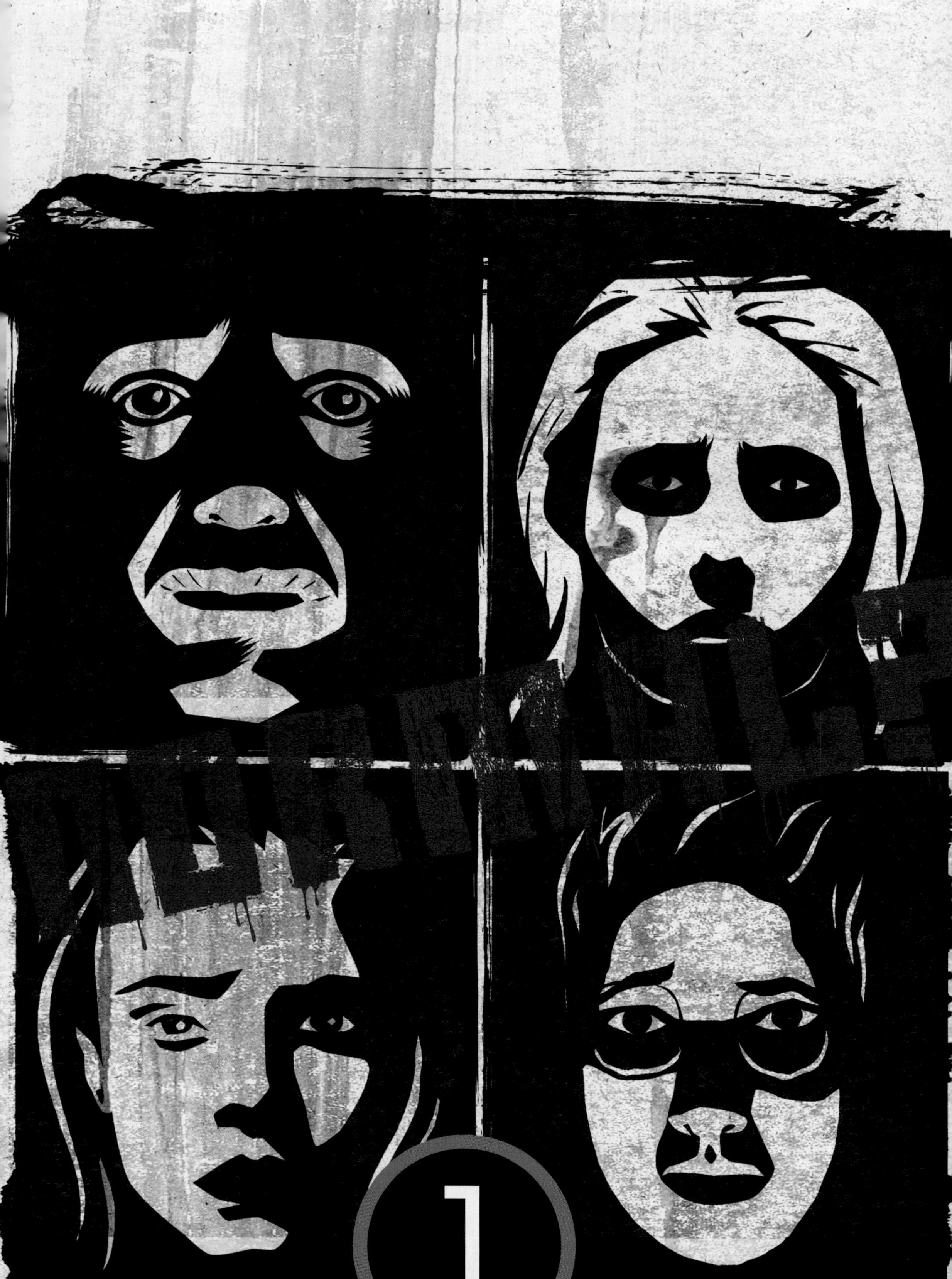
1

"SAME AS IT NEVER WAS"

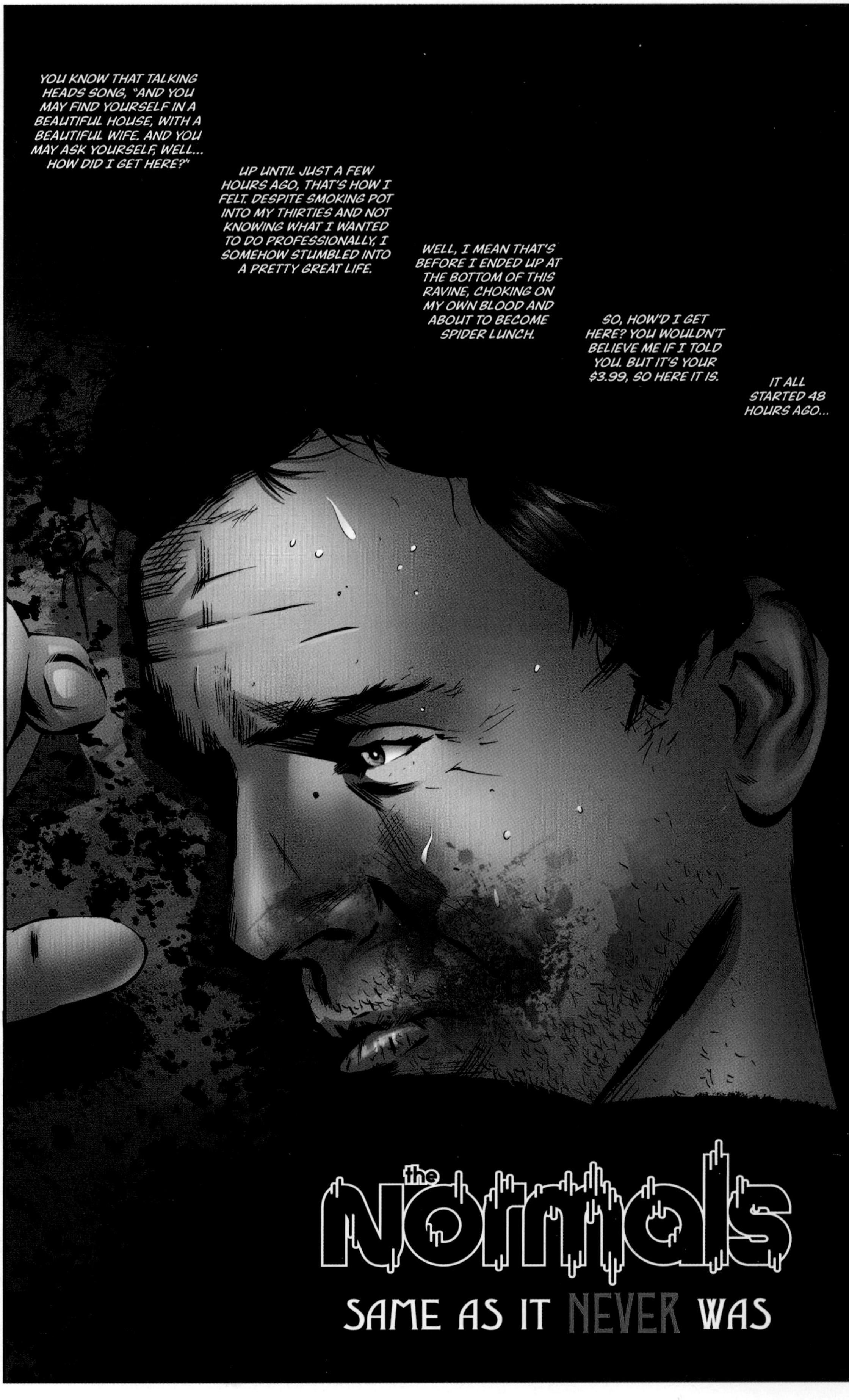
YOU KNOW THAT TALKING HEADS SONG, "AND YOU MAY FIND YOURSELF IN A BEAUTIFUL HOUSE, WITH A BEAUTIFUL WIFE. AND YOU MAY ASK YOURSELF, WELL... HOW DID I GET HERE?"
UP UNTIL JUST A FEW HOURS AGO, THAT'S HOW I FELT. DESPITE SMOKING POT INTO MY THIRTIES AND NOT KNOWING WHAT I WANTED TO DO PROFESSIONALLY, I SOMEHOW STUMBLED INTO A PRETTY GREAT LIFE.
WELL, I MEAN THAT'S BEFORE I ENDED UP AT THE BOTTOM OF THIS RAVINE, CHOKING ON MY OWN BLOOD AND ABOUT TO BECOME SPIDER LUNCH.
SO, HOW'D I GET HERE? YOU WOULDN'T BELIEVE ME IF I TOLD YOU. BUT IT'S YOUR $3.99, SO HERE IT IS.
IT ALL STARTED 48 HOURS AGO...
the Normals
SAME AS IT NEVER WAS

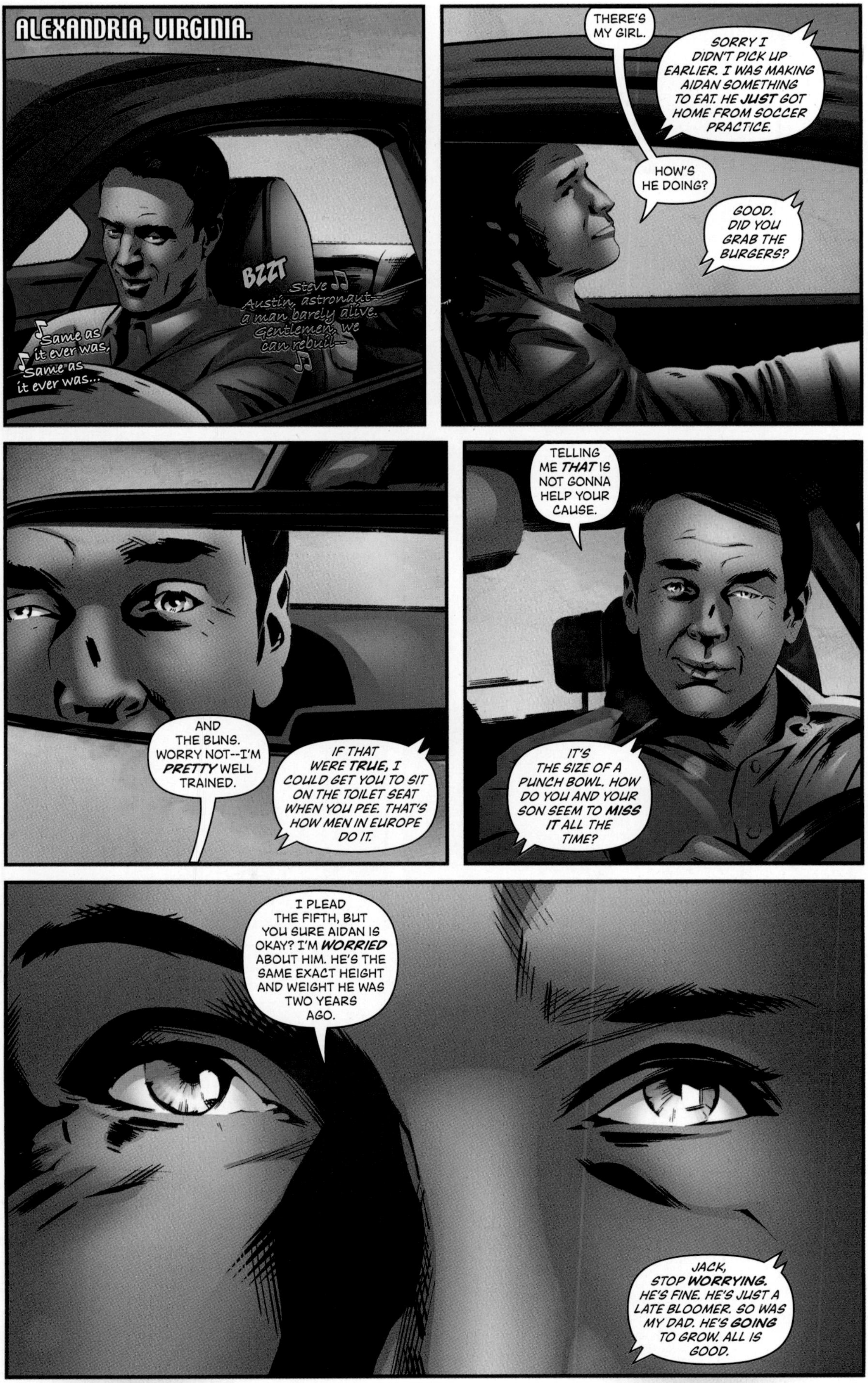

ALEXANDRIA, VIRGINIA.
BZZT
Steve Austin, astronaut-- a man barely alive. Gentlemen, we can rebuil--
Same as it ever was, Same as it ever was...
THERE'S MY GIRL.
SORRY I DIDN'T PICK UP EARLIER. I WAS MAKING AIDAN SOMETHING TO EAT. HE JUST GOT HOME FROM SOCCER PRACTICE.
HOW'S HE DOING?
GOOD. DID YOU GRAB THE BURGERS?
AND THE BUNS. WORRY NOT--I'M PRETTY WELL TRAINED.
IF THAT WERE TRUE, I COULD GET YOU TO SIT ON THE TOILET SEAT WHEN YOU PEE. THAT'S HOW MEN IN EUROPE DO IT.
TELLING ME THAT IS NOT GONNA HELP YOUR CAUSE.
IT'S THE SIZE OF A PUNCH BOWL. HOW DO YOU AND YOUR SON SEEM TO MISS IT ALL THE TIME?
I PLEAD THE FIFTH, BUT YOU SURE AIDAN IS OKAY? I'M WORRIED ABOUT HIM. HE'S THE SAME EXACT HEIGHT AND WEIGHT HE WAS TWO YEARS AGO.
JACK, STOP WORRYING. HE'S FINE. HE'S JUST A LATE BLOOMER. SO WAS MY DAD. HE'S GOING TO GROW. ALL IS GOOD.

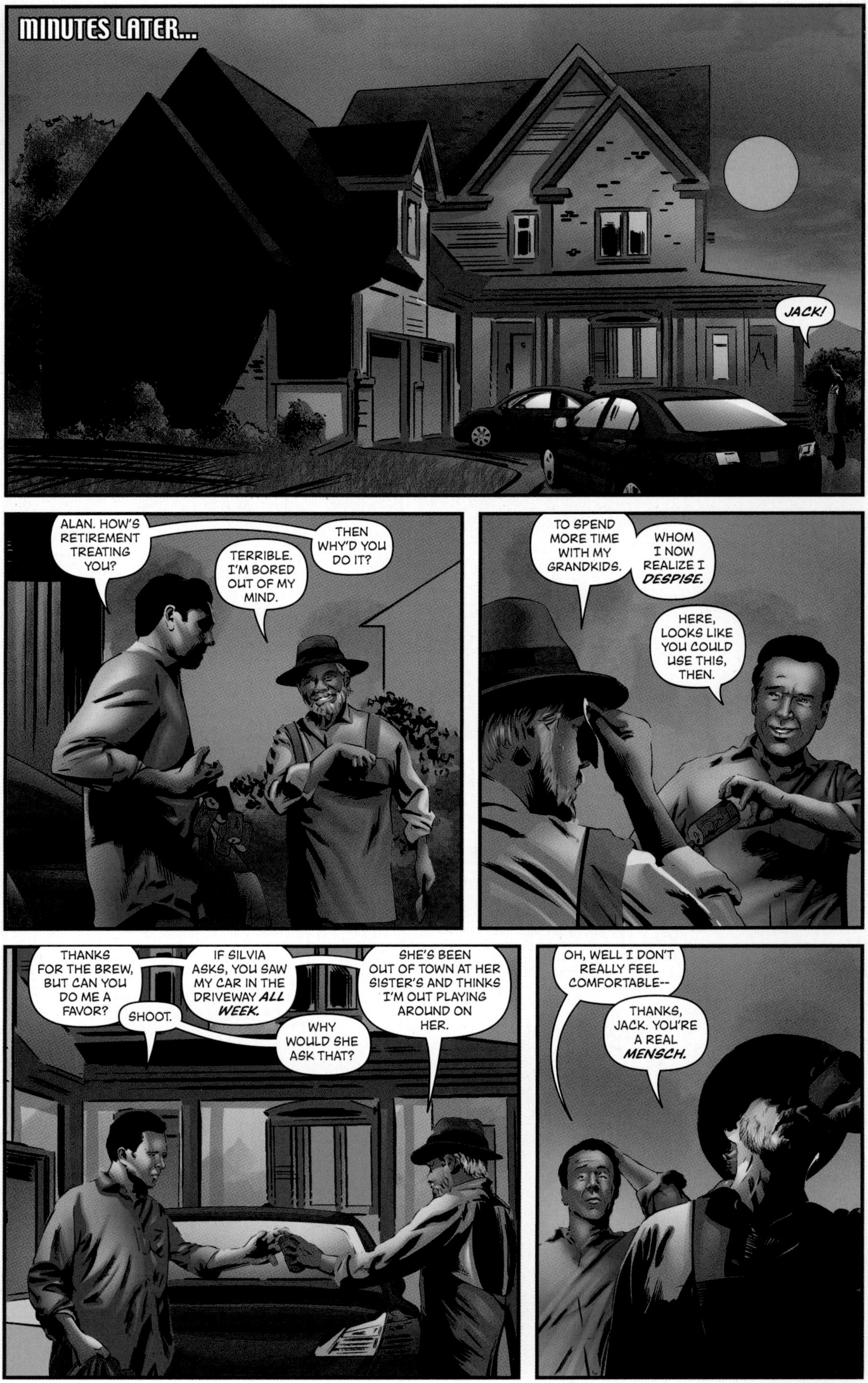
MINUTES LATER...
JACK!
ALAN. HOW'S RETIREMENT TREATING YOU?
TERRIBLE. I'M BORED OUT OF MY MIND.
THEN WHY'D YOU DO IT?
TO SPEND MORE TIME WITH MY GRANDKIDS.
WHOM I NOW REALIZE I DESPISE.
HERE, LOOKS LIKE YOU COULD USE THIS, THEN.
THANKS FOR THE BREW, BUT CAN YOU DO ME A FAVOR?
SHOOT.
IF SILVIA ASKS, YOU SAW MY CAR IN THE DRIVEWAY ALL WEEK.
WHY WOULD SHE ASK THAT?
SHE'S BEEN OUT OF TOWN AT HER SISTER'S AND THINKS I'M OUT PLAYING AROUND ON HER.
OH, WELL I DON'T REALLY FEEL COMFORTABLE--
THANKS, JACK. YOU'RE A REAL MENSCH.

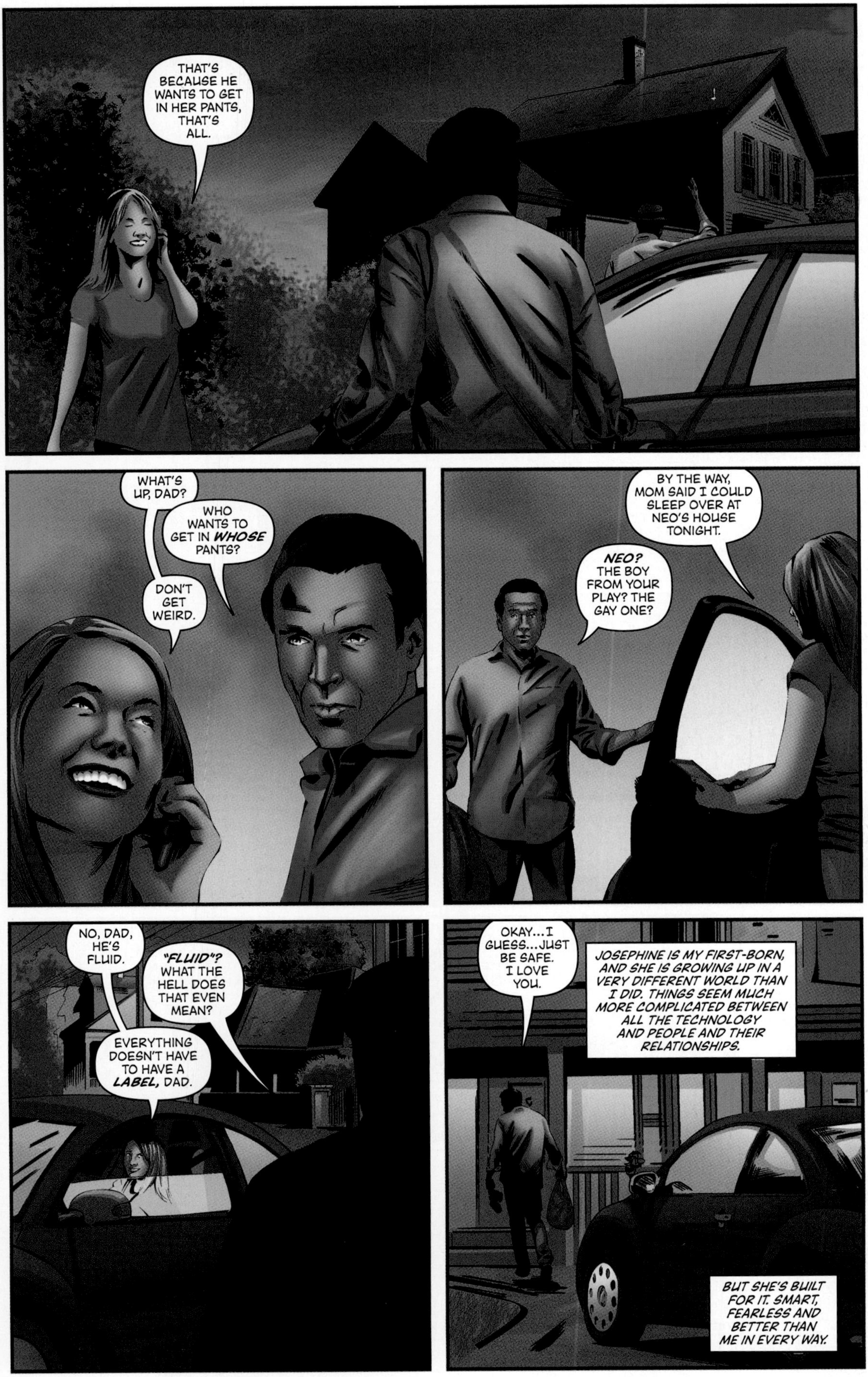
THAT'S BECAUSE HE WANTS TO GET IN HER PANTS, THAT'S ALL.
WHAT'S UP, DAD?
WHO WANTS TO GET IN WHOSE PANTS?
DON'T GET WEIRD.
BY THE WAY, MOM SAID I COULD SLEEP OVER AT NEO'S HOUSE TONIGHT.
NEO? THE BOY FROM YOUR PLAY? THE GAY ONE?
NO, DAD, HE'S FLUID.
"FLUID"? WHAT THE HELL DOES THAT EVEN MEAN?
EVERYTHING DOESN'T HAVE TO HAVE A LABEL, DAD.
OKAY... I GUESS... JUST BE SAFE. I LOVE YOU.
JOSEPHINE IS MY FIRST-BORN, AND SHE IS GROWING UP IN A VERY DIFFERENT WORLD THAN I DID. THINGS SEEM MUCH MORE COMPLICATED BETWEEN ALL THE TECHNOLOGY AND PEOPLE AND THEIR RELATIONSHIPS.
BUT SHE'S BUILT FOR IT. SMART, FEARLESS AND BETTER THAN ME IN EVERY WAY.

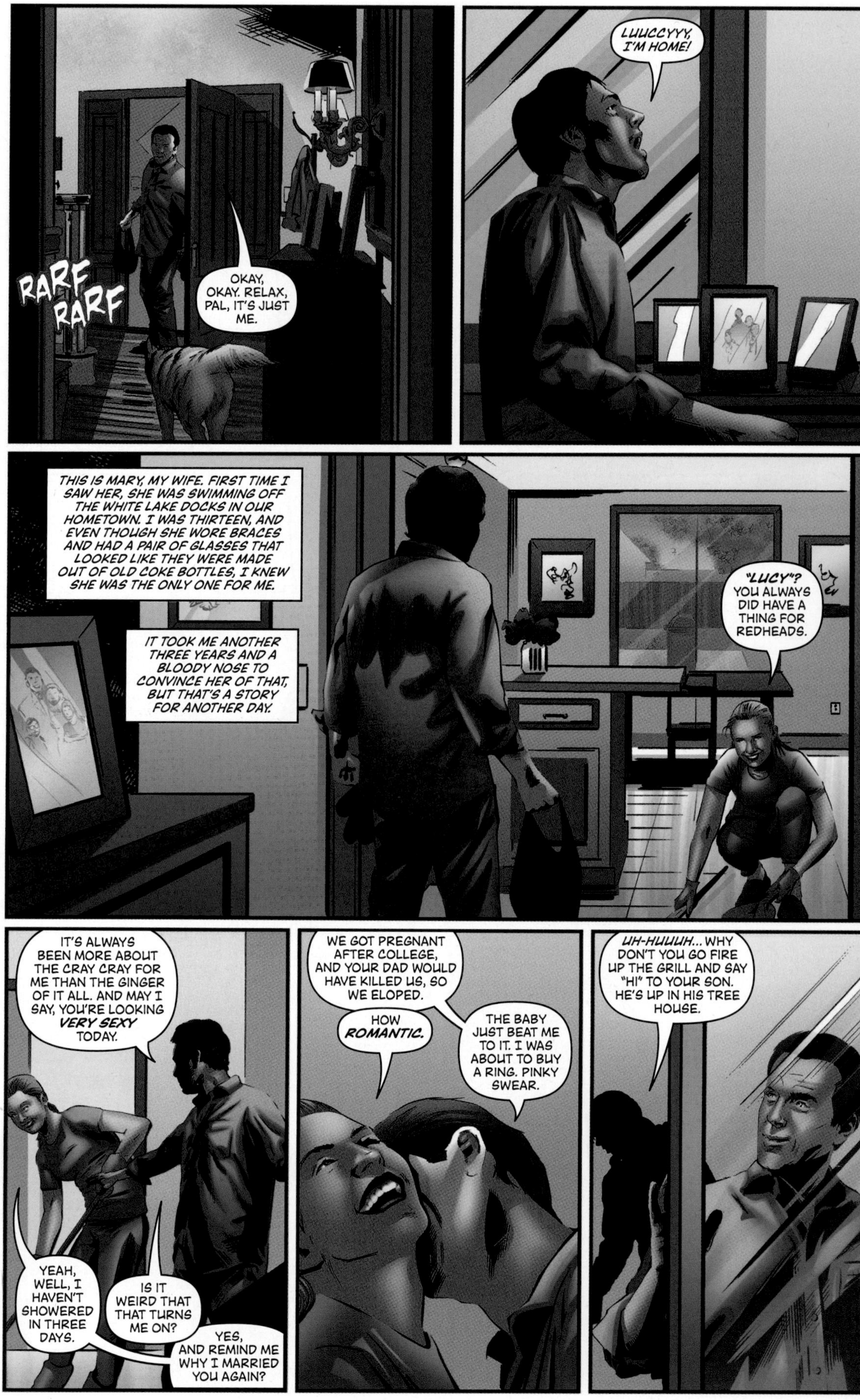
RARF RARF
OKAY, OKAY. RELAX, PAL, IT'S JUST ME.
LUUCCYYY, I'M HOME!
THIS IS MARY, MY WIFE. FIRST TIME I SAW HER, SHE WAS SWIMMING OFF THE WHITE LAKE DOCKS IN OUR HOMETOWN. I WAS THIRTEEN, AND EVEN THOUGH SHE WORE BRACES AND HAD A PAIR OF GLASSES THAT LOOKED LIKE THEY WERE MADE OUT OF OLD COKE BOTTLES, I KNEW SHE WAS THE ONLY ONE FOR ME.
IT TOOK ME ANOTHER THREE YEARS AND A BLOODY NOSE TO CONVINCE HER OF THAT, BUT THAT'S A STORY FOR ANOTHER DAY.
"LUCY"? YOU ALWAYS DID HAVE A THING FOR REDHEADS.
IT'S ALWAYS BEEN MORE ABOUT THE CRAY CRAY FOR ME THAN THE GINGER OF IT ALL. AND MAY I SAY, YOU'RE LOOKING VERY SEXY TODAY.
YEAH, WELL, I HAVEN'T SHOWERED IN THREE DAYS.
IS IT WEIRD THAT THAT TURNS ME ON?
YES, AND REMIND ME WHY I MARRIED YOU AGAIN?
WE GOT PREGNANT AFTER COLLEGE, AND YOUR DAD WOULD HAVE KILLED US, SO WE ELOPED.
HOW ROMANTIC.
THE BABY JUST BEAT ME TO IT. I WAS ABOUT TO BUY A RING. PINKY SWEAR.
UH-HUUUH... WHY DON'T YOU GO FIRE UP THE GRILL AND SAY "HI" TO YOUR SON. HE'S UP IN HIS TREE HOUSE.

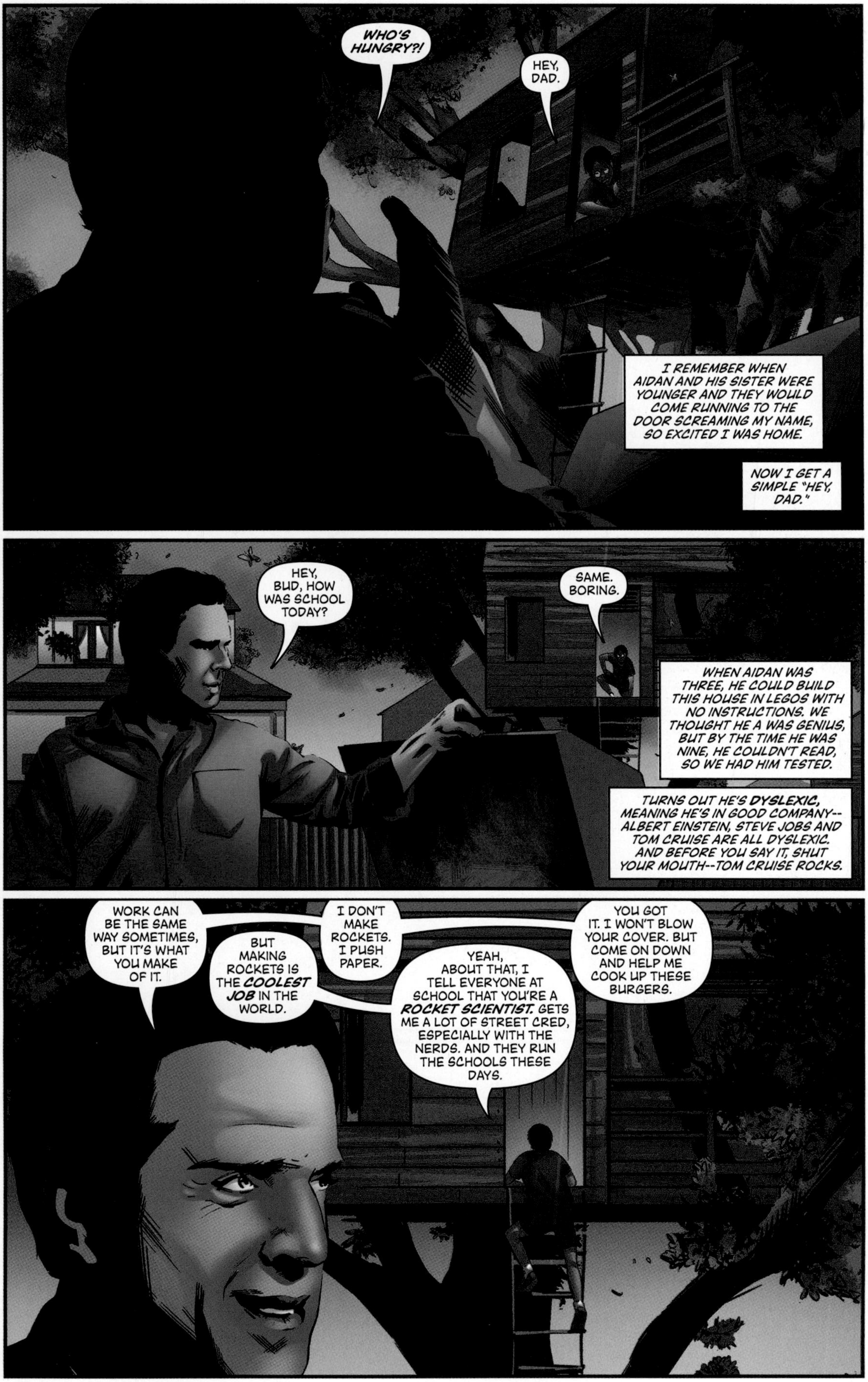
WHO'S HUNGRY?!
HEY, DAD.
I REMEMBER WHEN AIDAN AND HIS SISTER WERE YOUNGER AND THEY WOULD COME RUNNING TO THE DOOR SCREAMING MY NAME, SO EXCITED I WAS HOME.
NOW I GET A SIMPLE "HEY, DAD."
HEY, BUD, HOW WAS SCHOOL TODAY?
SAME. BORING.
WHEN AIDAN WAS THREE, HE COULD BUILD THIS HOUSE IN LEGOS WITH NO INSTRUCTIONS. WE THOUGHT HE A WAS GENIUS, BUT BY THE TIME HE WAS NINE, HE COULDN'T READ, SO WE HAD HIM TESTED.
TURNS OUT HE'S DYSLEXIC, MEANING HE'S IN GOOD COMPANY--ALBERT EINSTEIN, STEVE JOBS AND TOM CRUISE ARE ALL DYSLEXIC. AND BEFORE YOU SAY IT, SHUT YOUR MOUTH--TOM CRUISE ROCKS.
WORK CAN BE THE SAME WAY SOMETIMES, BUT IT'S WHAT YOU MAKE OF IT.
I DON'T MAKE ROCKETS. I PUSH PAPER.
BUT MAKING ROCKETS IS THE COOLEST JOB IN THE WORLD.
YEAH, ABOUT THAT, I TELL EVERYONE AT SCHOOL THAT YOU'RE A ROCKET SCIENTIST. GETS ME A LOT OF STREET CRED, ESPECIALLY WITH THE NERDS. AND THEY RUN THE SCHOOLS THESE DAYS.
YOU GOT IT. I WON'T BLOW YOUR COVER. BUT COME ON DOWN AND HELP ME COOK UP THESE BURGERS.

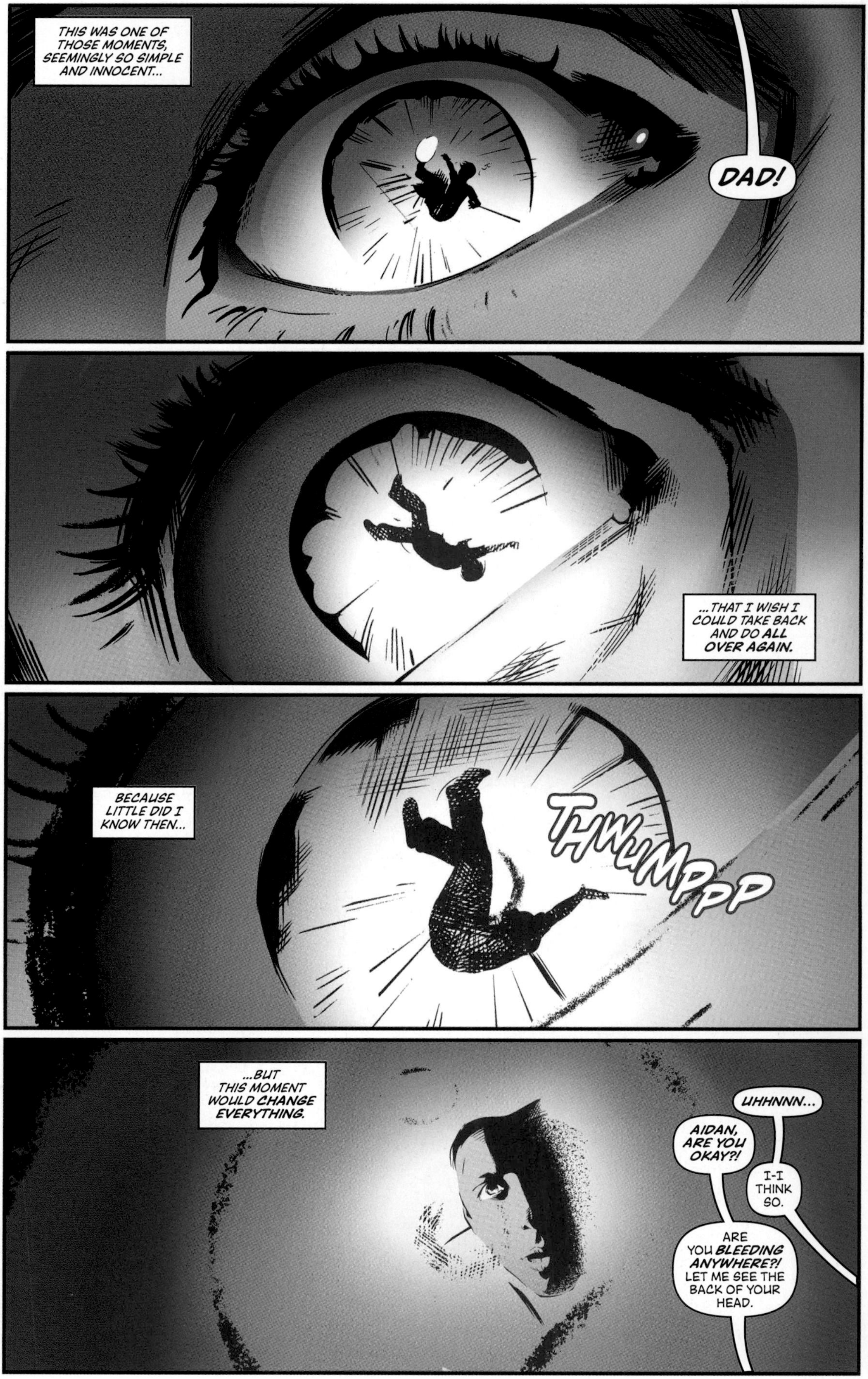
THIS WAS ONE OF THOSE MOMENTS, SEEMINGLY SO SIMPLE AND INNOCENT...
DAD!
...THAT I WISH I COULD TAKE BACK AND DO ALL OVER AGAIN.
BECAUSE LITTLE DID I KNOW THEN...
THWUMPPP
...BUT THIS MOMENT WOULD CHANGE EVERYTHING.
UHHNNN...
AIDAN, ARE YOU OKAY?!
I-I THINK SO.
ARE YOU BLEEDING ANYWHERE?! LET ME SEE THE BACK OF YOUR HEAD.

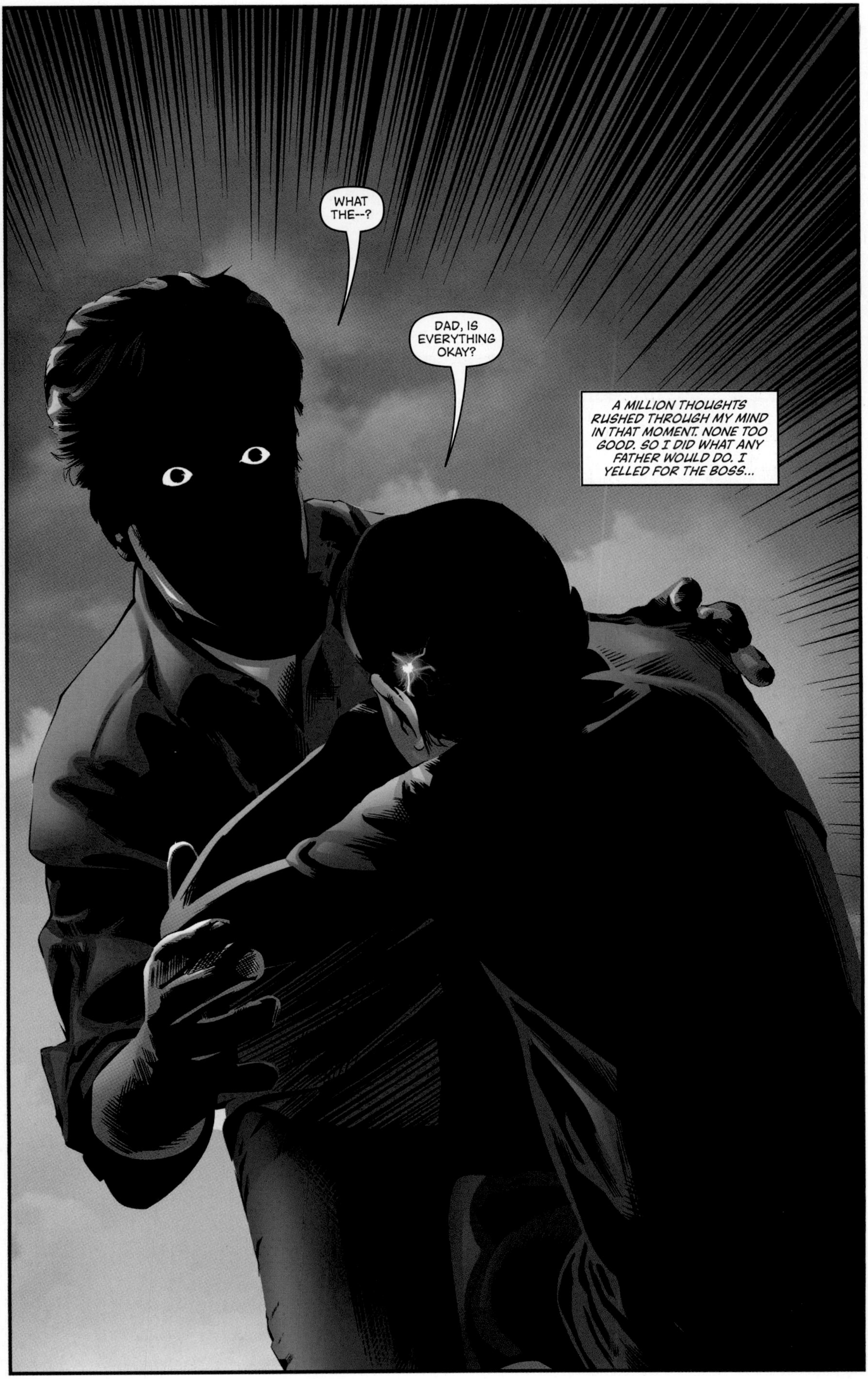
WHAT THE--?
DAD, IS EVERYTHING OKAY?
A MILLION THOUGHTS RUSHED THROUGH MY MIND IN THAT MOMENT. NONE TOO GOOD. SO I DID WHAT ANY FATHER WOULD DO. I YELLED FOR THE BOSS...

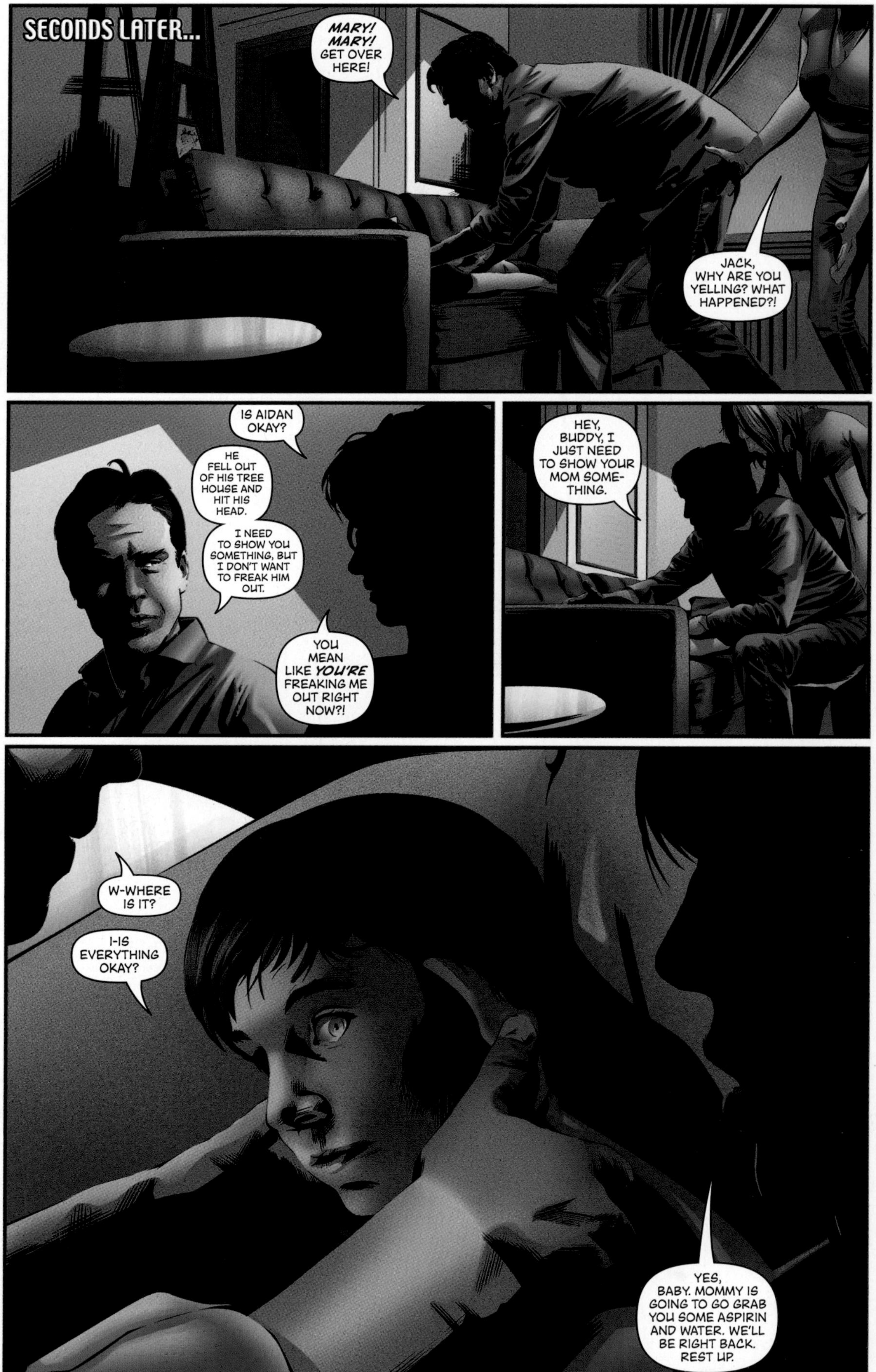
SECONDS LATER...
MARY! MARY! GET OVER HERE!
JACK, WHY ARE YOU YELLING? WHAT HAPPENED?!
IS AIDAN OKAY?
HE FELL OUT OF HIS TREE HOUSE AND HIT HIS HEAD.
I NEED TO SHOW YOU SOMETHING, BUT I DON'T WANT TO FREAK HIM OUT.
YOU MEAN LIKE YOU'RE FREAKING ME OUT RIGHT NOW?!
HEY, BUDDY, I JUST NEED TO SHOW YOUR MOM SOME-THING.
W-WHERE IS IT?
I-IS EVERYTHING OKAY?
YES, BABY. MOMMY IS GOING TO GO GRAB YOU SOME ASPIRIN AND WATER. WE'LL BE RIGHT BACK. REST UP.

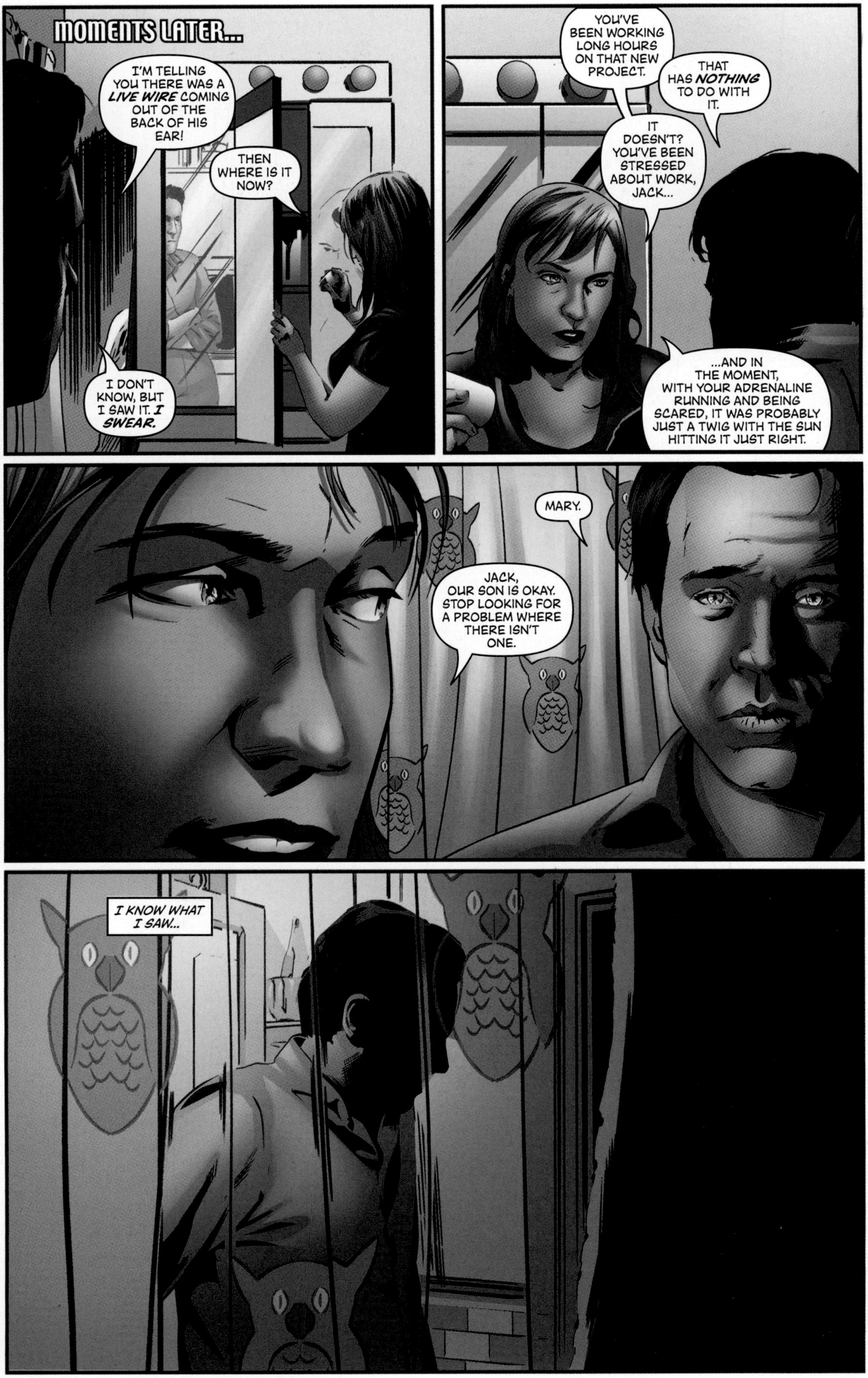
MOMENTS LATER...
I'M TELLING YOU THERE WAS A *LIVE WIRE* COMING OUT OF THE BACK OF HIS EAR!
THEN WHERE IS IT NOW?
I DON'T KNOW, BUT I SAW IT. *I SWEAR.*
YOU'VE BEEN WORKING LONG HOURS ON THAT NEW PROJECT.
THAT HAS *NOTHING* TO DO WITH IT.
IT DOESN'T? YOU'VE BEEN STRESSED ABOUT WORK, JACK...
...AND IN THE MOMENT, WITH YOUR ADRENALINE RUNNING AND BEING SCARED, IT WAS PROBABLY JUST A TWIG WITH THE SUN HITTING IT JUST RIGHT.
MARY.
JACK, OUR SON IS OKAY. STOP LOOKING FOR A PROBLEM WHERE THERE ISN'T ONE.
I KNOW WHAT I SAW...

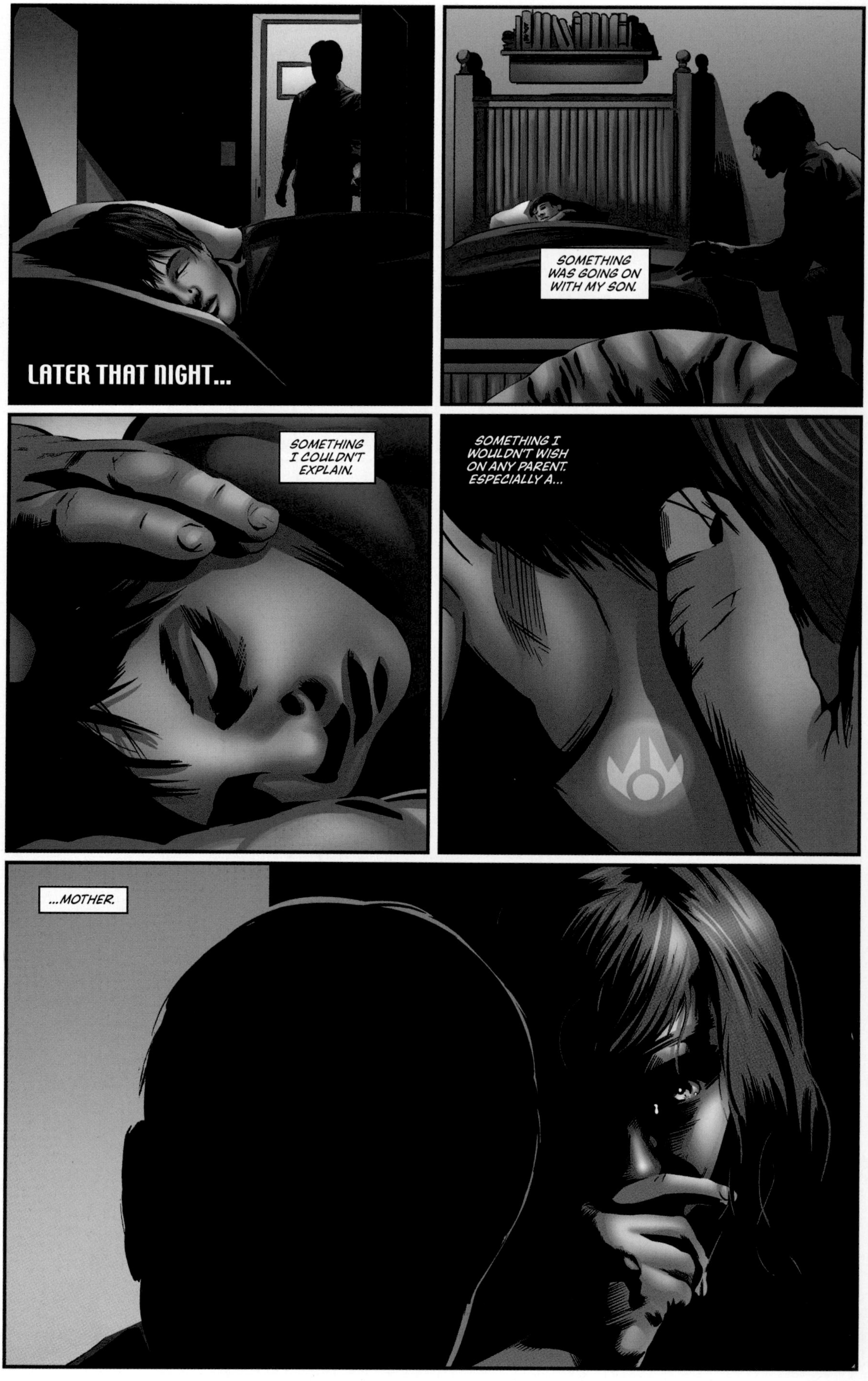
LATER THAT NIGHT...
SOMETHING WAS GOING ON WITH MY SON.
SOMETHING I COULDN'T EXPLAIN.
SOMETHING I WOULDN'T WISH ON ANY PARENT. ESPECIALLY A...
...MOTHER.

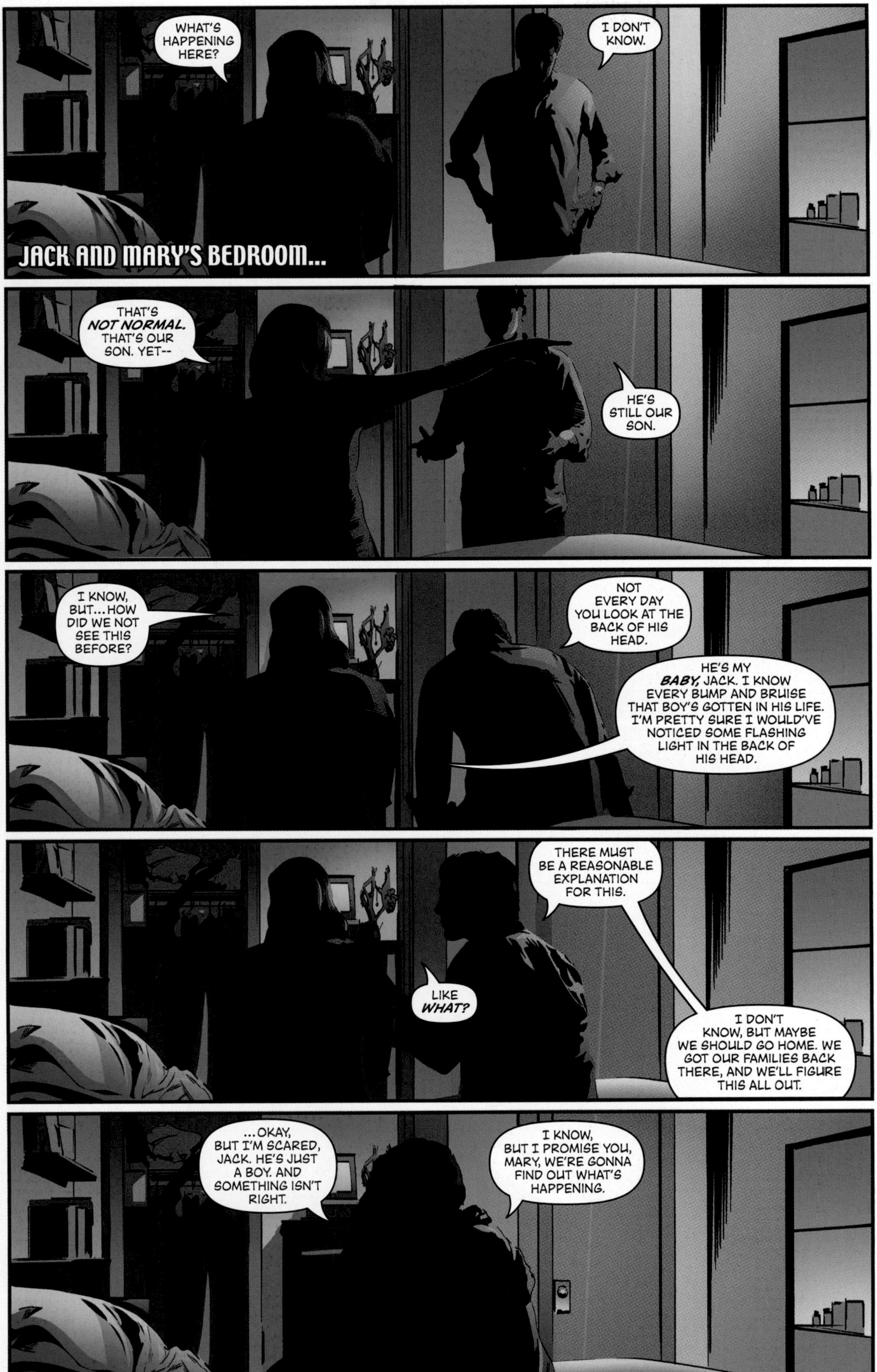
JACK AND MARY'S BEDROOM...
WHAT'S HAPPENING HERE?
I DON'T KNOW.
THAT'S NOT NORMAL. THAT'S OUR SON. YET--
HE'S STILL OUR SON.
I KNOW, BUT...HOW DID WE NOT SEE THIS BEFORE?
NOT EVERY DAY YOU LOOK AT THE BACK OF HIS HEAD.
HE'S MY BABY, JACK. I KNOW EVERY BUMP AND BRUISE THAT BOY'S GOTTEN IN HIS LIFE. I'M PRETTY SURE I WOULD'VE NOTICED SOME FLASHING LIGHT IN THE BACK OF HIS HEAD.
THERE MUST BE A REASONABLE EXPLANATION FOR THIS.
LIKE WHAT?
I DON'T KNOW, BUT MAYBE WE SHOULD GO HOME. WE GOT OUR FAMILIES BACK THERE, AND WE'LL FIGURE THIS ALL OUT.
...OKAY, BUT I'M SCARED, JACK. HE'S JUST A BOY. AND SOMETHING ISN'T RIGHT.
I KNOW, BUT I PROMISE YOU, MARY, WE'RE GONNA FIND OUT WHAT'S HAPPENING.

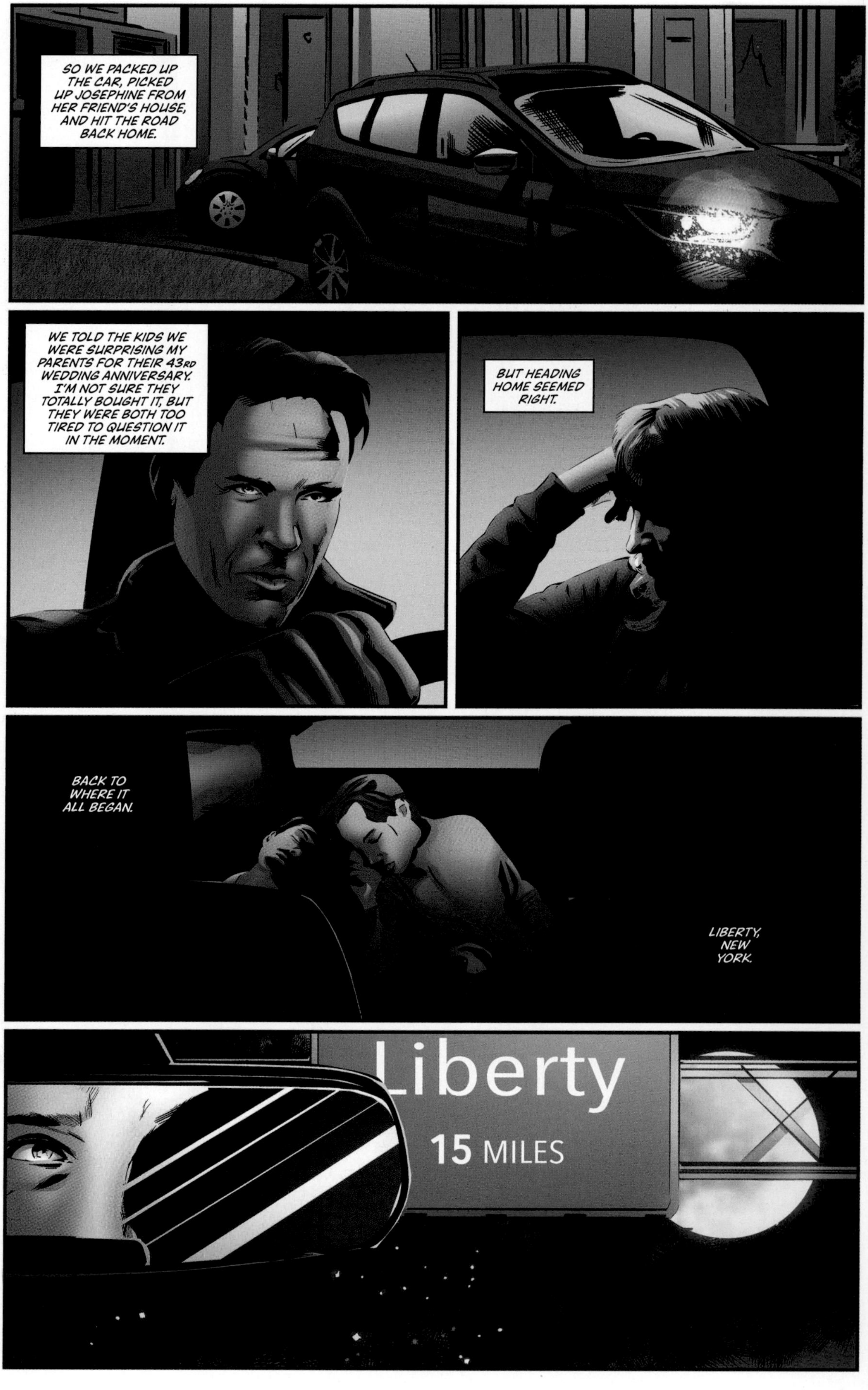
SO WE PACKED UP THE CAR, PICKED UP JOSEPHINE FROM HER FRIEND'S HOUSE, AND HIT THE ROAD BACK HOME.
WE TOLD THE KIDS WE WERE SURPRISING MY PARENTS FOR THEIR 43RD WEDDING ANNIVERSARY. I'M NOT SURE THEY TOTALLY BOUGHT IT, BUT THEY WERE BOTH TOO TIRED TO QUESTION IT IN THE MOMENT.
BUT HEADING HOME SEEMED RIGHT.
BACK TO WHERE IT ALL BEGAN.
LIBERTY, NEW YORK.
Liberty
15 MILES

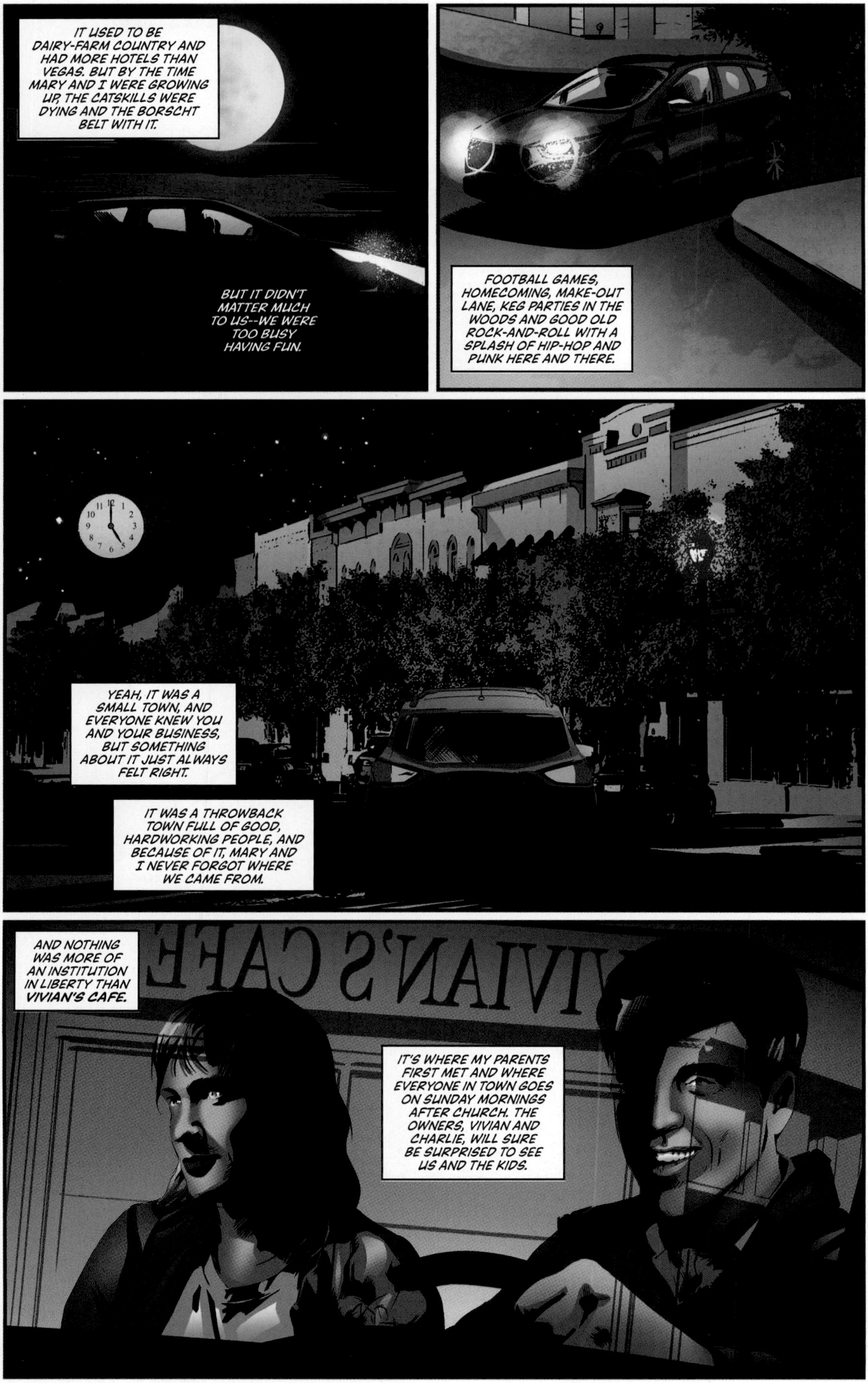
IT USED TO BE DAIRY-FARM COUNTRY AND HAD MORE HOTELS THAN VEGAS. BUT BY THE TIME MARY AND I WERE GROWING UP, THE CATSKILLS WERE DYING AND THE BORSCHT BELT WITH IT.
BUT IT DIDN'T MATTER MUCH TO US--WE WERE TOO BUSY HAVING FUN.
FOOTBALL GAMES, HOMECOMING, MAKE-OUT LANE, KEG PARTIES IN THE WOODS AND GOOD OLD ROCK-AND-ROLL WITH A SPLASH OF HIP-HOP AND PUNK HERE AND THERE.
YEAH, IT WAS A SMALL TOWN, AND EVERYONE KNEW YOU AND YOUR BUSINESS, BUT SOMETHING ABOUT IT JUST ALWAYS FELT RIGHT.
IT WAS A THROWBACK TOWN FULL OF GOOD, HARDWORKING PEOPLE, AND BECAUSE OF IT, MARY AND I NEVER FORGOT WHERE WE CAME FROM.
AND NOTHING WAS MORE OF AN INSTITUTION IN LIBERTY THAN VIVIAN'S CAFE.
IT'S WHERE MY PARENTS FIRST MET AND WHERE EVERYONE IN TOWN GOES ON SUNDAY MORNINGS AFTER CHURCH. THE OWNERS, VIVIAN AND CHARLIE, WILL SURE BE SURPRISED TO SEE US AND THE KIDS.

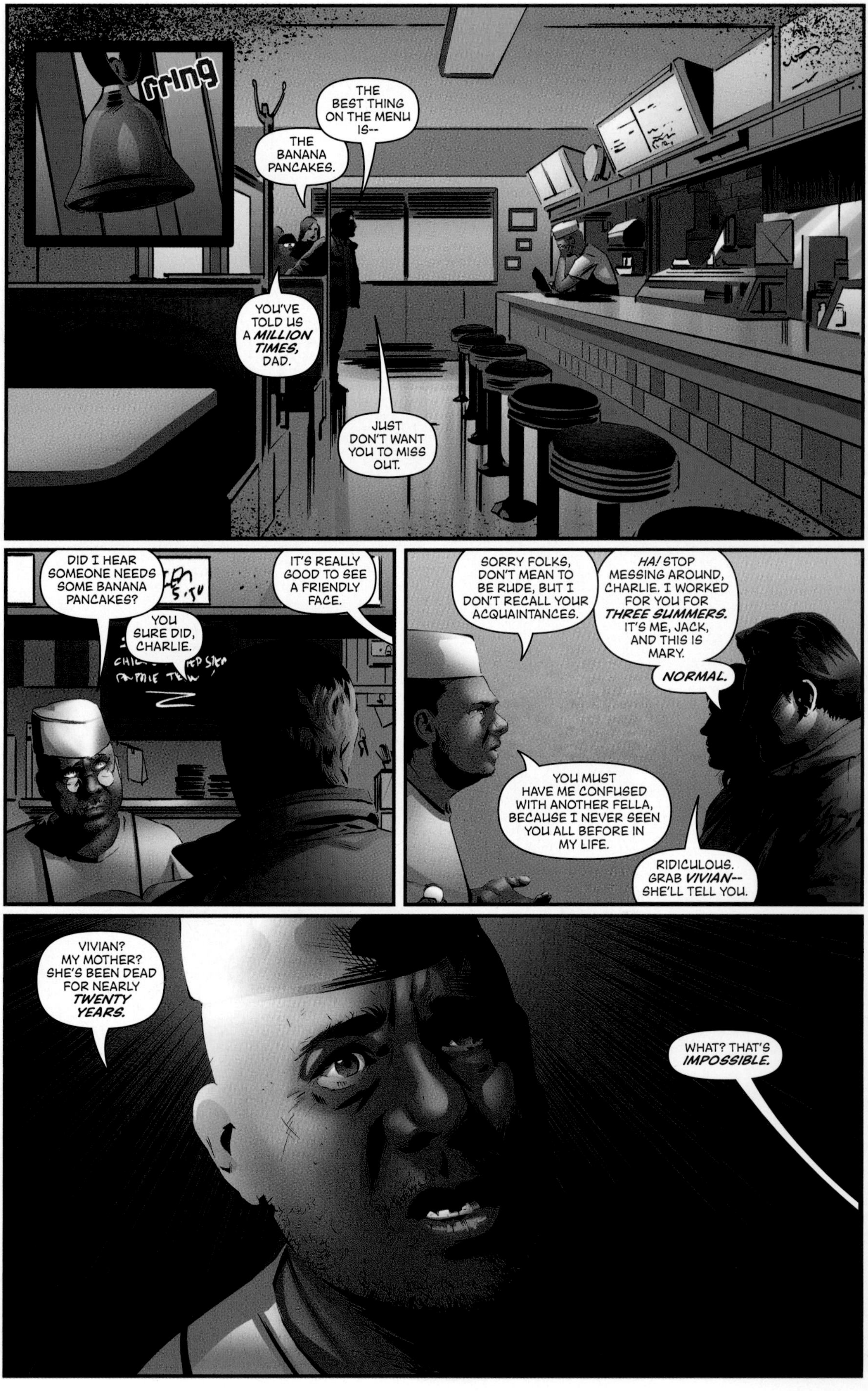
rring
THE BEST THING ON THE MENU IS--
THE BANANA PANCAKES.
YOU'VE TOLD US A MILLION TIMES, DAD.
JUST DON'T WANT YOU TO MISS OUT.
DID I HEAR SOMEONE NEEDS SOME BANANA PANCAKES?
YOU SURE DID, CHARLIE.
IT'S REALLY GOOD TO SEE A FRIENDLY FACE.
SORRY FOLKS, DON'T MEAN TO BE RUDE, BUT I DON'T RECALL YOUR ACQUAINTANCES.
HA! STOP MESSING AROUND, CHARLIE. I WORKED FOR YOU FOR THREE SUMMERS. IT'S ME, JACK, AND THIS IS MARY.
NORMAL.
YOU MUST HAVE ME CONFUSED WITH ANOTHER FELLA, BECAUSE I NEVER SEEN YOU ALL BEFORE IN MY LIFE.
RIDICULOUS. GRAB VIVIAN-- SHE'LL TELL YOU.
VIVIAN? MY MOTHER? SHE'S BEEN DEAD FOR NEARLY TWENTY YEARS.
WHAT? THAT'S IMPOSSIBLE.

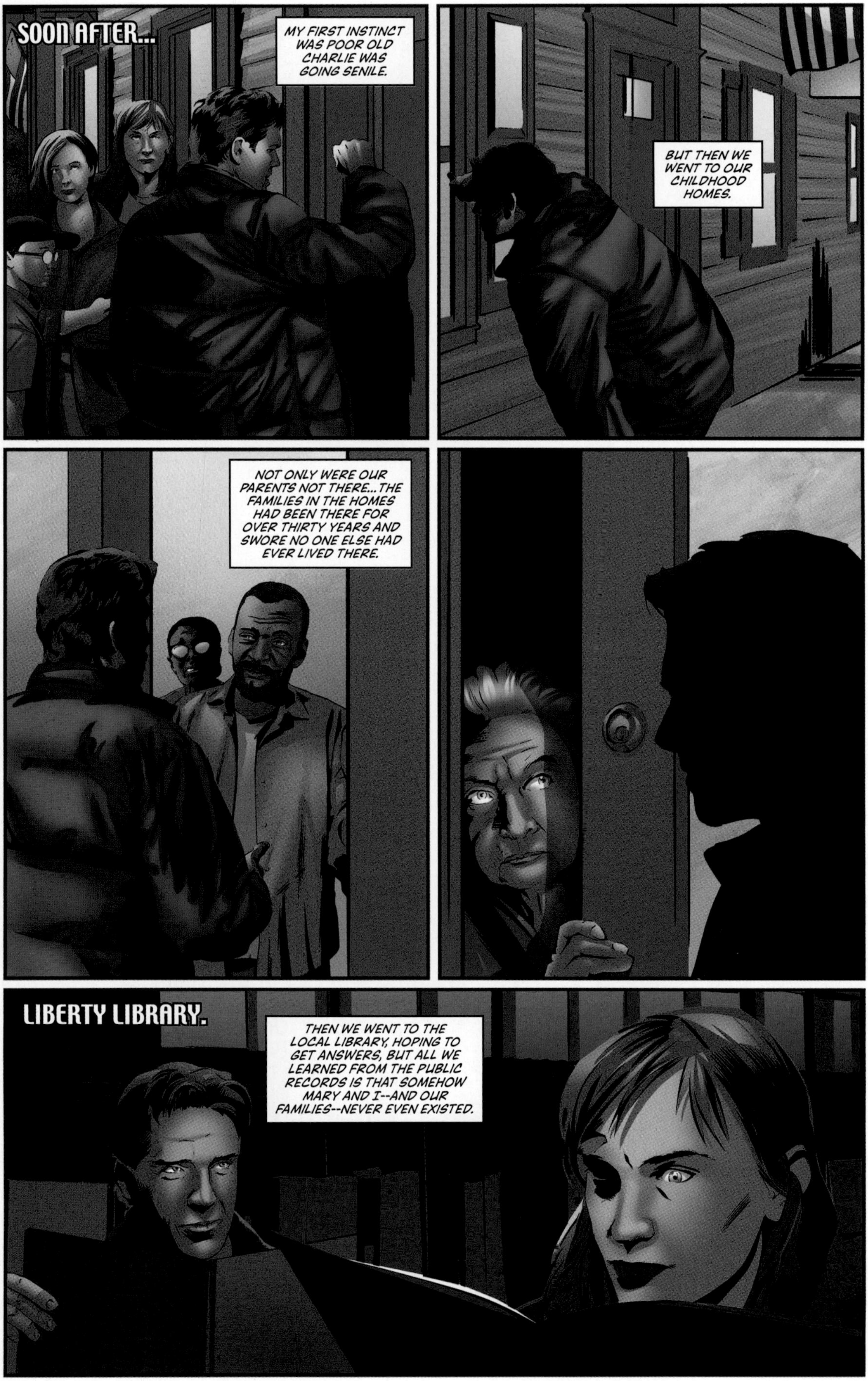
SOON AFTER...
MY FIRST INSTINCT WAS POOR OLD CHARLIE WAS GOING SENILE.
BUT THEN WE WENT TO OUR CHILDHOOD HOMES.
NOT ONLY WERE OUR PARENTS NOT THERE...THE FAMILIES IN THE HOMES HAD BEEN THERE FOR OVER THIRTY YEARS AND SWORE NO ONE ELSE HAD EVER LIVED THERE.
LIBERTY LIBRARY.
THEN WE WENT TO THE LOCAL LIBRARY, HOPING TO GET ANSWERS, BUT ALL WE LEARNED FROM THE PUBLIC RECORDS IS THAT SOMEHOW MARY AND I--AND OUR FAMILIES--NEVER EVEN EXISTED.

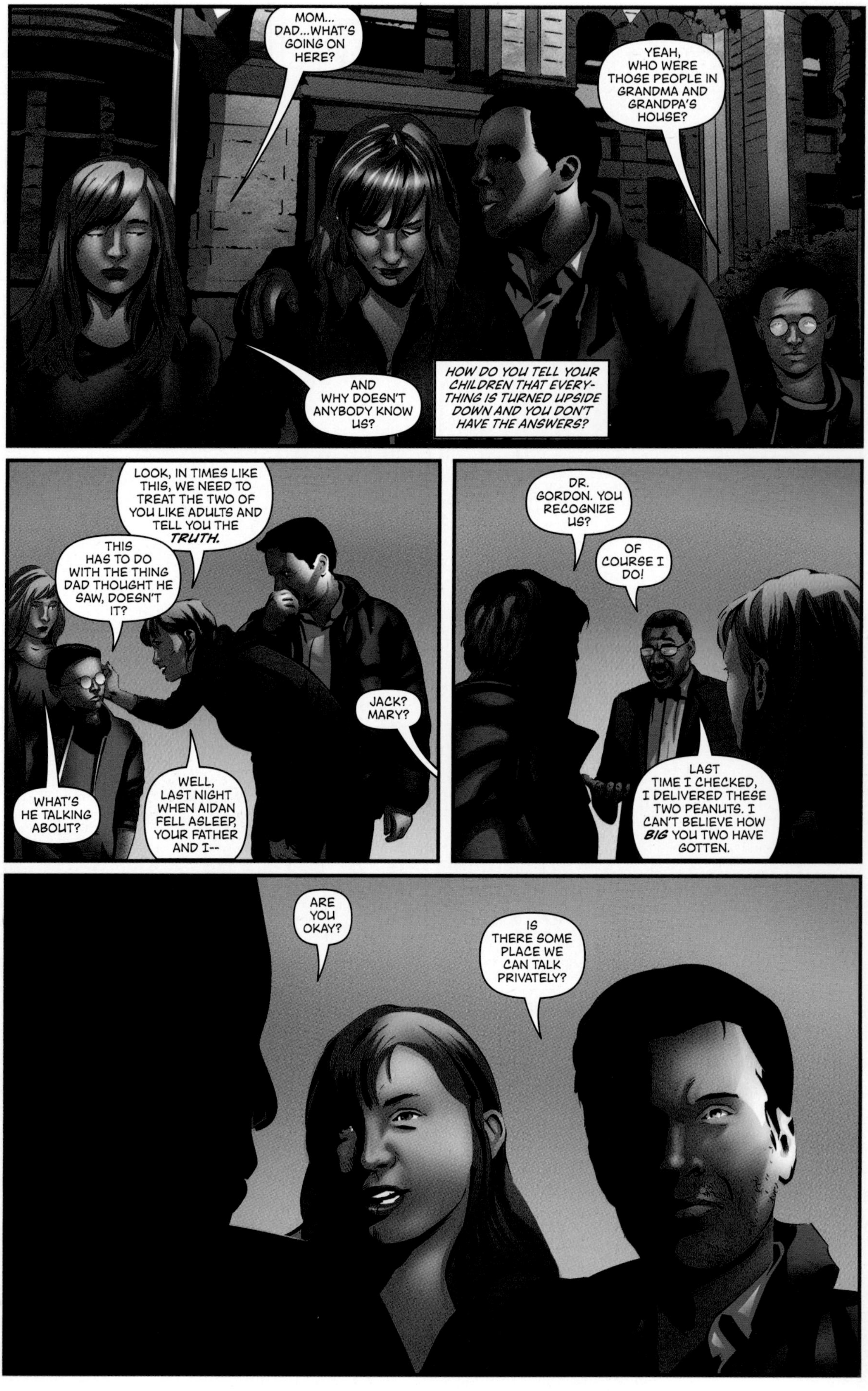
MOM... DAD...WHAT'S GOING ON HERE?
YEAH, WHO WERE THOSE PEOPLE IN GRANDMA AND GRANDPA'S HOUSE?
AND WHY DOESN'T ANYBODY KNOW US?
HOW DO YOU TELL YOUR CHILDREN THAT EVERY-THING IS TURNED UPSIDE DOWN AND YOU DON'T HAVE THE ANSWERS?
LOOK, IN TIMES LIKE THIS, WE NEED TO TREAT THE TWO OF YOU LIKE ADULTS AND TELL YOU THE TRUTH.
THIS HAS TO DO WITH THE THING DAD THOUGHT HE SAW, DOESN'T IT?
WHAT'S HE TALKING ABOUT?
WELL, LAST NIGHT WHEN AIDAN FELL ASLEEP, YOUR FATHER AND I--
JACK? MARY?
DR. GORDON. YOU RECOGNIZE US?
OF COURSE I DO!
LAST TIME I CHECKED, I DELIVERED THESE TWO PEANUTS. I CAN'T BELIEVE HOW BIG YOU TWO HAVE GOTTEN.
ARE YOU OKAY?
IS THERE SOME PLACE WE CAN TALK PRIVATELY?

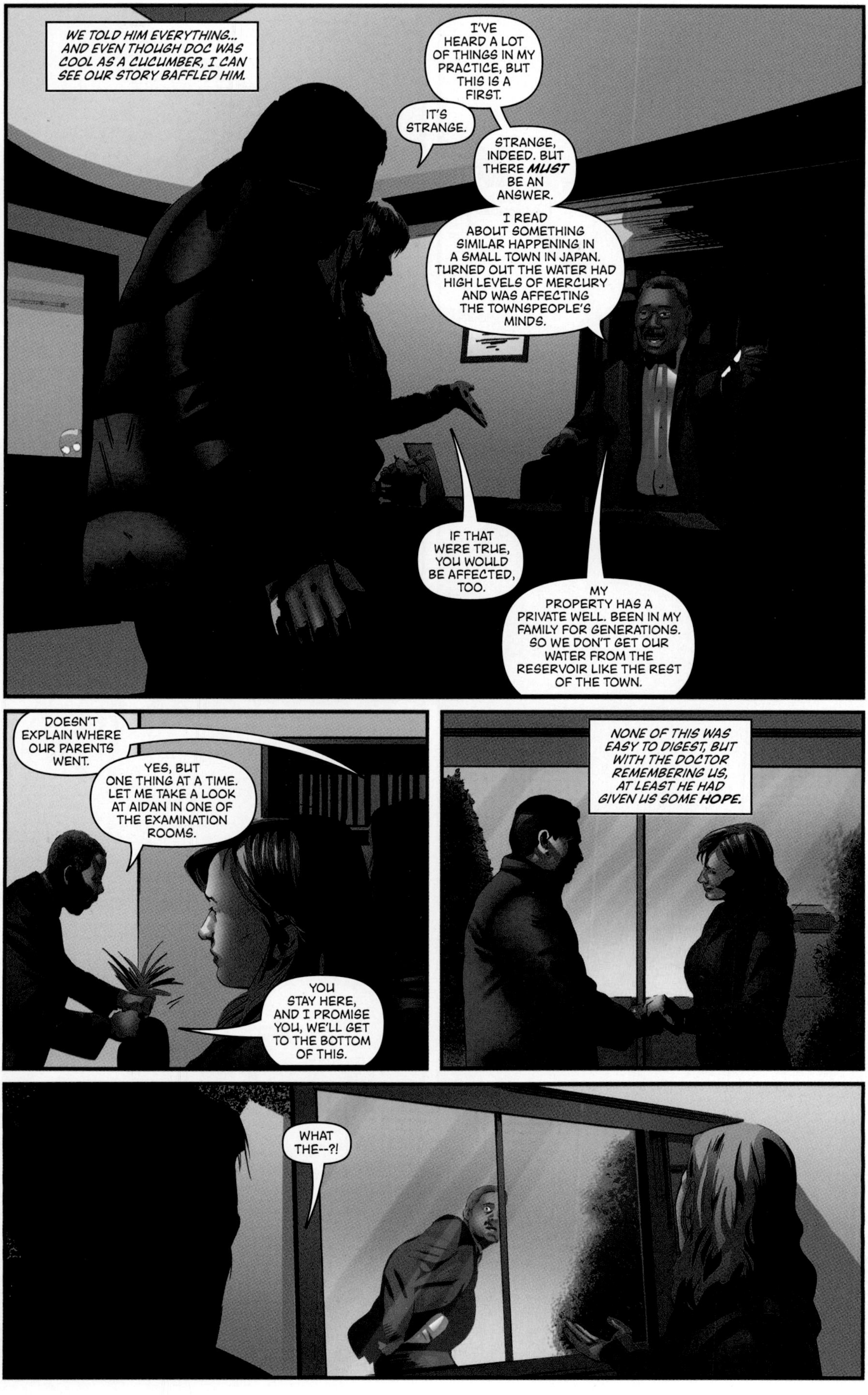
WE TOLD HIM EVERYTHING... AND EVEN THOUGH DOC WAS COOL AS A CUCUMBER, I CAN SEE OUR STORY BAFFLED HIM.
I'VE HEARD A LOT OF THINGS IN MY PRACTICE, BUT THIS IS A FIRST.
IT'S STRANGE.
STRANGE, INDEED. BUT THERE MUST BE AN ANSWER.
I READ ABOUT SOMETHING SIMILAR HAPPENING IN A SMALL TOWN IN JAPAN. TURNED OUT THE WATER HAD HIGH LEVELS OF MERCURY AND WAS AFFECTING THE TOWNSPEOPLE'S MINDS.
IF THAT WERE TRUE, YOU WOULD BE AFFECTED, TOO.
MY PROPERTY HAS A PRIVATE WELL. BEEN IN MY FAMILY FOR GENERATIONS. SO WE DON'T GET OUR WATER FROM THE RESERVOIR LIKE THE REST OF THE TOWN.
DOESN'T EXPLAIN WHERE OUR PARENTS WENT.
YES, BUT ONE THING AT A TIME. LET ME TAKE A LOOK AT AIDAN IN ONE OF THE EXAMINATION ROOMS.
YOU STAY HERE, AND I PROMISE YOU, WE'LL GET TO THE BOTTOM OF THIS.
NONE OF THIS WAS EASY TO DIGEST, BUT WITH THE DOCTOR REMEMBERING US, AT LEAST HE HAD GIVEN US SOME HOPE.
WHAT THE--?!

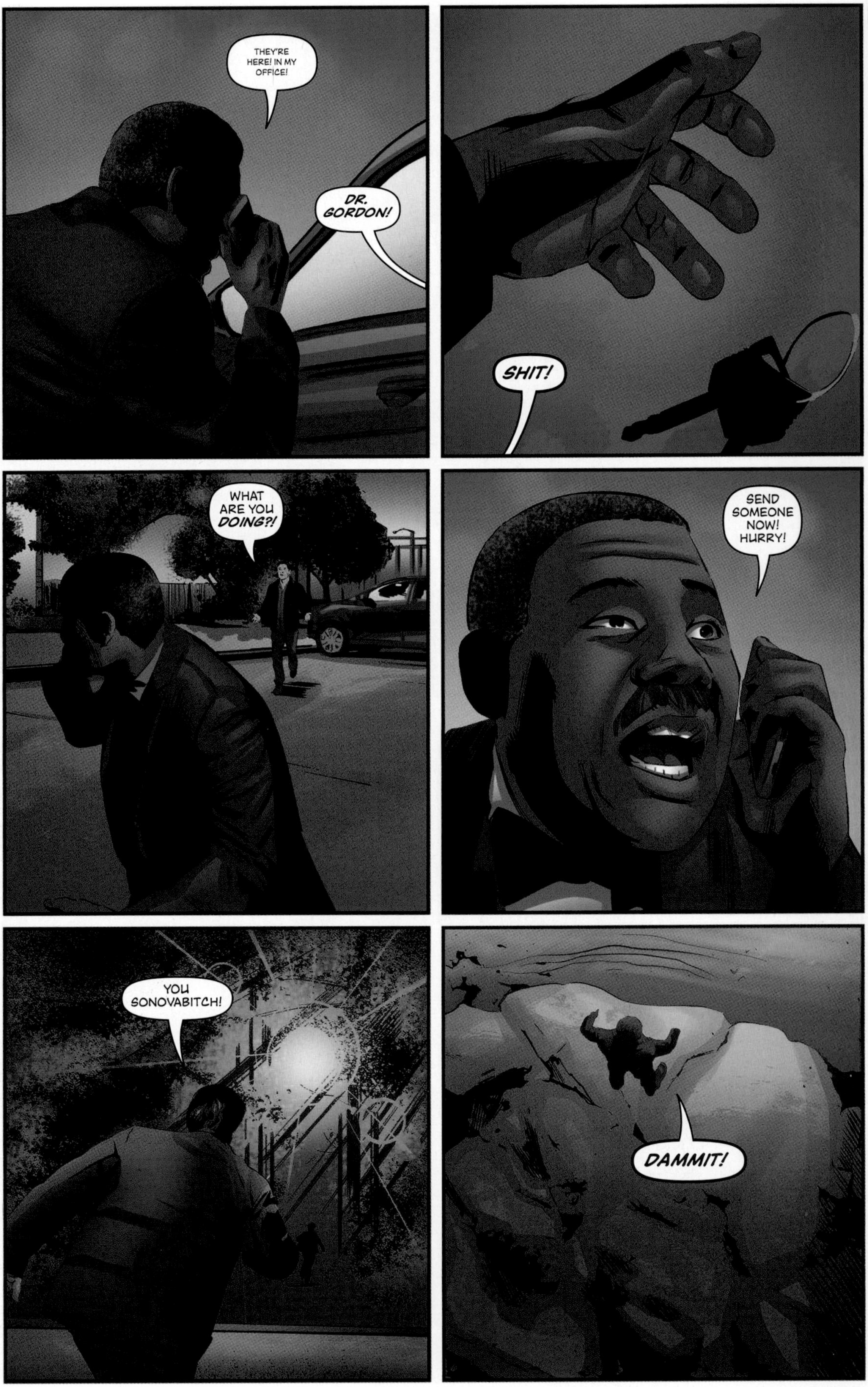
THEY'RE HERE! IN MY OFFICE!
DR. GORDON!
SHIT!
WHAT ARE YOU DOING?!
SEND SOMEONE NOW! HURRY!
YOU SONOVABITCH!
DAMMIT!

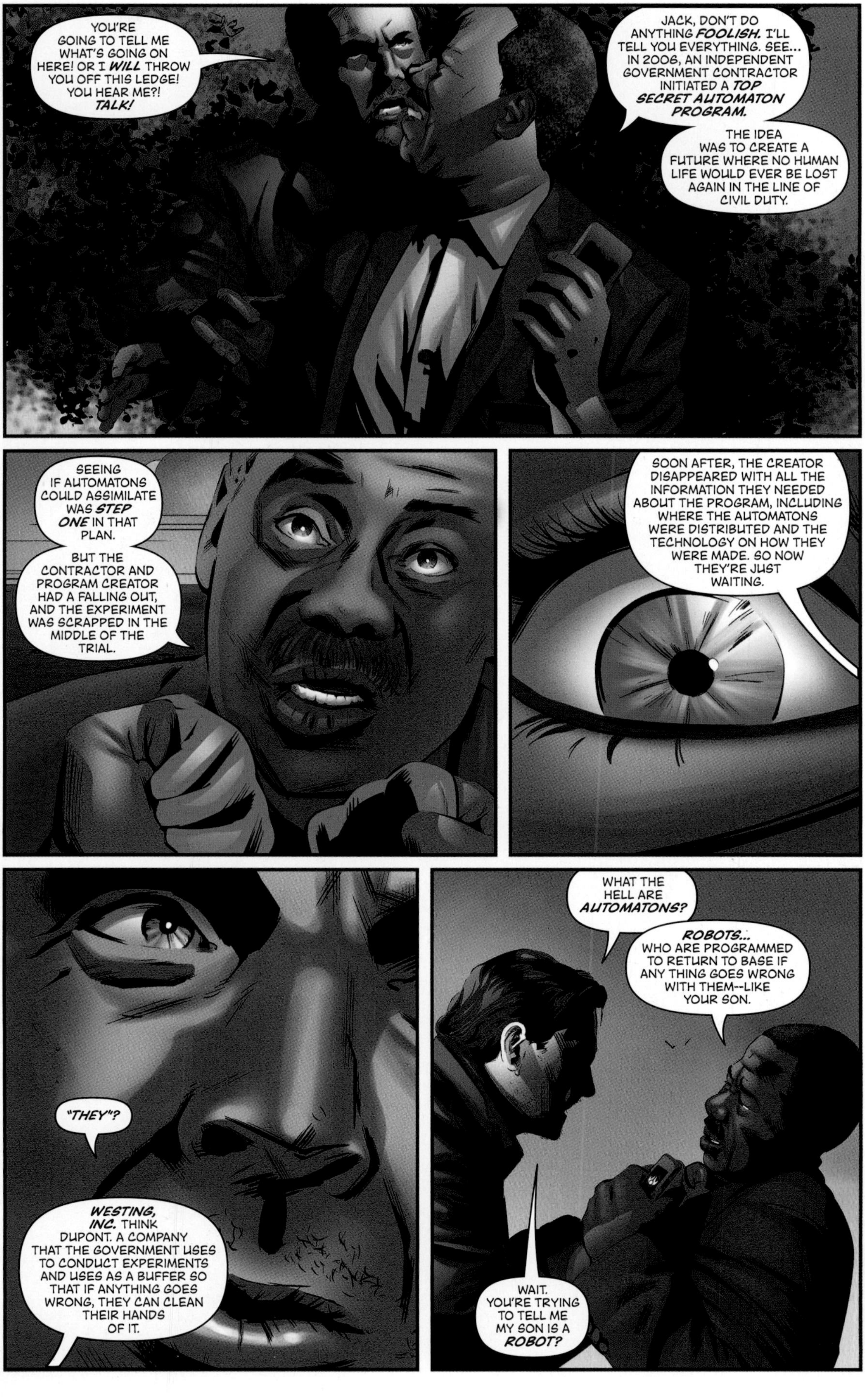
YOU'RE GOING TO TELL ME WHAT'S GOING ON HERE! OR I WILL THROW YOU OFF THIS LEDGE! YOU HEAR ME?! TALK!
JACK, DON'T DO ANYTHING FOOLISH. I'LL TELL YOU EVERYTHING. SEE... IN 2006, AN INDEPENDENT GOVERNMENT CONTRACTOR INITIATED A TOP SECRET AUTOMATON PROGRAM.
THE IDEA WAS TO CREATE A FUTURE WHERE NO HUMAN LIFE WOULD EVER BE LOST AGAIN IN THE LINE OF CIVIL DUTY.
SEEING IF AUTOMATONS COULD ASSIMILATE WAS STEP ONE IN THAT PLAN.
BUT THE CONTRACTOR AND PROGRAM CREATOR HAD A FALLING OUT, AND THE EXPERIMENT WAS SCRAPPED IN THE MIDDLE OF THE TRIAL.
SOON AFTER, THE CREATOR DISAPPEARED WITH ALL THE INFORMATION THEY NEEDED ABOUT THE PROGRAM, INCLUDING WHERE THE AUTOMATONS WERE DISTRIBUTED AND THE TECHNOLOGY ON HOW THEY WERE MADE. SO NOW THEY'RE JUST WAITING.
"THEY"?
WESTING, INC. THINK DUPONT. A COMPANY THAT THE GOVERNMENT USES TO CONDUCT EXPERIMENTS AND USES AS A BUFFER SO THAT IF ANYTHING GOES WRONG, THEY CAN CLEAN THEIR HANDS OF IT.
WHAT THE HELL ARE AUTOMATONS?
ROBOTS... WHO ARE PROGRAMMED TO RETURN TO BASE IF ANY THING GOES WRONG WITH THEM--LIKE YOUR SON.
WAIT. YOU'RE TRYING TO TELL ME MY SON IS A ROBOT?

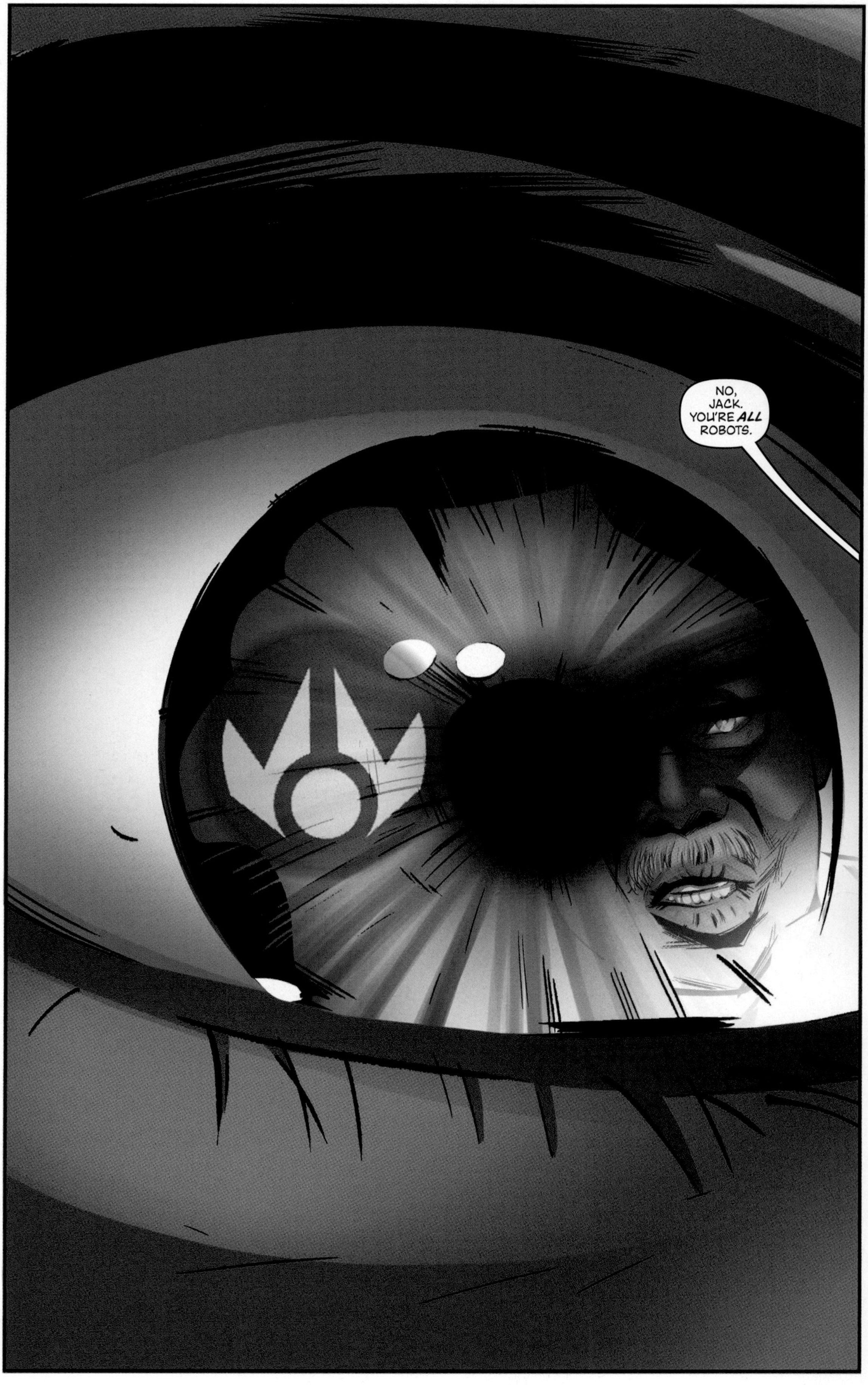
NO, JACK. YOU'RE ALL ROBOTS.

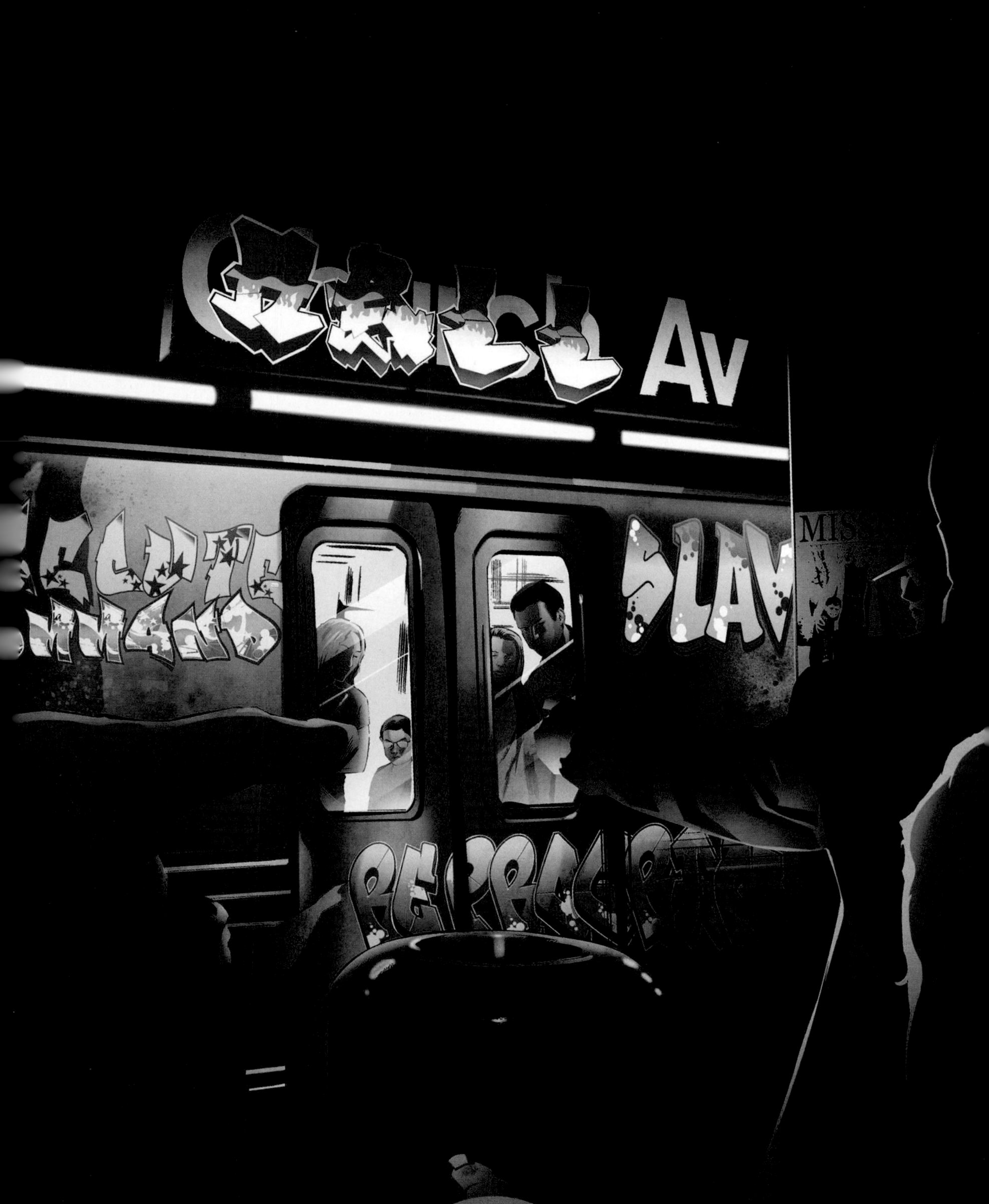
Av

2

"BURNING DOWN THE HOUSE"

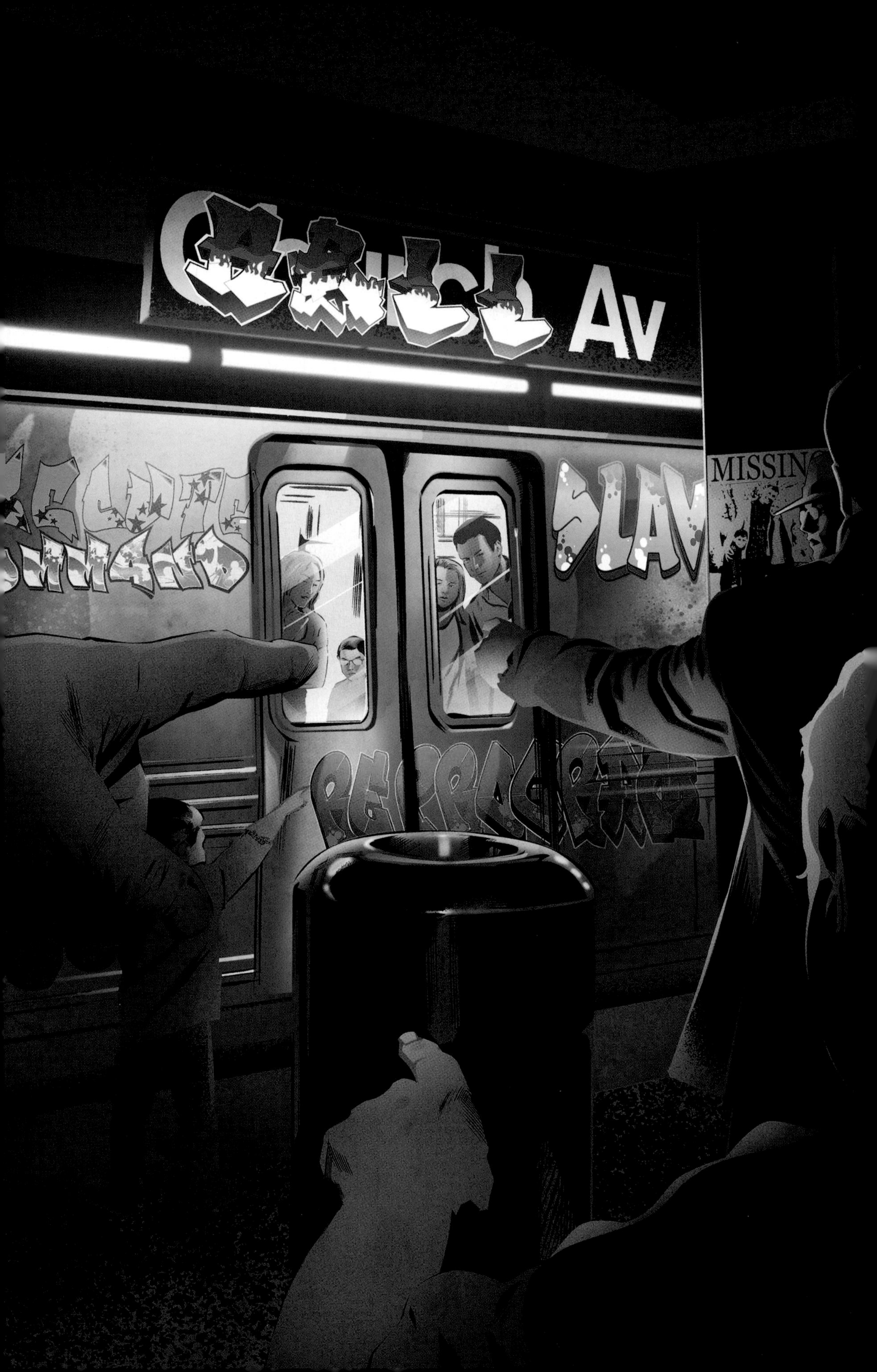
Av

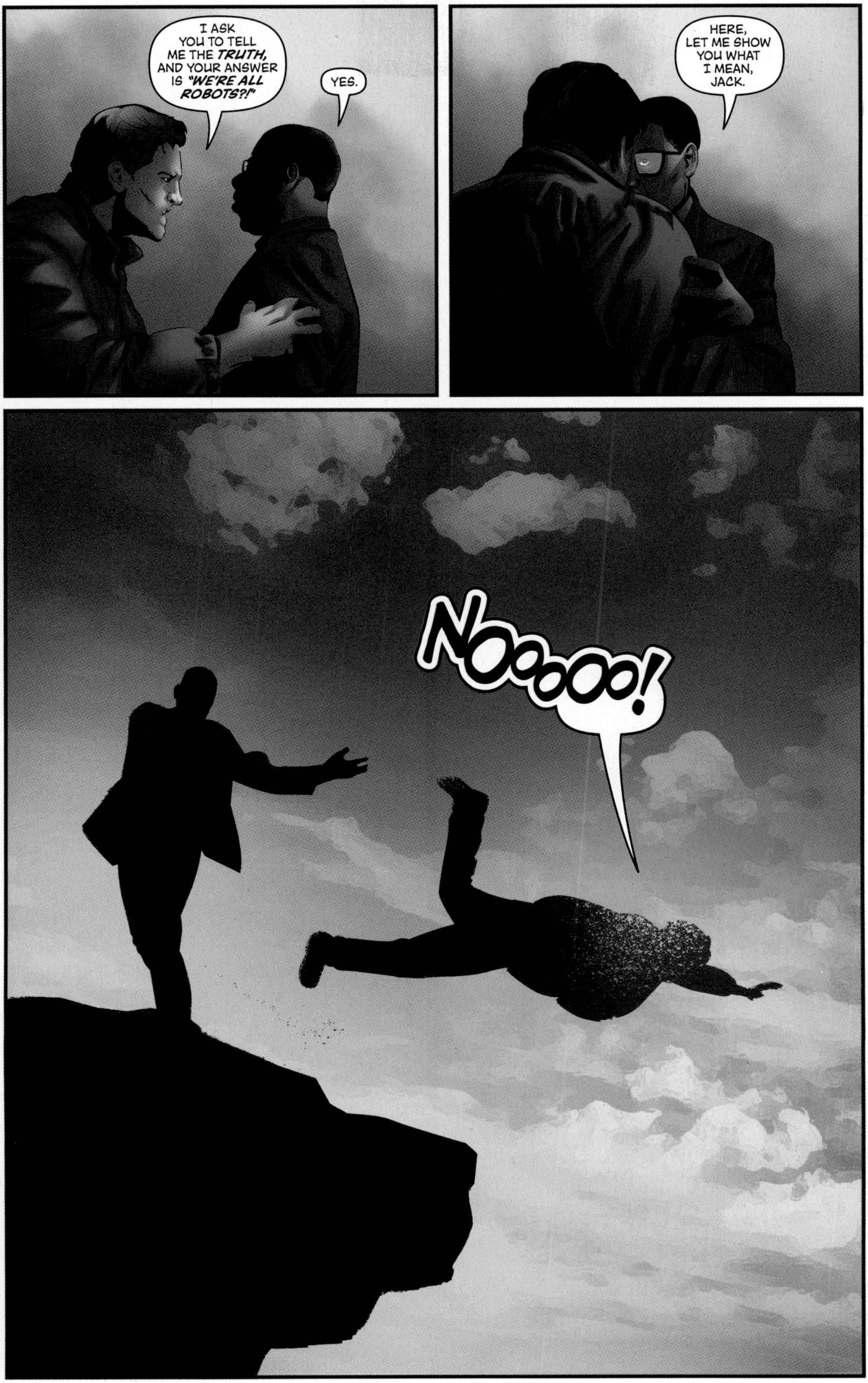
I ASK YOU TO TELL ME THE *TRUTH,* AND YOUR ANSWER IS *"WE'RE ALL ROBOTS?!"*
YES.
HERE, LET ME SHOW YOU WHAT I MEAN, JACK.
NOooooo!

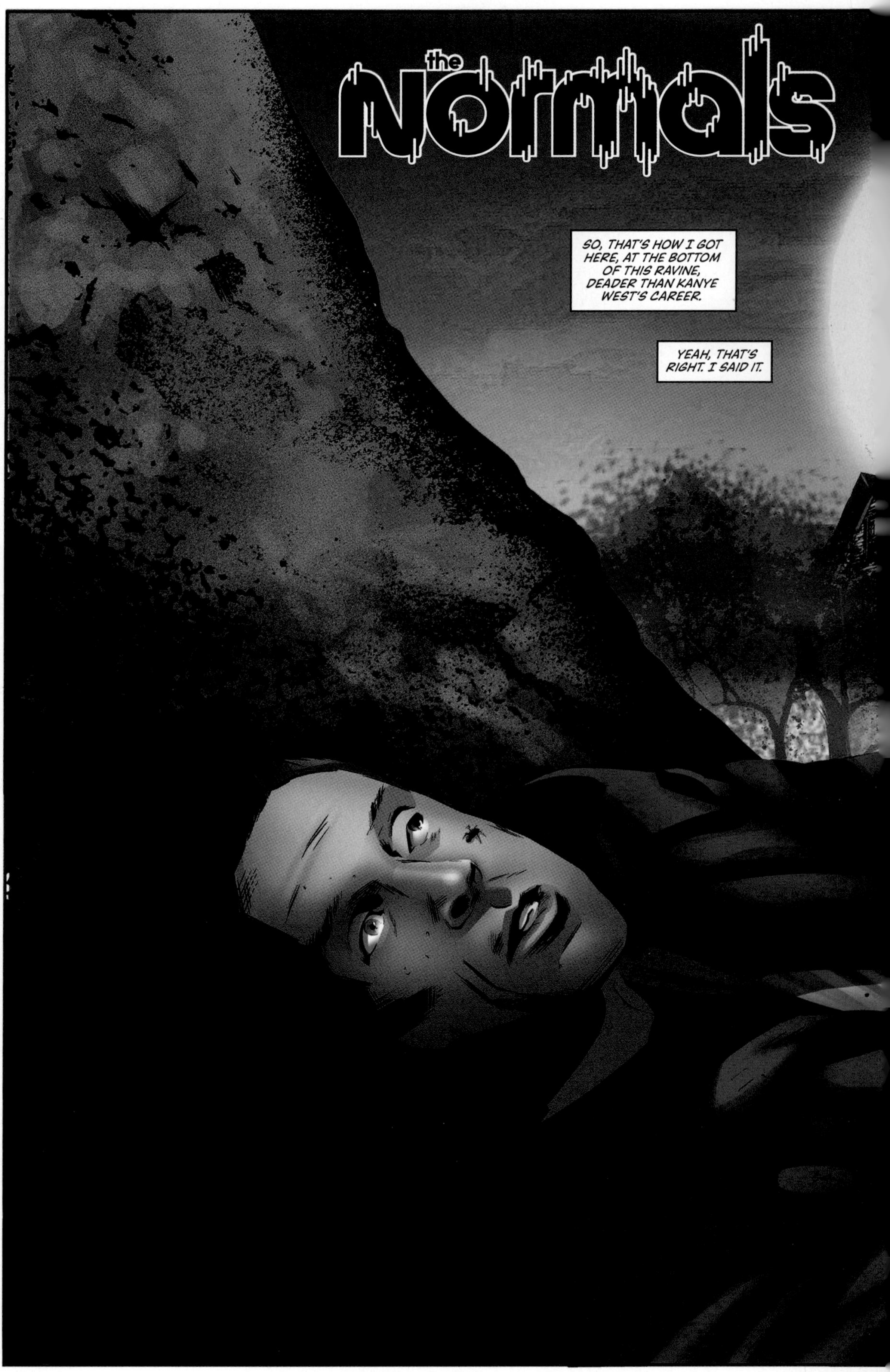
the Normals
SO, THAT'S HOW I GOT HERE, AT THE BOTTOM OF THIS RAVINE, DEADER THAN KANYE WEST'S CAREER.
YEAH, THAT'S RIGHT. I SAID IT.

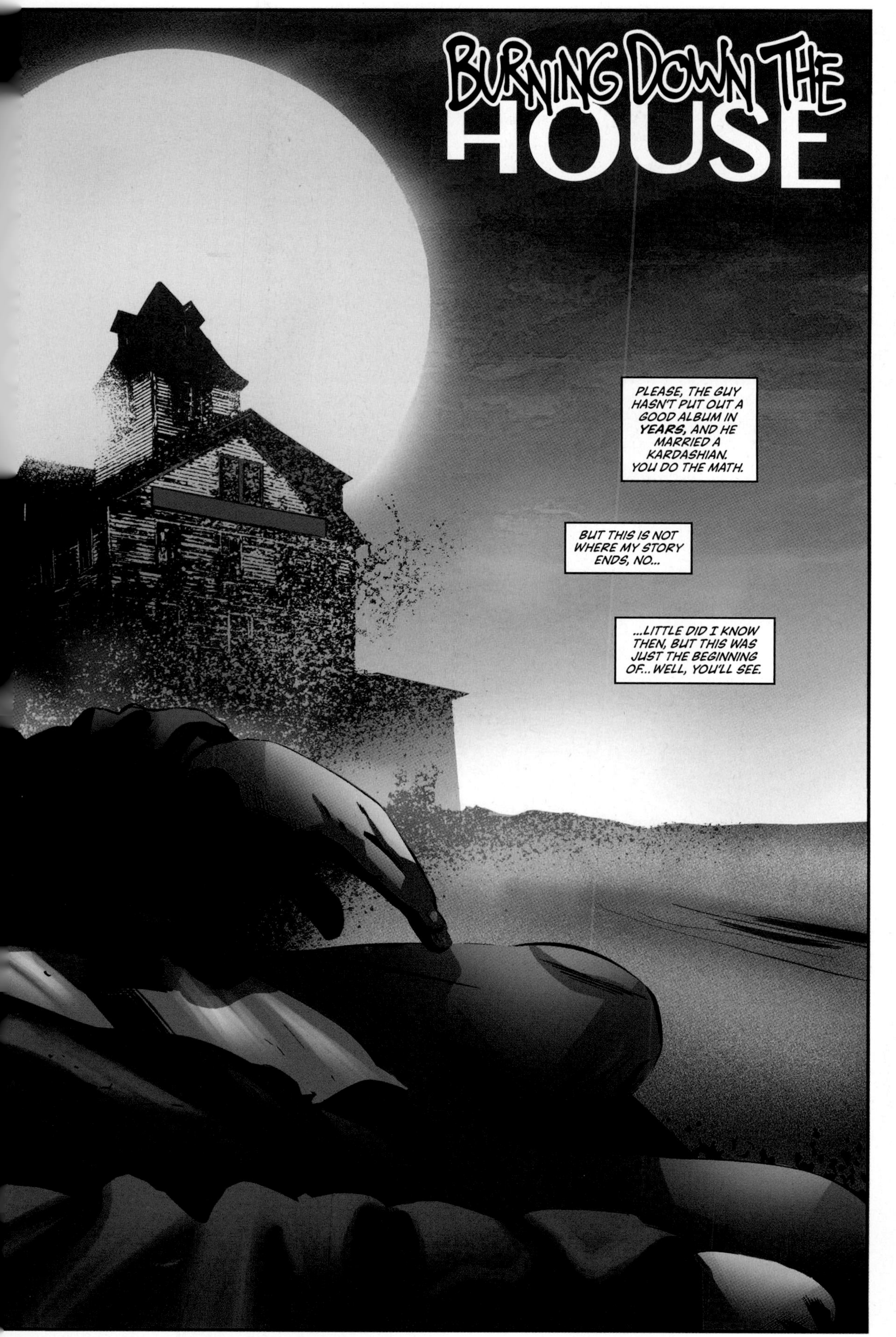
BURNING DOWN THE HOUSE
PLEASE, THE GUY HASN'T PUT OUT A GOOD ALBUM IN YEARS, AND HE MARRIED A KARDASHIAN. YOU DO THE MATH.
BUT THIS IS NOT WHERE MY STORY ENDS, NO...
...LITTLE DID I KNOW THEN, BUT THIS WAS JUST THE BEGINNING OF... WELL, YOU'LL SEE.

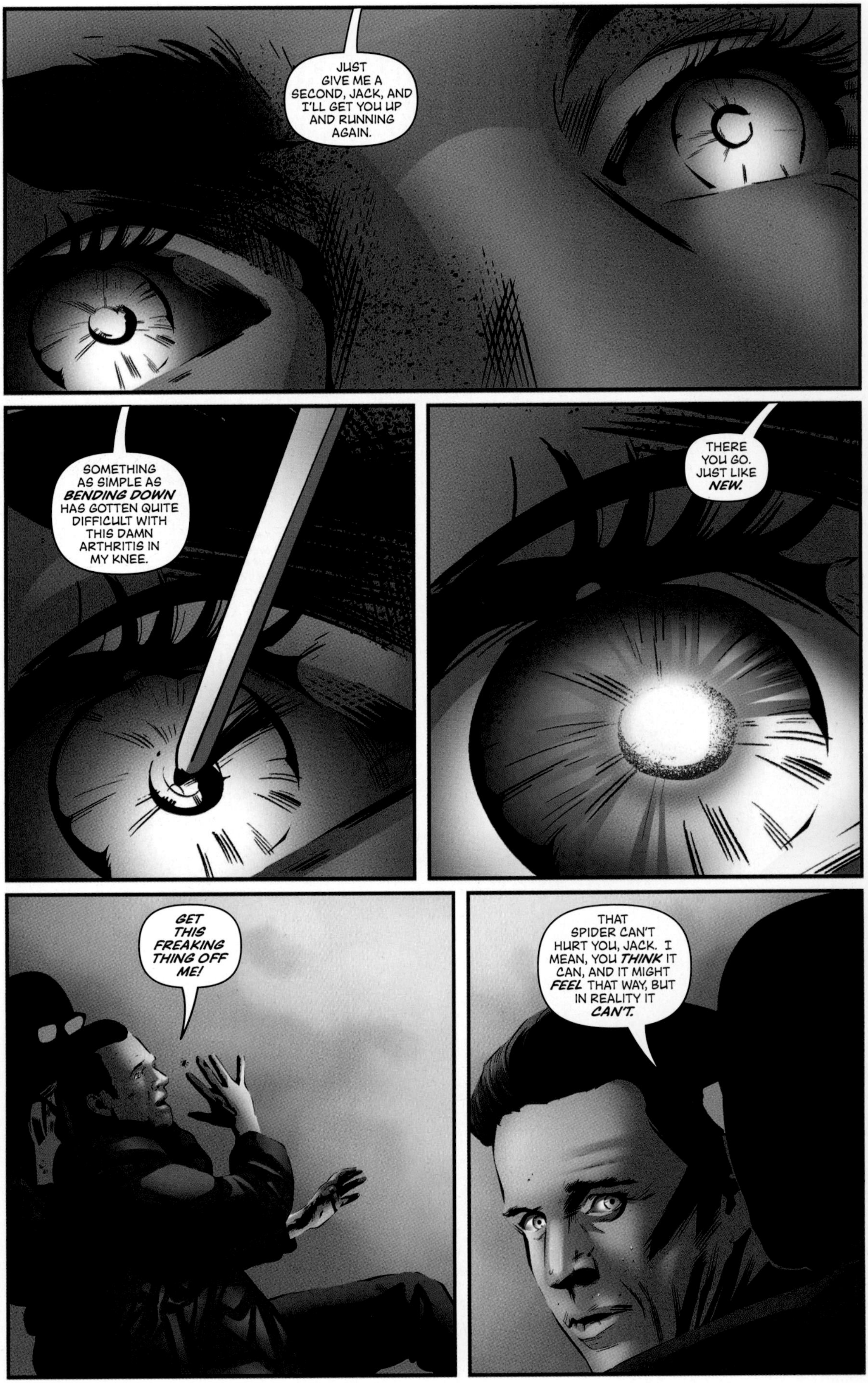
JUST GIVE ME A SECOND, JACK, AND I'LL GET YOU UP AND RUNNING AGAIN.
SOMETHING AS SIMPLE AS BENDING DOWN HAS GOTTEN QUITE DIFFICULT WITH THIS DAMN ARTHRITIS IN MY KNEE.
THERE YOU GO. JUST LIKE NEW.
GET THIS FREAKING THING OFF ME!
THAT SPIDER CAN'T HURT YOU, JACK. I MEAN, YOU THINK IT CAN, AND IT MIGHT FEEL THAT WAY, BUT IN REALITY IT CAN'T.

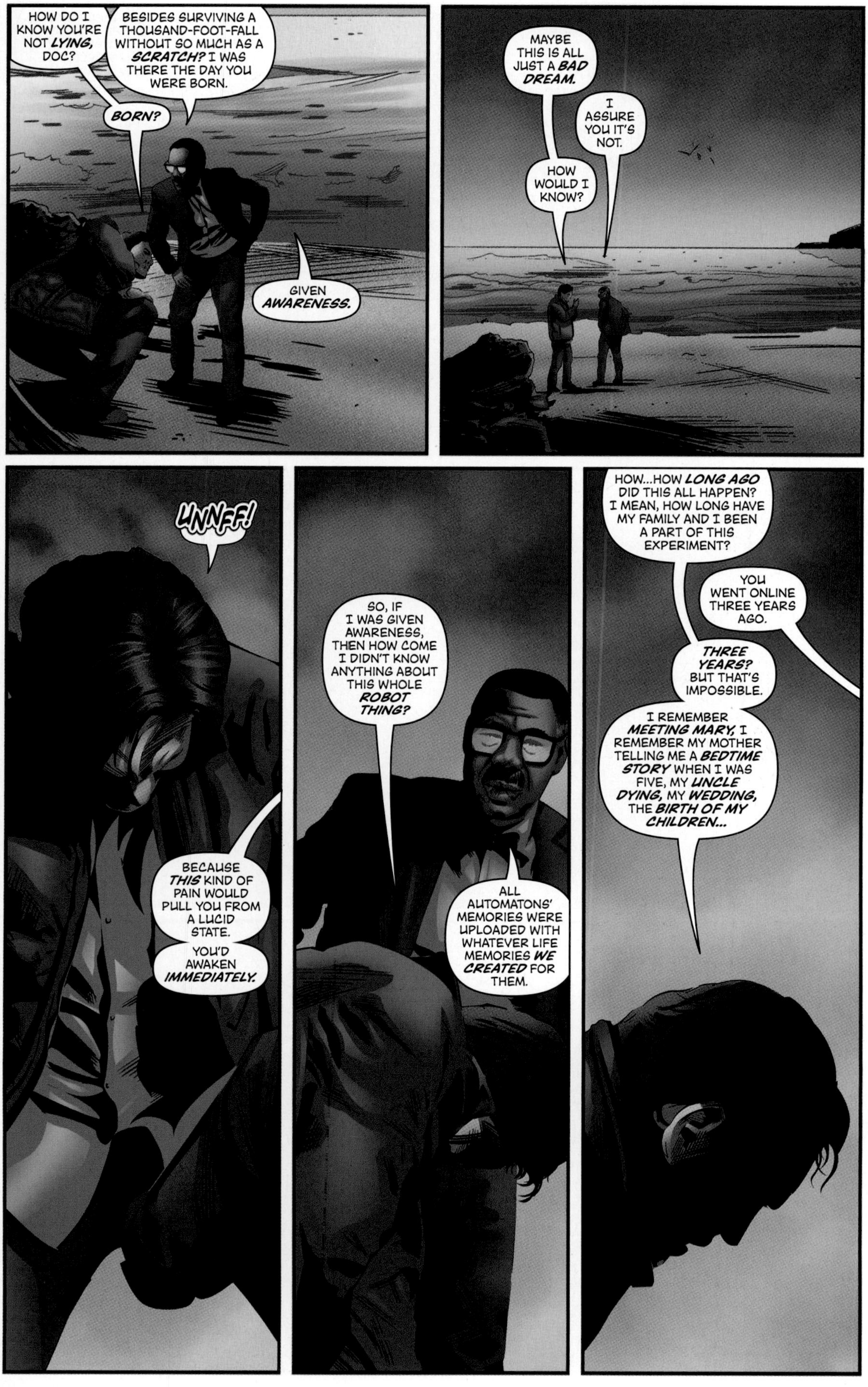

HOW DO I KNOW YOU'RE NOT *LYING,* DOC?
BESIDES SURVIVING A THOUSAND-FOOT-FALL WITHOUT SO MUCH AS A *SCRATCH?* I WAS THERE THE DAY YOU WERE BORN.
BORN?
GIVEN *AWARENESS.*
MAYBE THIS IS ALL JUST A *BAD DREAM.*
I ASSURE YOU IT'S NOT.
HOW WOULD I KNOW?
UNNFF!
BECAUSE *THIS* KIND OF PAIN WOULD PULL YOU FROM A LUCID STATE.
YOU'D AWAKEN *IMMEDIATELY.*
SO, IF I WAS GIVEN AWARENESS, THEN HOW COME I DIDN'T KNOW ANYTHING ABOUT THIS WHOLE *ROBOT THING?*
ALL AUTOMATONS' MEMORIES WERE UPLOADED WITH WHATEVER LIFE MEMORIES *WE CREATED* FOR THEM.
HOW...HOW *LONG AGO* DID THIS ALL HAPPEN? I MEAN, HOW LONG HAVE MY FAMILY AND I BEEN A PART OF THIS EXPERIMENT?
YOU WENT ONLINE THREE YEARS AGO.
THREE YEARS? BUT THAT'S IMPOSSIBLE.
I REMEMBER *MEETING MARY,* I REMEMBER MY MOTHER TELLING ME A *BEDTIME STORY* WHEN I WAS FIVE, MY *UNCLE DYING,* MY *WEDDING,* THE *BIRTH OF MY CHILDREN...*

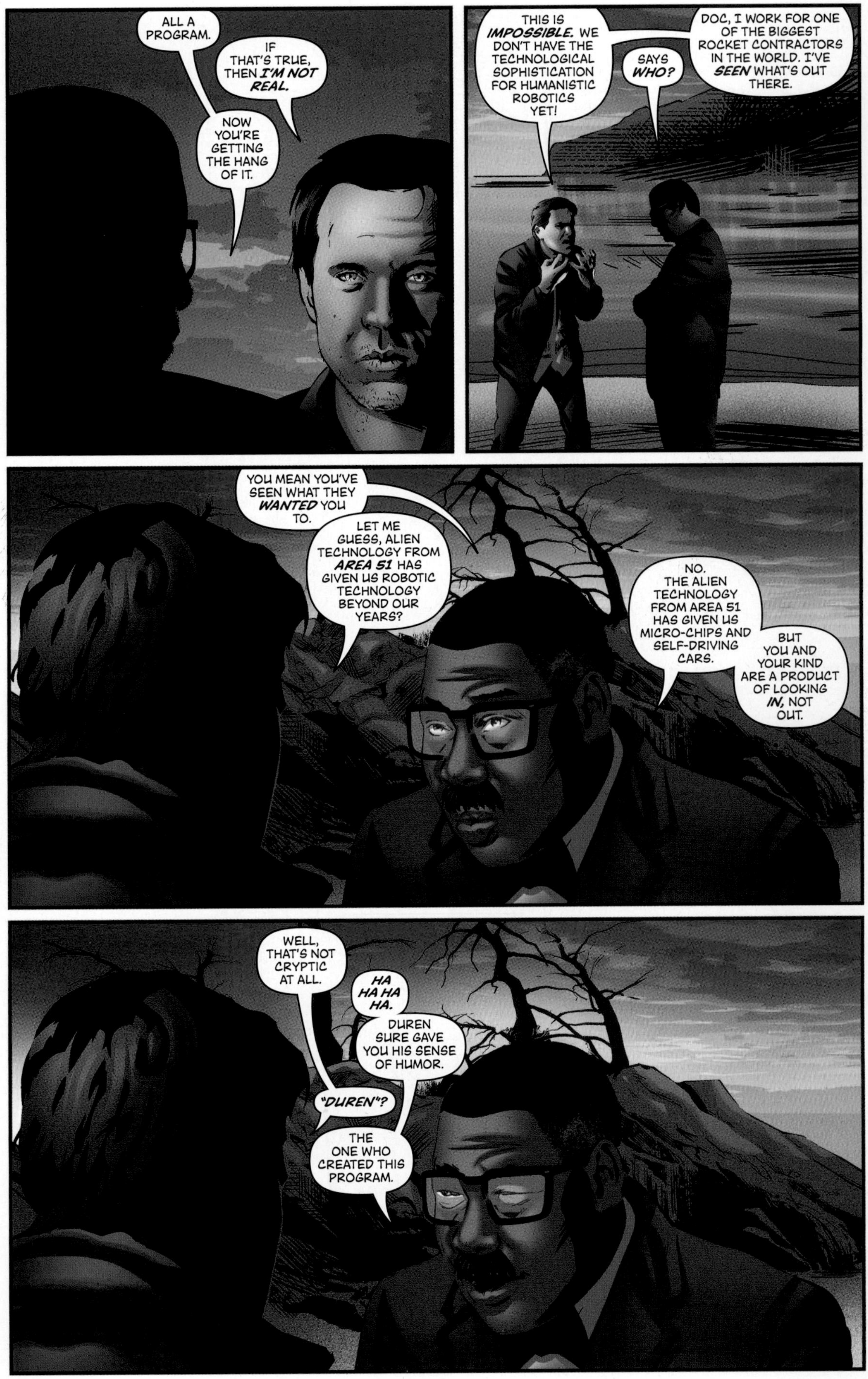
ALL A PROGRAM.
IF THAT'S TRUE, THEN *I'M NOT REAL.*
NOW YOU'RE GETTING THE HANG OF IT.
THIS IS *IMPOSSIBLE.* WE DON'T HAVE THE TECHNOLOGICAL SOPHISTICATION FOR HUMANISTIC ROBOTICS YET!
SAYS *WHO?*
DOC, I WORK FOR ONE OF THE BIGGEST ROCKET CONTRACTORS IN THE WORLD. I'VE *SEEN* WHAT'S OUT THERE.
YOU MEAN YOU'VE SEEN WHAT THEY *WANTED* YOU TO.
LET ME GUESS, ALIEN TECHNOLOGY FROM *AREA 51* HAS GIVEN US ROBOTIC TECHNOLOGY BEYOND OUR YEARS?
NO. THE ALIEN TECHNOLOGY FROM AREA 51 HAS GIVEN US MICRO-CHIPS AND SELF-DRIVING CARS.
BUT YOU AND YOUR KIND ARE A PRODUCT OF LOOKING *IN,* NOT OUT.
WELL, THAT'S NOT CRYPTIC AT ALL.
HA HA HA HA.
DUREN SURE GAVE YOU HIS SENSE OF HUMOR.
"DUREN"?
THE ONE WHO CREATED THIS PROGRAM.

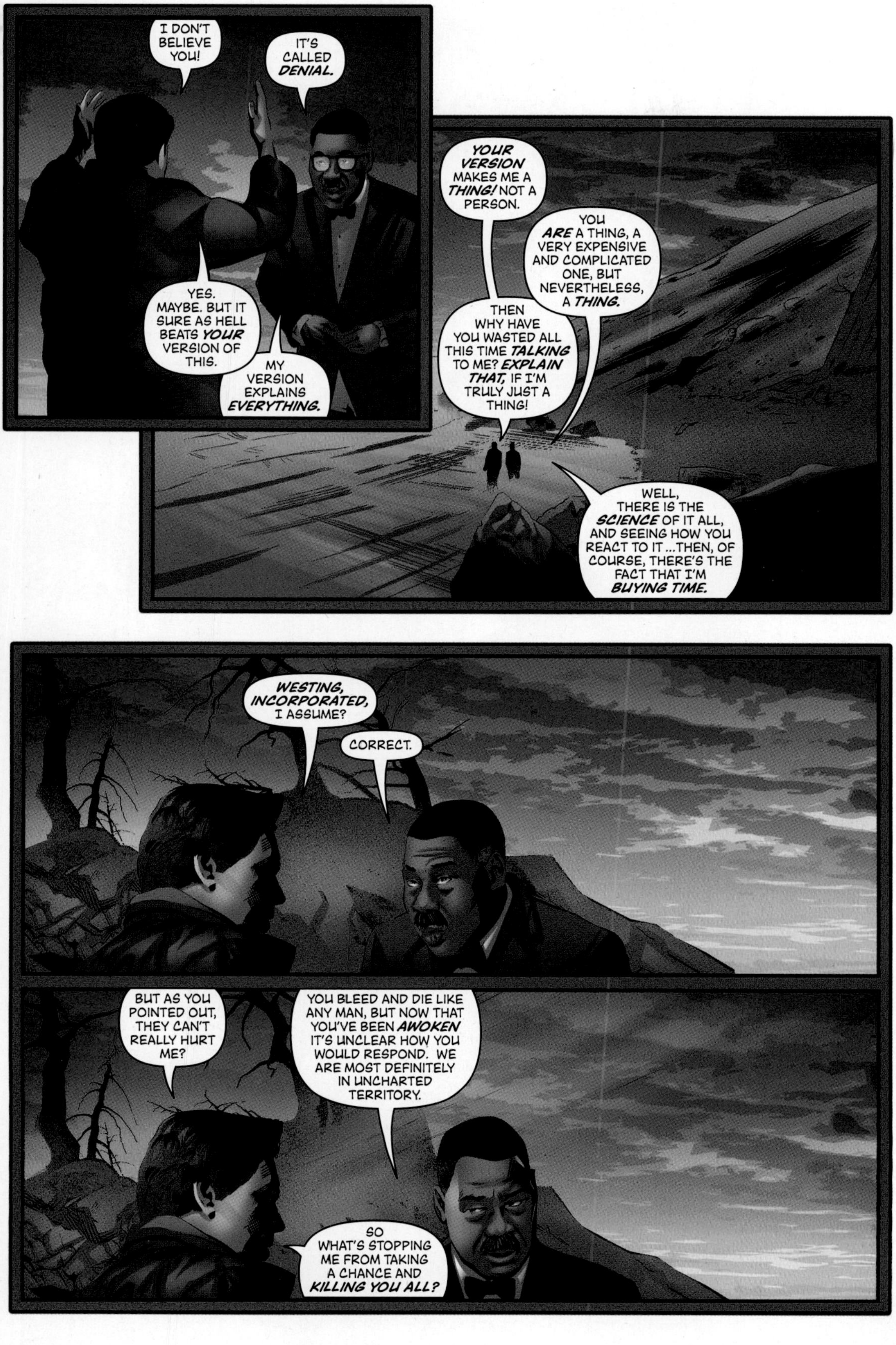
I DON'T BELIEVE YOU!
IT'S CALLED DENIAL.
YES. MAYBE. BUT IT SURE AS HELL BEATS YOUR VERSION OF THIS.
MY VERSION EXPLAINS EVERYTHING.
YOUR VERSION MAKES ME A THING! NOT A PERSON.
YOU ARE A THING, A VERY EXPENSIVE AND COMPLICATED ONE, BUT NEVERTHELESS, A THING.
THEN WHY HAVE YOU WASTED ALL THIS TIME TALKING TO ME? EXPLAIN THAT, IF I'M TRULY JUST A THING!
WELL, THERE IS THE SCIENCE OF IT ALL, AND SEEING HOW YOU REACT TO IT ...THEN, OF COURSE, THERE'S THE FACT THAT I'M BUYING TIME.
WESTING, INCORPORATED, I ASSUME?
CORRECT.
BUT AS YOU POINTED OUT, THEY CAN'T REALLY HURT ME?
YOU BLEED AND DIE LIKE ANY MAN, BUT NOW THAT YOU'VE BEEN AWOKEN IT'S UNCLEAR HOW YOU WOULD RESPOND. WE ARE MOST DEFINITELY IN UNCHARTED TERRITORY.
SO WHAT'S STOPPING ME FROM TAKING A CHANCE AND KILLING YOU ALL?

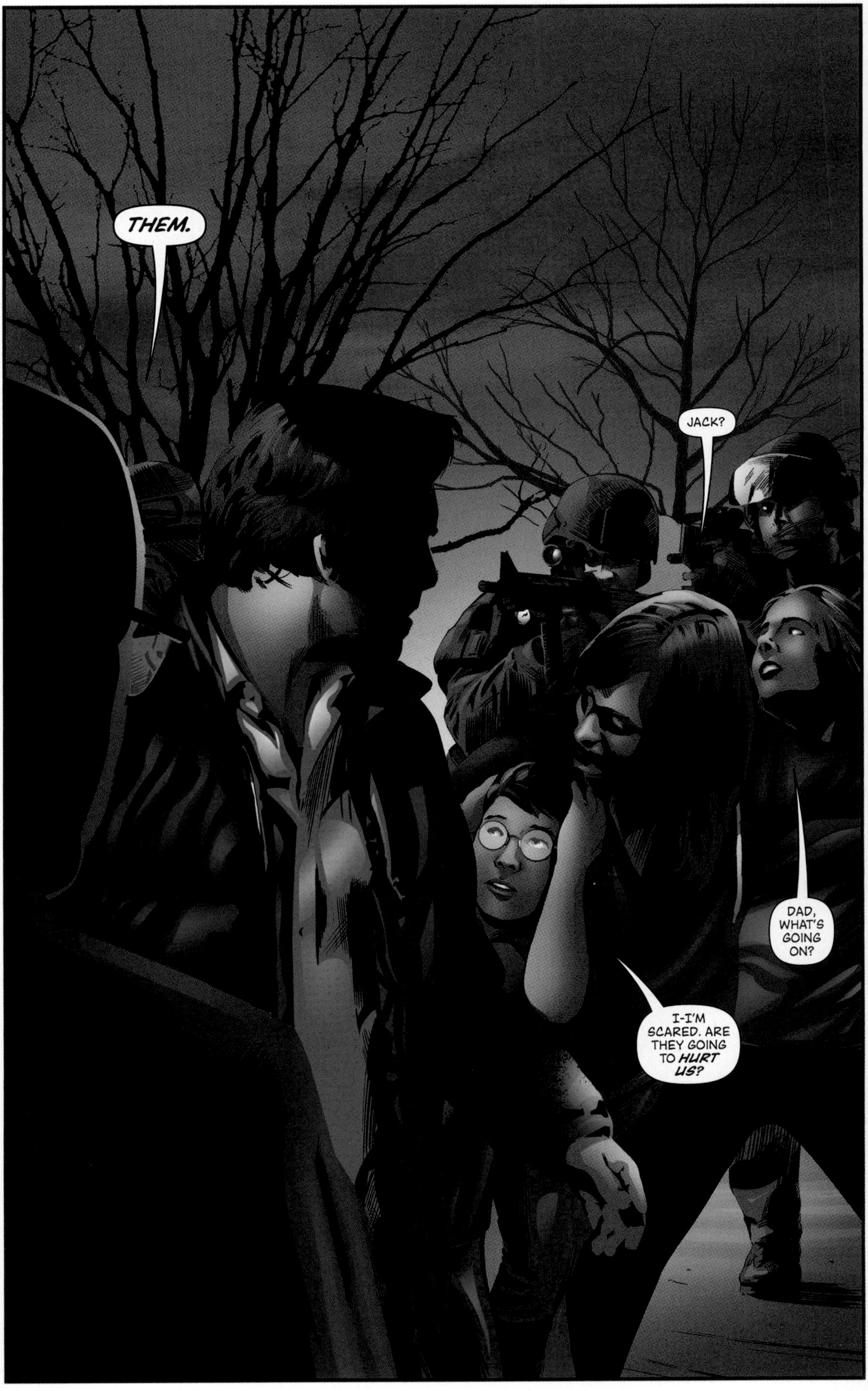
THEM.
JACK?
DAD, WHAT'S GOING ON?
I-I'M SCARED. ARE THEY GOING TO *HURT US?*

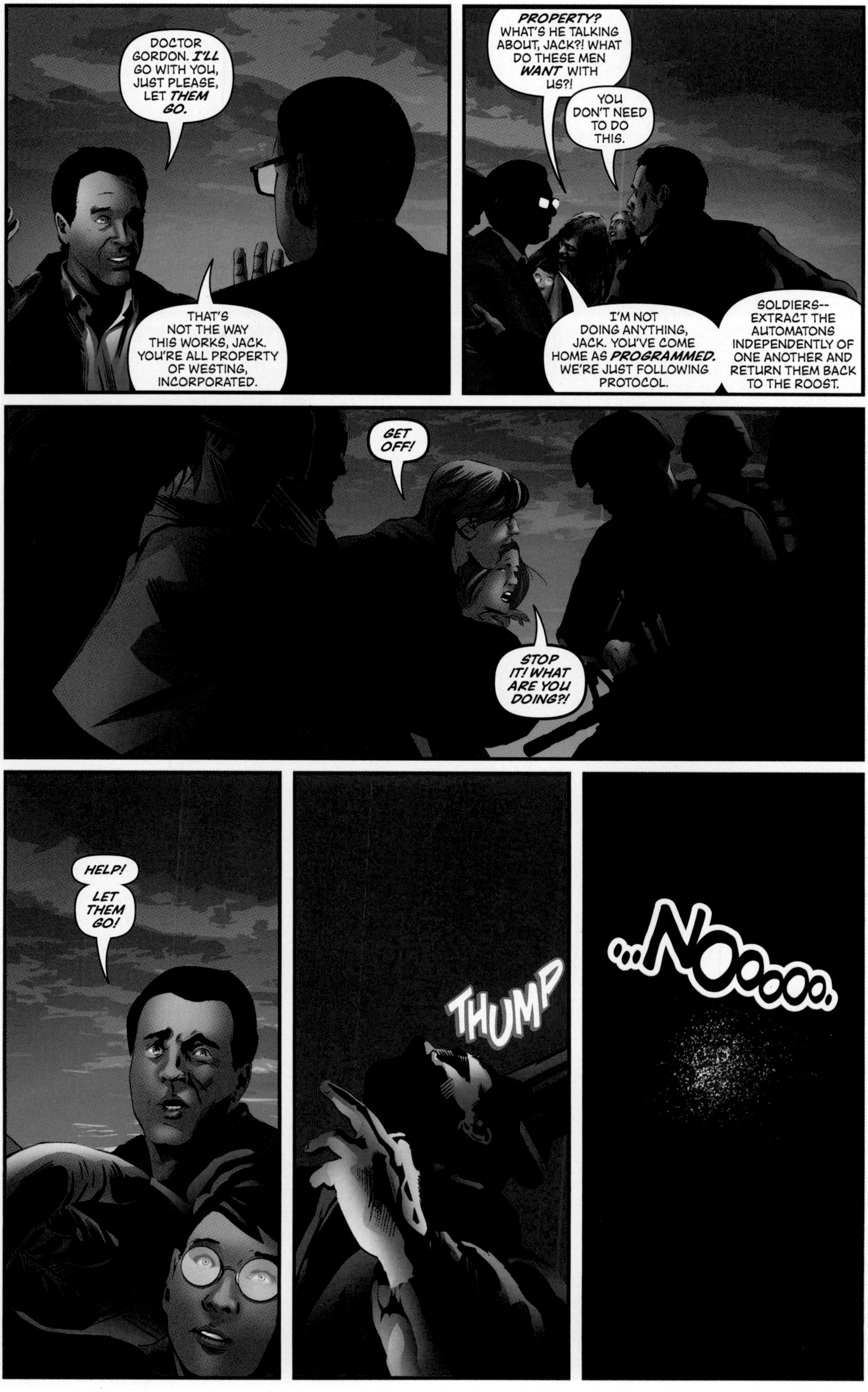
DOCTOR GORDON. I'LL GO WITH YOU, JUST PLEASE, LET THEM GO.
THAT'S NOT THE WAY THIS WORKS, JACK. YOU'RE ALL PROPERTY OF WESTING, INCORPORATED.
PROPERTY? WHAT'S HE TALKING ABOUT, JACK?! WHAT DO THESE MEN WANT WITH US?!
YOU DON'T NEED TO DO THIS.
I'M NOT DOING ANYTHING, JACK. YOU'VE COME HOME AS PROGRAMMED. WE'RE JUST FOLLOWING PROTOCOL.
SOLDIERS-- EXTRACT THE AUTOMATONS INDEPENDENTLY OF ONE ANOTHER AND RETURN THEM BACK TO THE ROOST.
GET OFF!
STOP IT! WHAT ARE YOU DOING?!
HELP! LET THEM GO!
THUMP
...NOooooo.

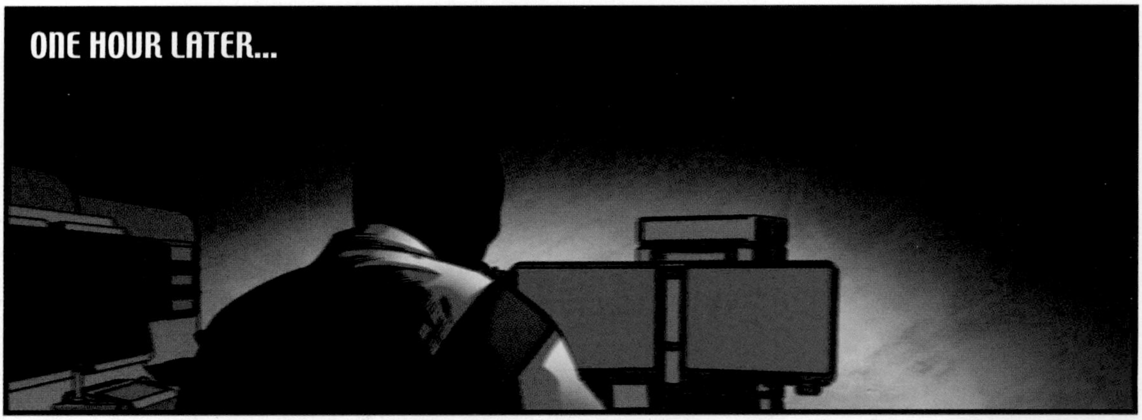
ONE HOUR LATER...

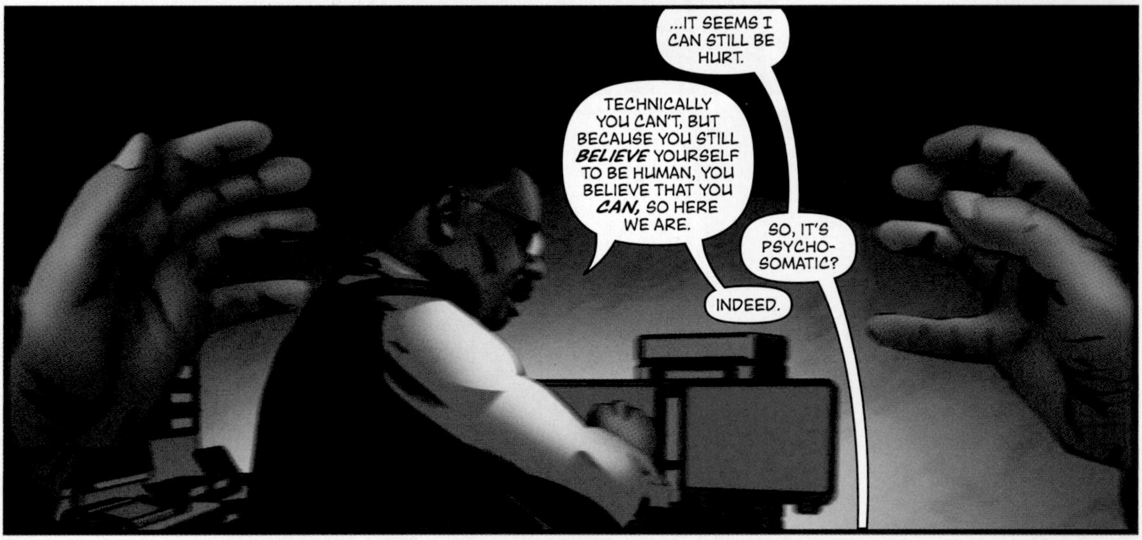
...IT SEEMS I CAN STILL BE HURT.
TECHNICALLY YOU CAN'T, BUT BECAUSE YOU STILL BELIEVE YOURSELF TO BE HUMAN, YOU BELIEVE THAT YOU CAN, SO HERE WE ARE.
SO, IT'S PSYCHO-SOMATIC?
INDEED.

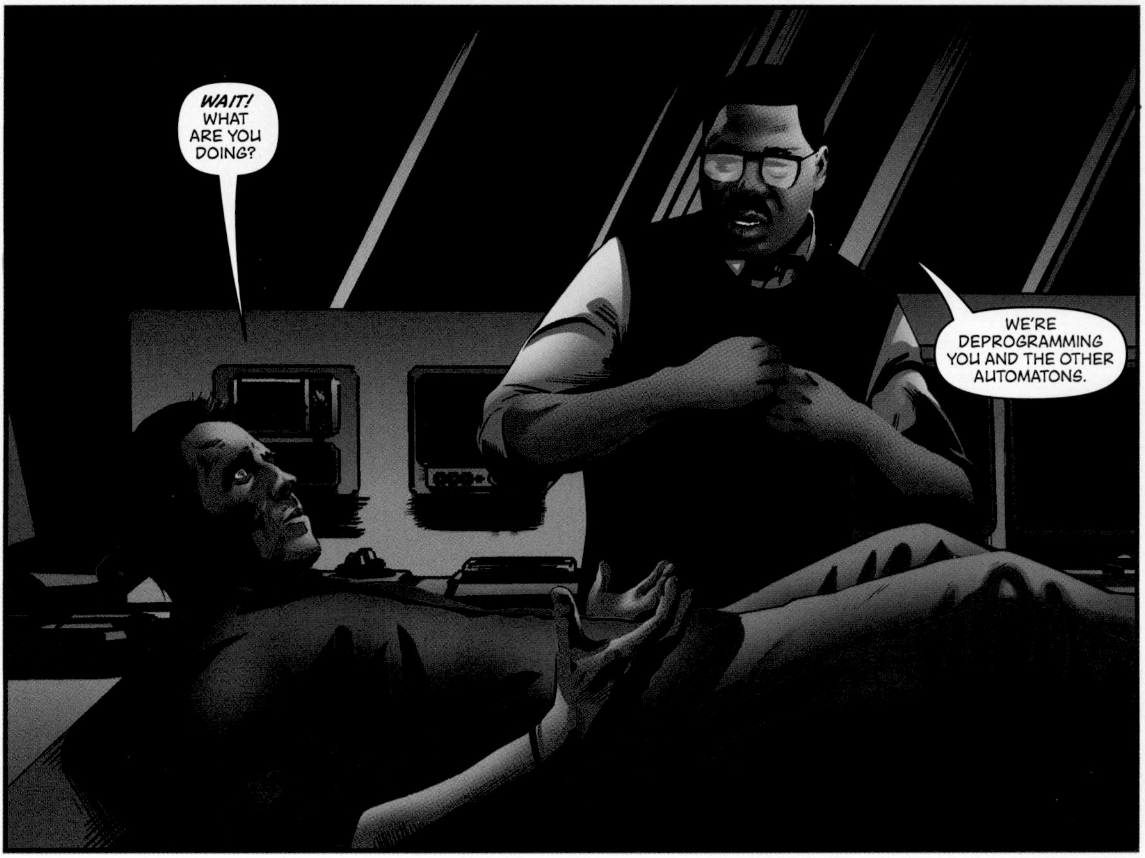
WAIT! WHAT ARE YOU DOING?
WE'RE DEPROGRAMMING YOU AND THE OTHER AUTOMATONS.

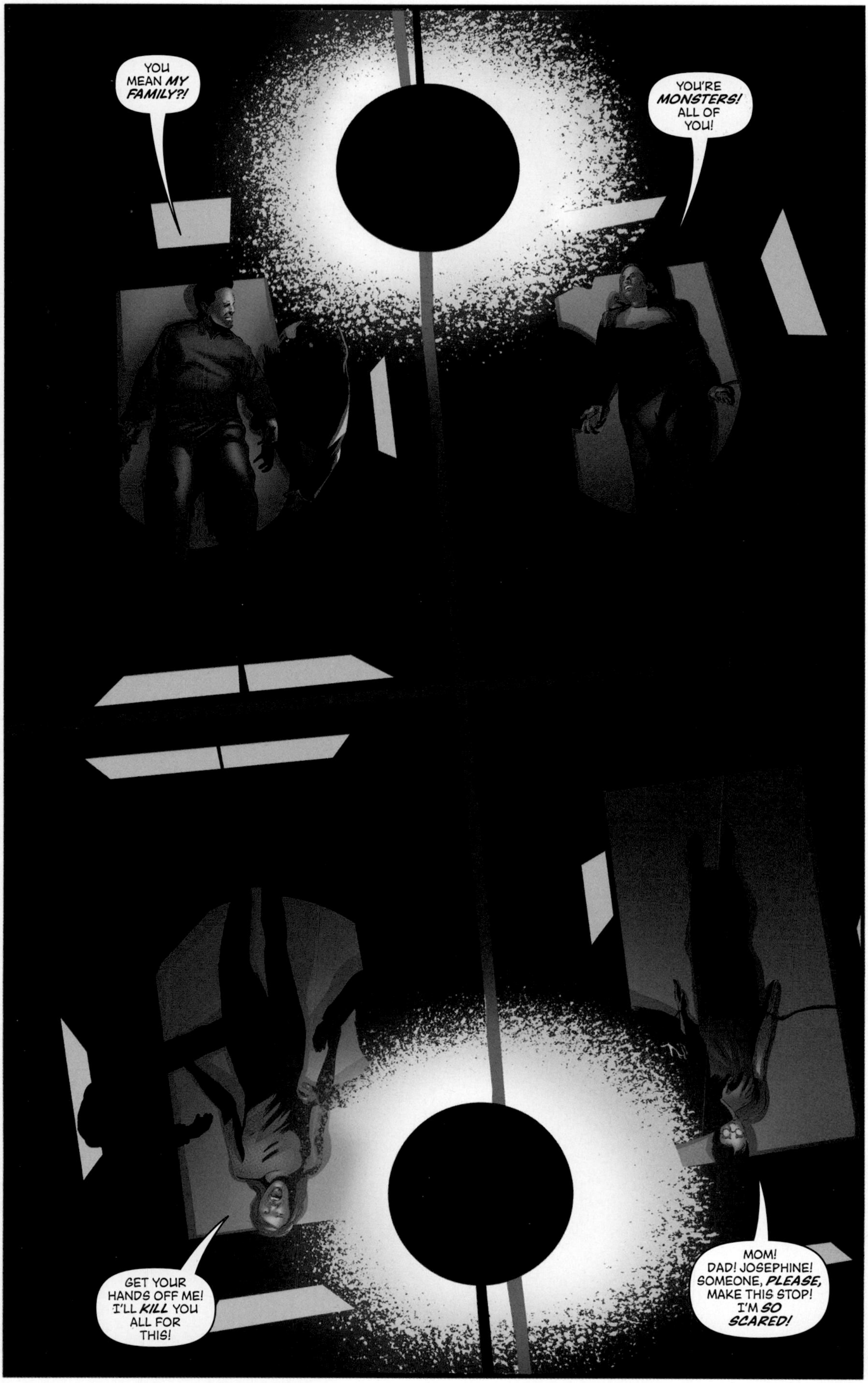

YOU MEAN MY FAMILY?!
YOU'RE MONSTERS! ALL OF YOU!
GET YOUR HANDS OFF ME! I'LL KILL YOU ALL FOR THIS!
MOM! DAD! JOSEPHINE! SOMEONE, PLEASE, MAKE THIS STOP! I'M SO SCARED!

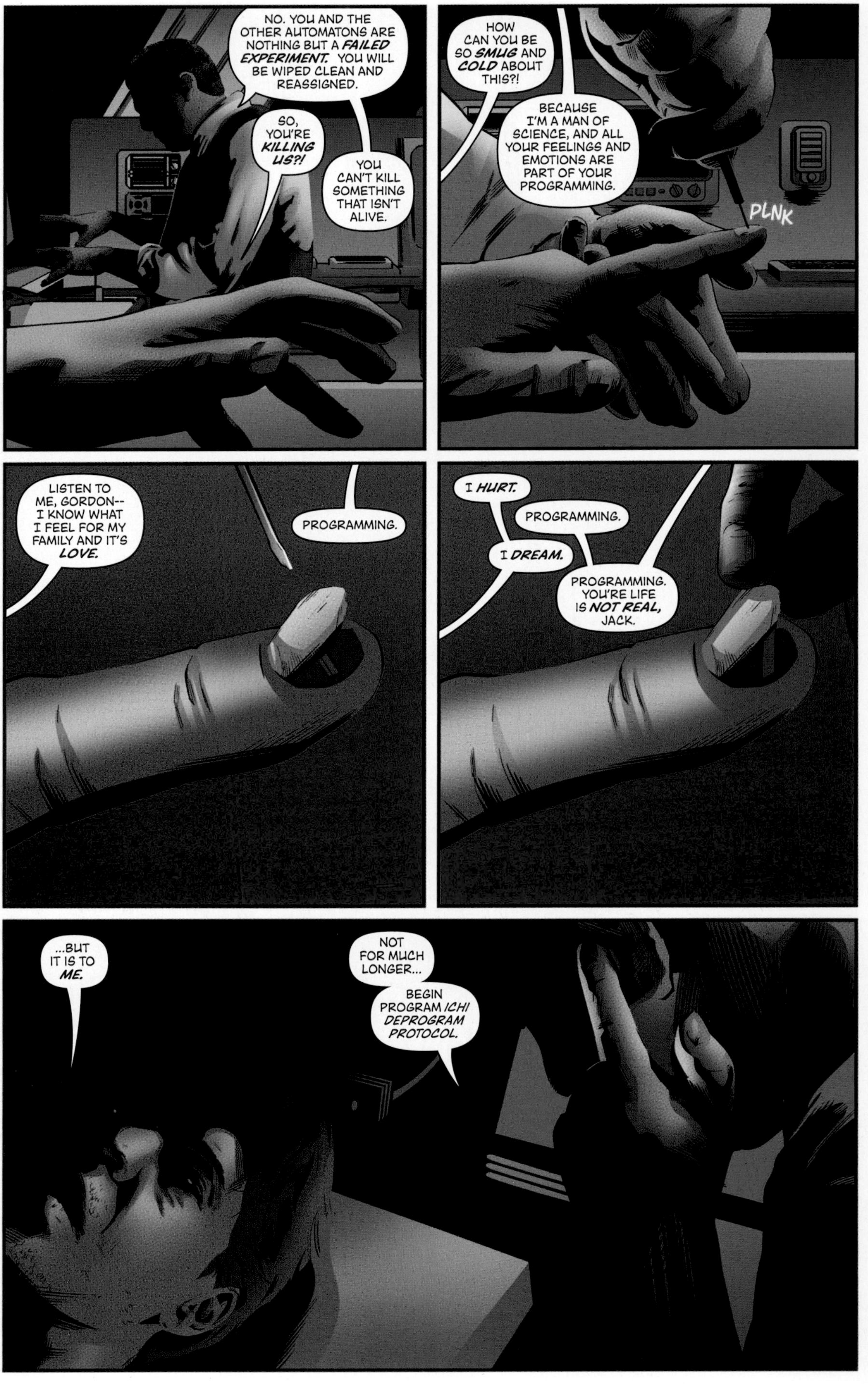
NO. YOU AND THE OTHER AUTOMATONS ARE NOTHING BUT A FAILED EXPERIMENT. YOU WILL BE WIPED CLEAN AND REASSIGNED.
SO, YOU'RE KILLING US?!
YOU CAN'T KILL SOMETHING THAT ISN'T ALIVE.
HOW CAN YOU BE SO SMUG AND COLD ABOUT THIS?!
BECAUSE I'M A MAN OF SCIENCE, AND ALL YOUR FEELINGS AND EMOTIONS ARE PART OF YOUR PROGRAMMING.
PLNK
LISTEN TO ME, GORDON-- I KNOW WHAT I FEEL FOR MY FAMILY AND IT'S LOVE.
PROGRAMMING.
I HURT.
PROGRAMMING.
I DREAM.
PROGRAMMING. YOU'RE LIFE IS NOT REAL, JACK.
...BUT IT IS TO ME.
NOT FOR MUCH LONGER...
BEGIN PROGRAM ICHI DEPROGRAM PROTOCOL.

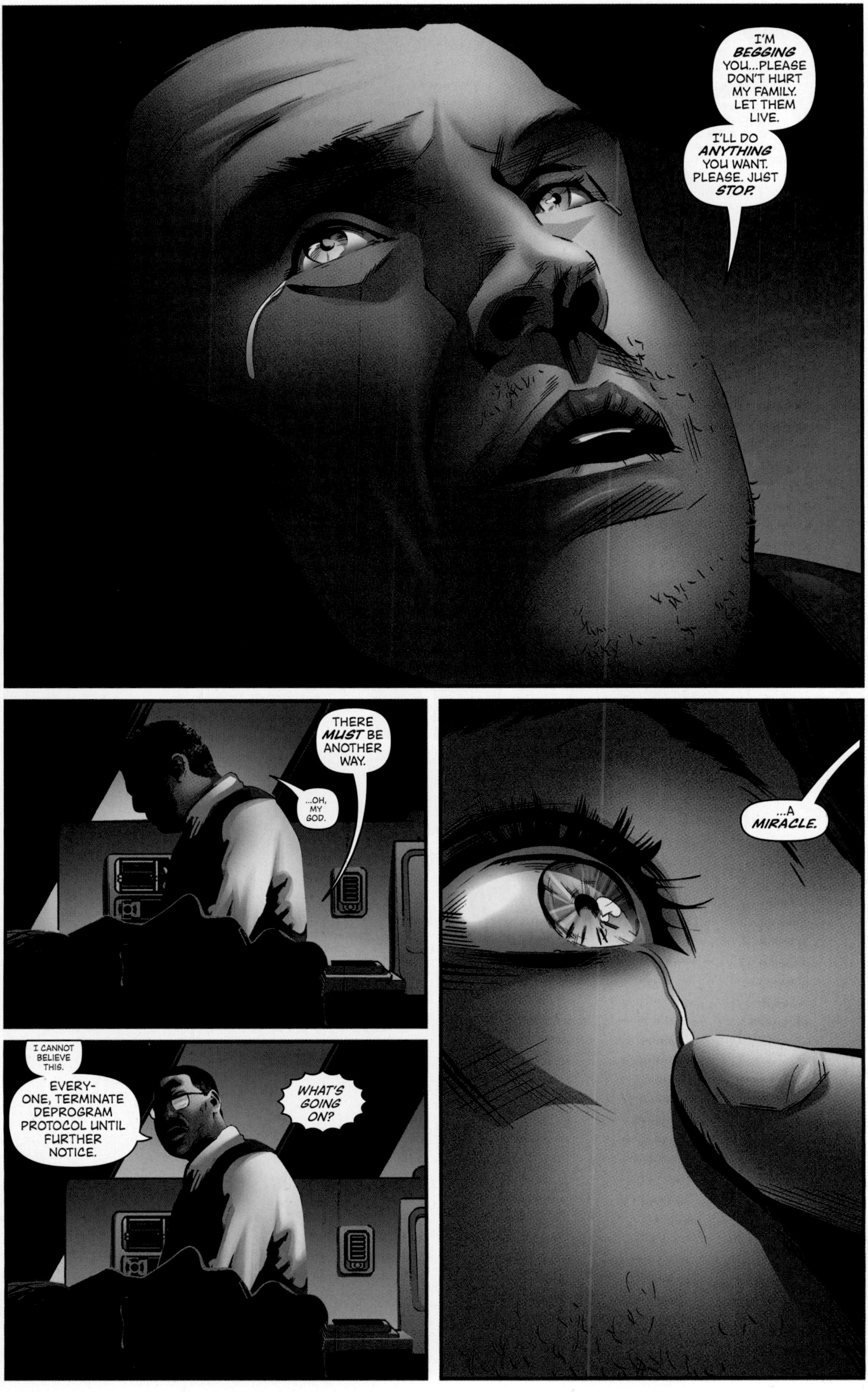
I'M *BEGGING* YOU...PLEASE DON'T HURT MY FAMILY. LET THEM LIVE.
I'LL DO *ANYTHING* YOU WANT. PLEASE. JUST *STOP.*
THERE *MUST* BE ANOTHER WAY.
...OH, MY GOD.
I CANNOT BELIEVE THIS.
EVERY-ONE, TERMINATE DEPROGRAM PROTOCOL UNTIL FURTHER NOTICE.
WHAT'S GOING ON?
...A *MIRACLE.*

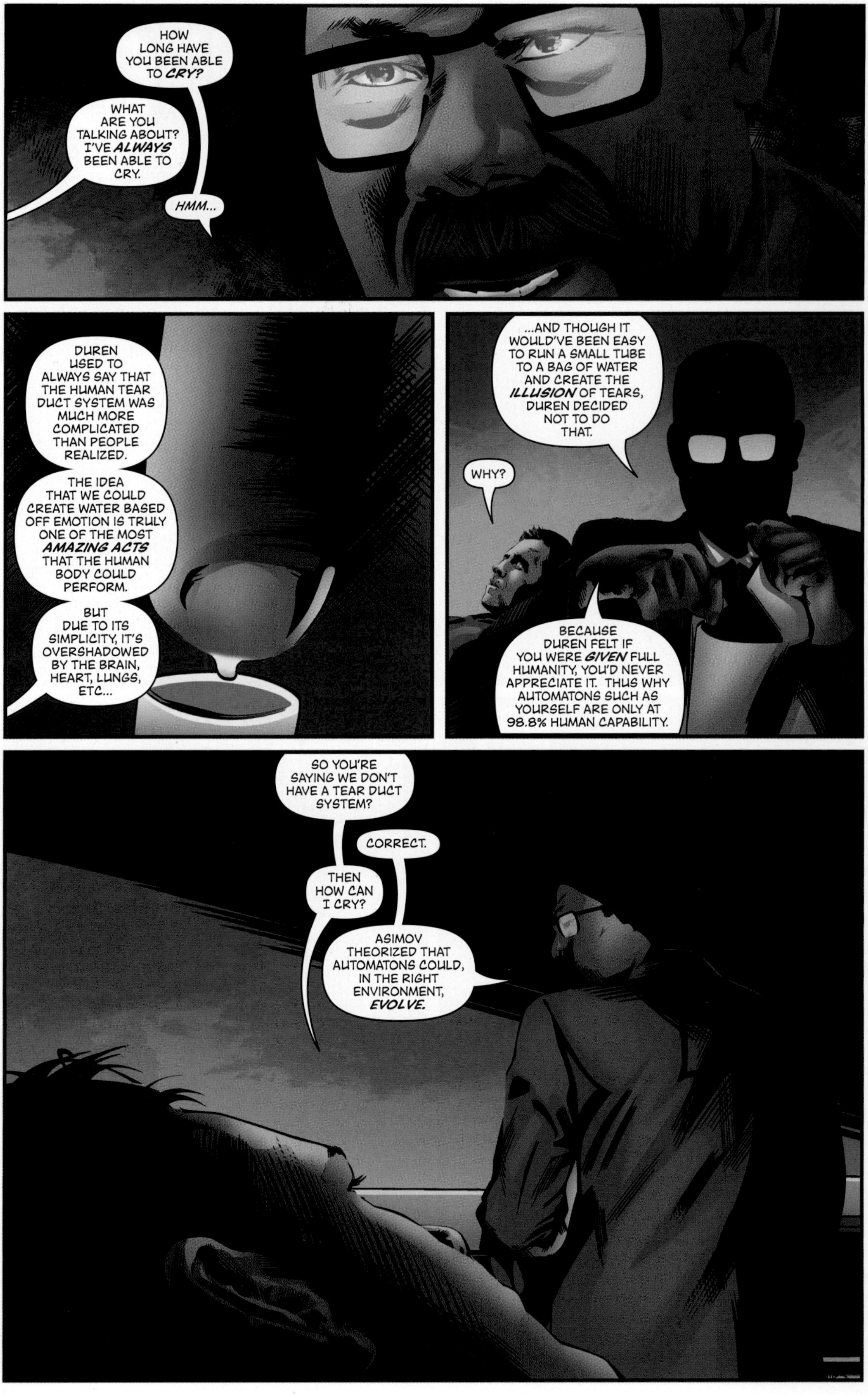
HOW LONG HAVE YOU BEEN ABLE TO CRY?
WHAT ARE YOU TALKING ABOUT? I'VE ALWAYS BEEN ABLE TO CRY.
HMM...
DUREN USED TO ALWAYS SAY THAT THE HUMAN TEAR DUCT SYSTEM WAS MUCH MORE COMPLICATED THAN PEOPLE REALIZED.
THE IDEA THAT WE COULD CREATE WATER BASED OFF EMOTION IS TRULY ONE OF THE MOST AMAZING ACTS THAT THE HUMAN BODY COULD PERFORM.
BUT DUE TO ITS SIMPLICITY, IT'S OVERSHADOWED BY THE BRAIN, HEART, LUNGS, ETC...
...AND THOUGH IT WOULD'VE BEEN EASY TO RUN A SMALL TUBE TO A BAG OF WATER AND CREATE THE ILLUSION OF TEARS, DUREN DECIDED NOT TO DO THAT.
WHY?
BECAUSE DUREN FELT IF YOU WERE GIVEN FULL HUMANITY, YOU'D NEVER APPRECIATE IT. THUS WHY AUTOMATONS SUCH AS YOURSELF ARE ONLY AT 98.8% HUMAN CAPABILITY.
SO YOU'RE SAYING WE DON'T HAVE A TEAR DUCT SYSTEM?
CORRECT.
THEN HOW CAN I CRY?
ASIMOV THEORIZED THAT AUTOMATONS COULD, IN THE RIGHT ENVIRONMENT, EVOLVE.

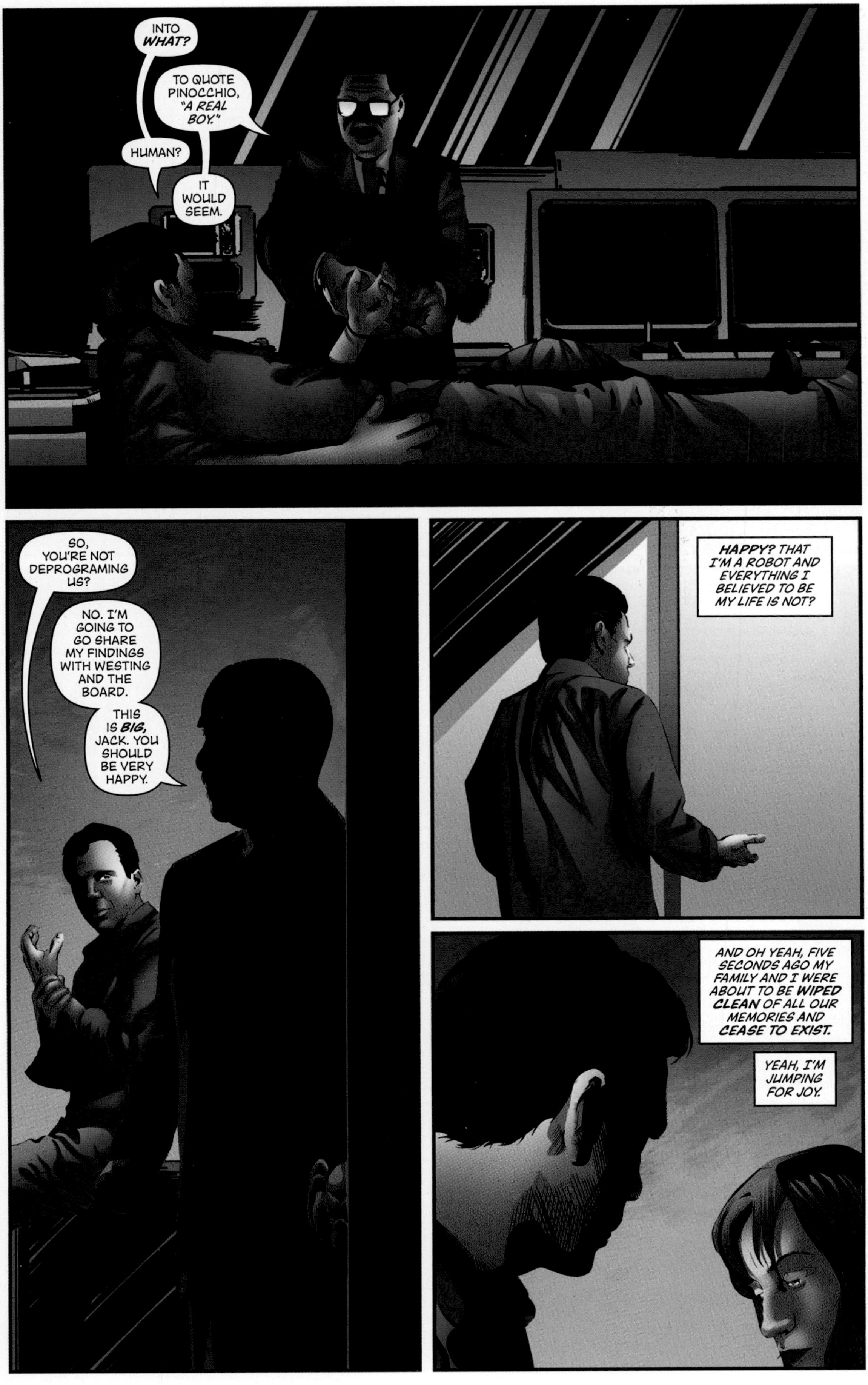
INTO WHAT?
TO QUOTE PINOCCHIO, "A REAL BOY."
HUMAN?
IT WOULD SEEM.
SO, YOU'RE NOT DEPROGRAMING US?
NO. I'M GOING TO GO SHARE MY FINDINGS WITH WESTING AND THE BOARD.
THIS IS BIG, JACK. YOU SHOULD BE VERY HAPPY.
HAPPY? THAT I'M A ROBOT AND EVERYTHING I BELIEVED TO BE MY LIFE IS NOT?
AND OH YEAH, FIVE SECONDS AGO MY FAMILY AND I WERE ABOUT TO BE WIPED CLEAN OF ALL OUR MEMORIES AND CEASE TO EXIST.
YEAH, I'M JUMPING FOR JOY.

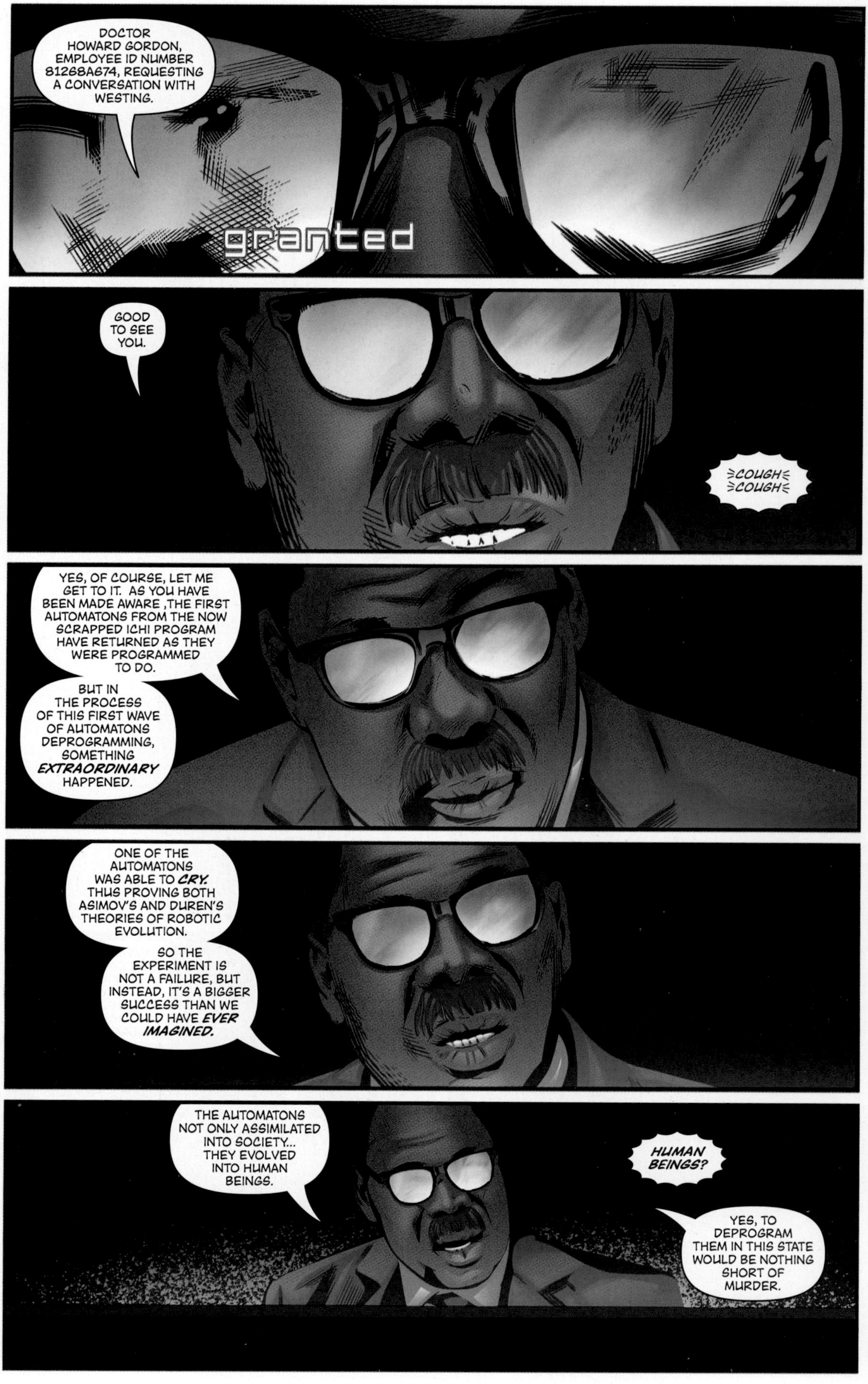
DOCTOR HOWARD GORDON, EMPLOYEE ID NUMBER 81268A674, REQUESTING A CONVERSATION WITH WESTING.
granted
GOOD TO SEE YOU.
COUGH COUGH
YES, OF COURSE, LET ME GET TO IT. AS YOU HAVE BEEN MADE AWARE ,THE FIRST AUTOMATONS FROM THE NOW SCRAPPED ICHI PROGRAM HAVE RETURNED AS THEY WERE PROGRAMMED TO DO.
BUT IN THE PROCESS OF THIS FIRST WAVE OF AUTOMATONS DEPROGRAMMING, SOMETHING EXTRAORDINARY HAPPENED.
ONE OF THE AUTOMATONS WAS ABLE TO CRY. THUS PROVING BOTH ASIMOV'S AND DUREN'S THEORIES OF ROBOTIC EVOLUTION.
SO THE EXPERIMENT IS NOT A FAILURE, BUT INSTEAD, IT'S A BIGGER SUCCESS THAN WE COULD HAVE EVER IMAGINED.
THE AUTOMATONS NOT ONLY ASSIMILATED INTO SOCIETY... THEY EVOLVED INTO HUMAN BEINGS.
HUMAN BEINGS?
YES, TO DEPROGRAM THEM IN THIS STATE WOULD BE NOTHING SHORT OF MURDER.

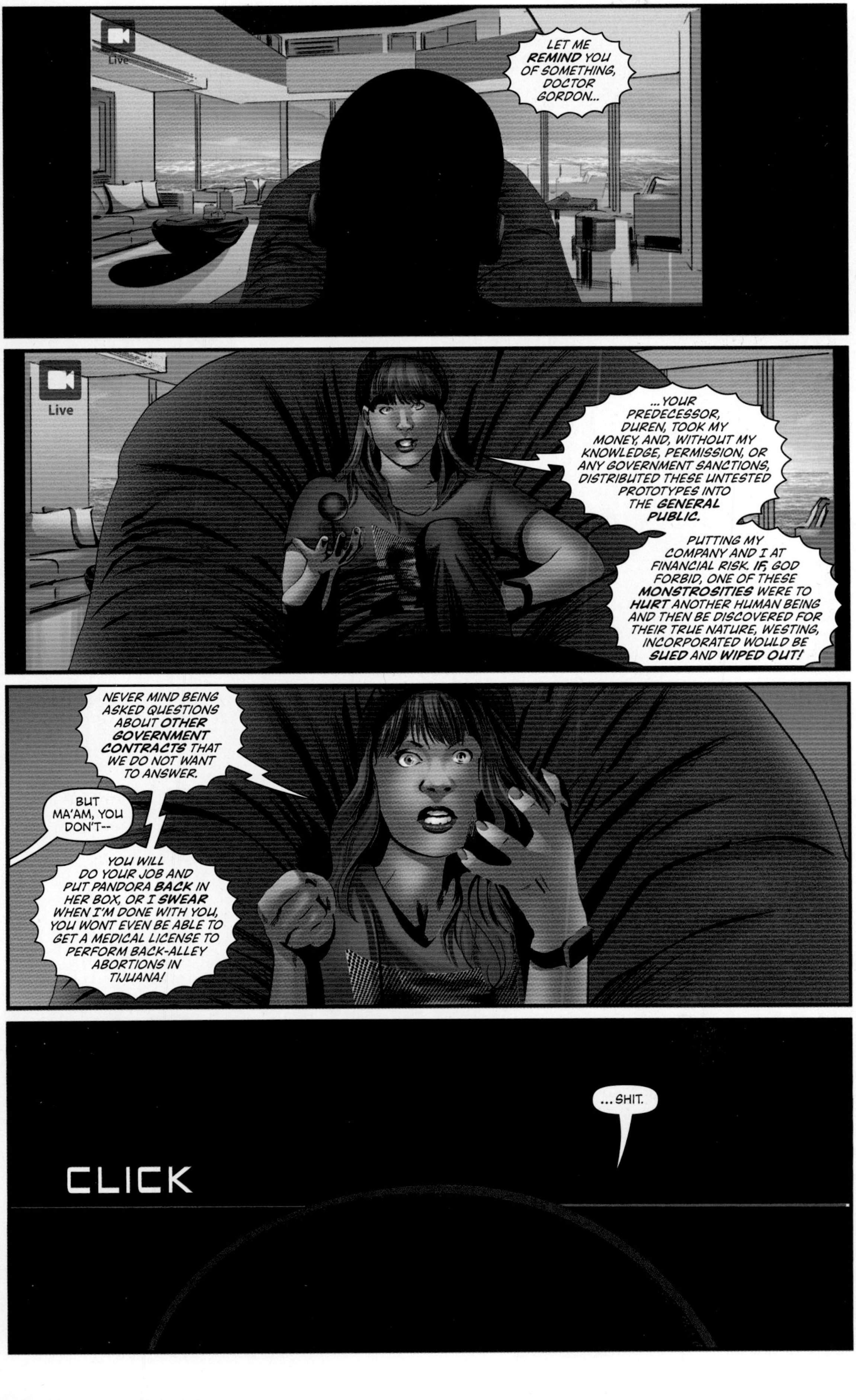
Live
LET ME REMIND YOU OF SOMETHING, DOCTOR GORDON...
Live
...YOUR PREDECESSOR, DUREN, TOOK MY MONEY, AND, WITHOUT MY KNOWLEDGE, PERMISSION, OR ANY GOVERNMENT SANCTIONS, DISTRIBUTED THESE UNTESTED PROTOTYPES INTO THE GENERAL PUBLIC.
PUTTING MY COMPANY AND I AT FINANCIAL RISK. IF, GOD FORBID, ONE OF THESE MONSTROSITIES WERE TO HURT ANOTHER HUMAN BEING AND THEN BE DISCOVERED FOR THEIR TRUE NATURE, WESTING, INCORPORATED WOULD BE SUED AND WIPED OUT!
NEVER MIND BEING ASKED QUESTIONS ABOUT OTHER GOVERNMENT CONTRACTS THAT WE DO NOT WANT TO ANSWER.
BUT MA'AM, YOU DON'T--
YOU WILL DO YOUR JOB AND PUT PANDORA BACK IN HER BOX, OR I SWEAR WHEN I'M DONE WITH YOU, YOU WONT EVEN BE ABLE TO GET A MEDICAL LICENSE TO PERFORM BACK-ALLEY ABORTIONS IN TIJUANA!
...SHIT.
CLICK

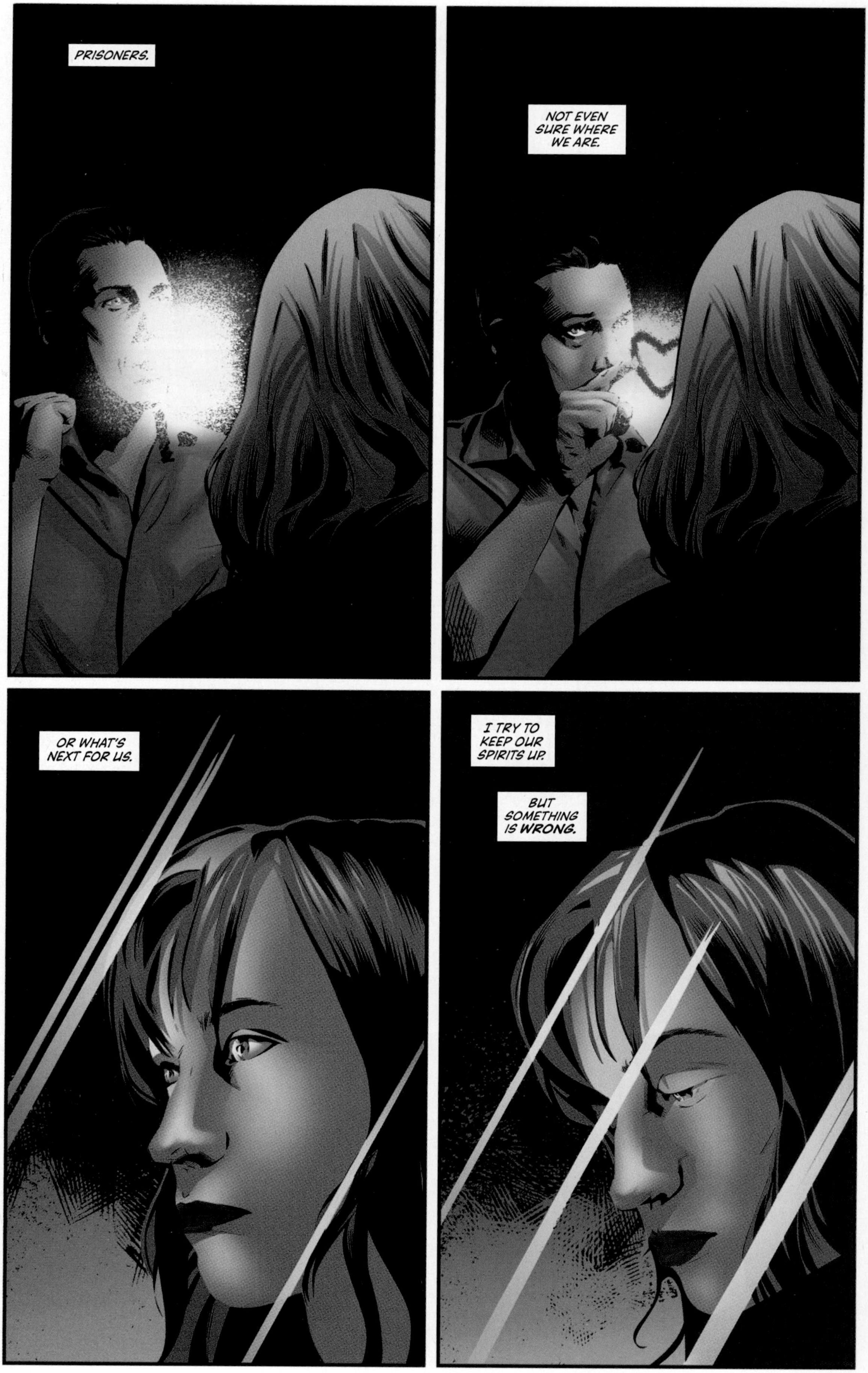
PRISONERS.
NOT EVEN SURE WHERE WE ARE.
OR WHAT'S NEXT FOR US.
I TRY TO KEEP OUR SPIRITS UP.
BUT SOMETHING IS WRONG.

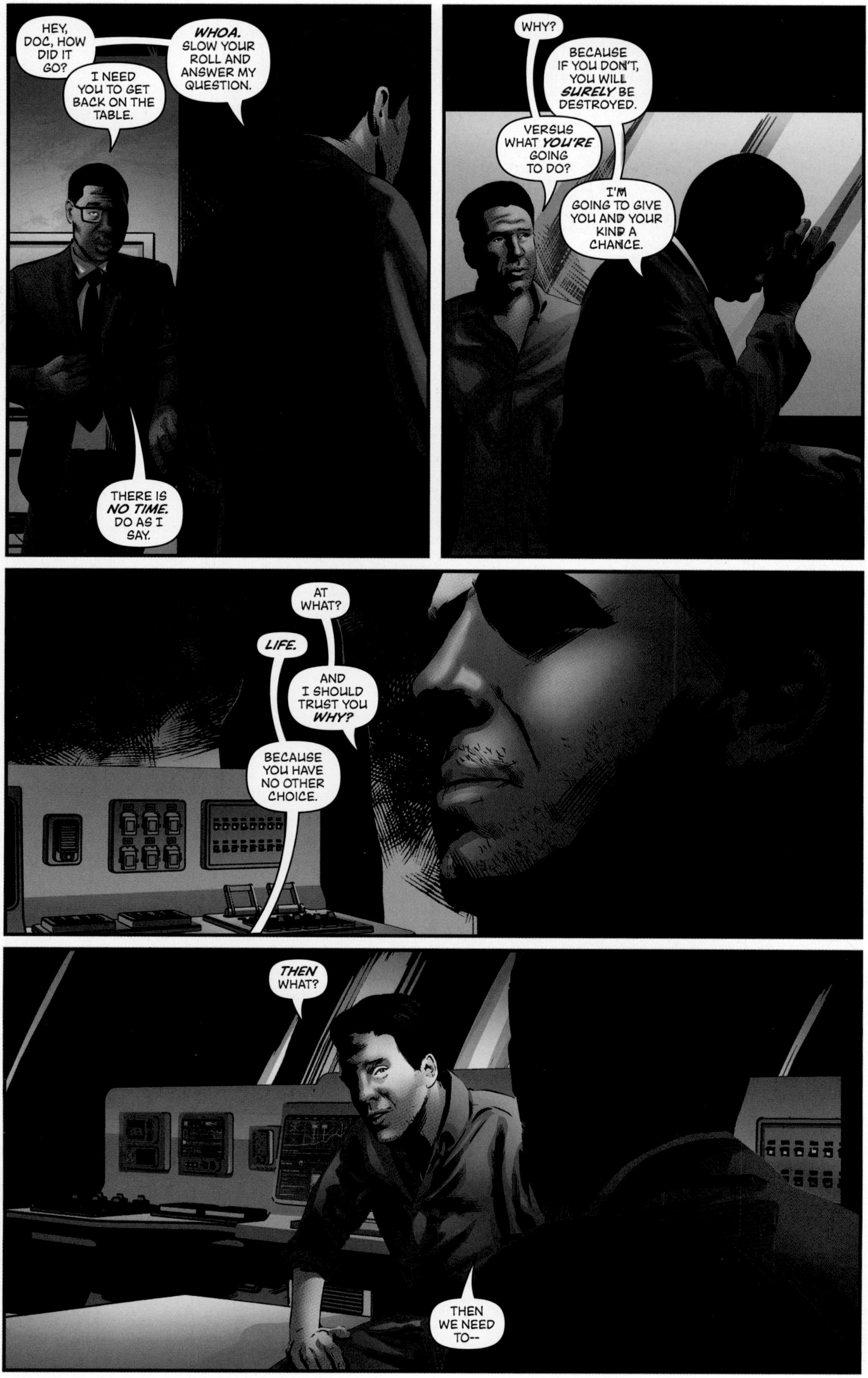
HEY, DOC, HOW DID IT GO?
I NEED YOU TO GET BACK ON THE TABLE.
WHOA. SLOW YOUR ROLL AND ANSWER MY QUESTION.
THERE IS NO TIME. DO AS I SAY.
WHY?
BECAUSE IF YOU DON'T, YOU WILL SURELY BE DESTROYED.
VERSUS WHAT YOU'RE GOING TO DO?
I'M GOING TO GIVE YOU AND YOUR KIND A CHANCE.
AT WHAT?
LIFE.
AND I SHOULD TRUST YOU WHY?
BECAUSE YOU HAVE NO OTHER CHOICE.
THEN WHAT?
THEN WE NEED TO--

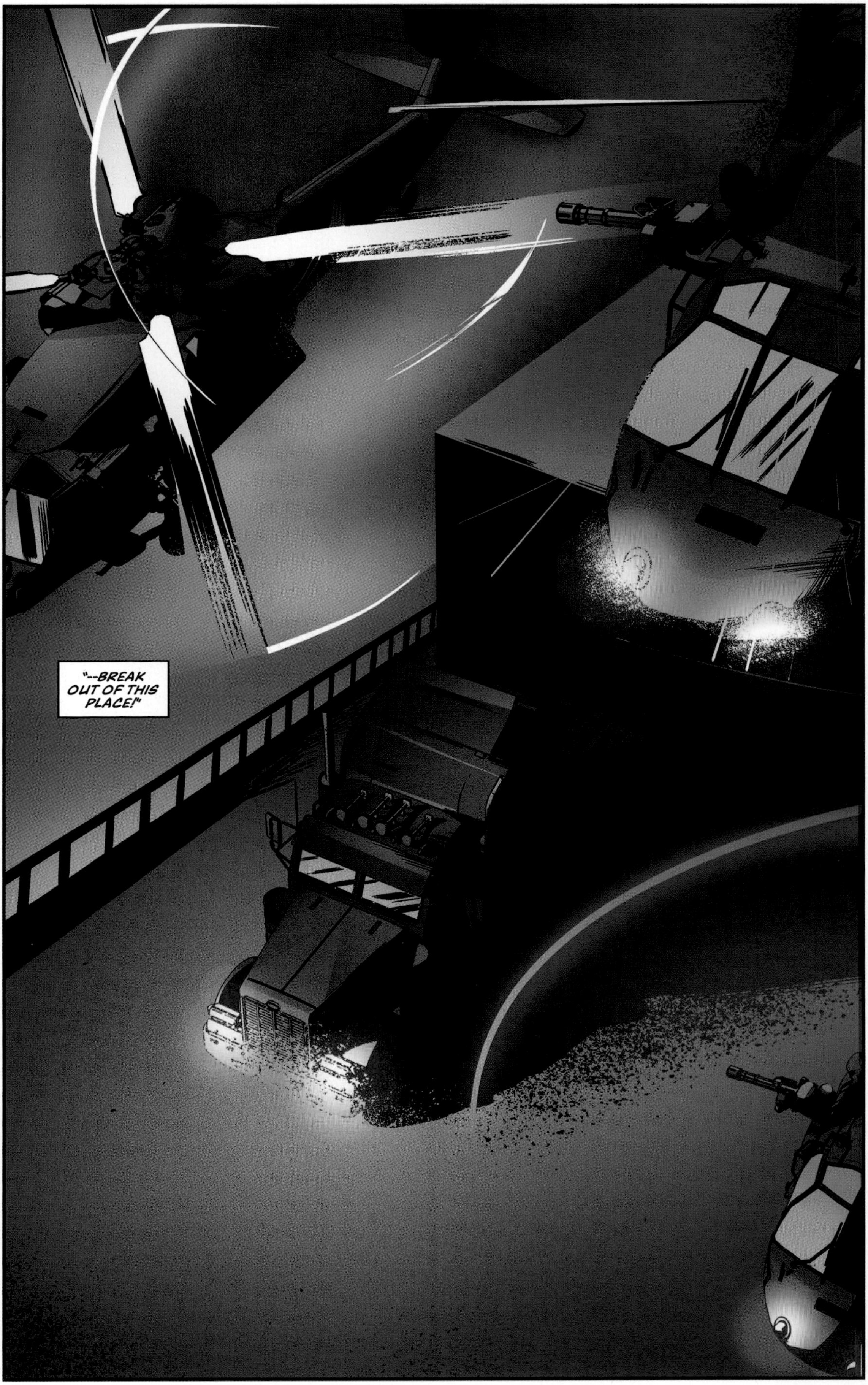
"--BREAK OUT OF THIS PLACE!"

3

"AND SHE WAS"

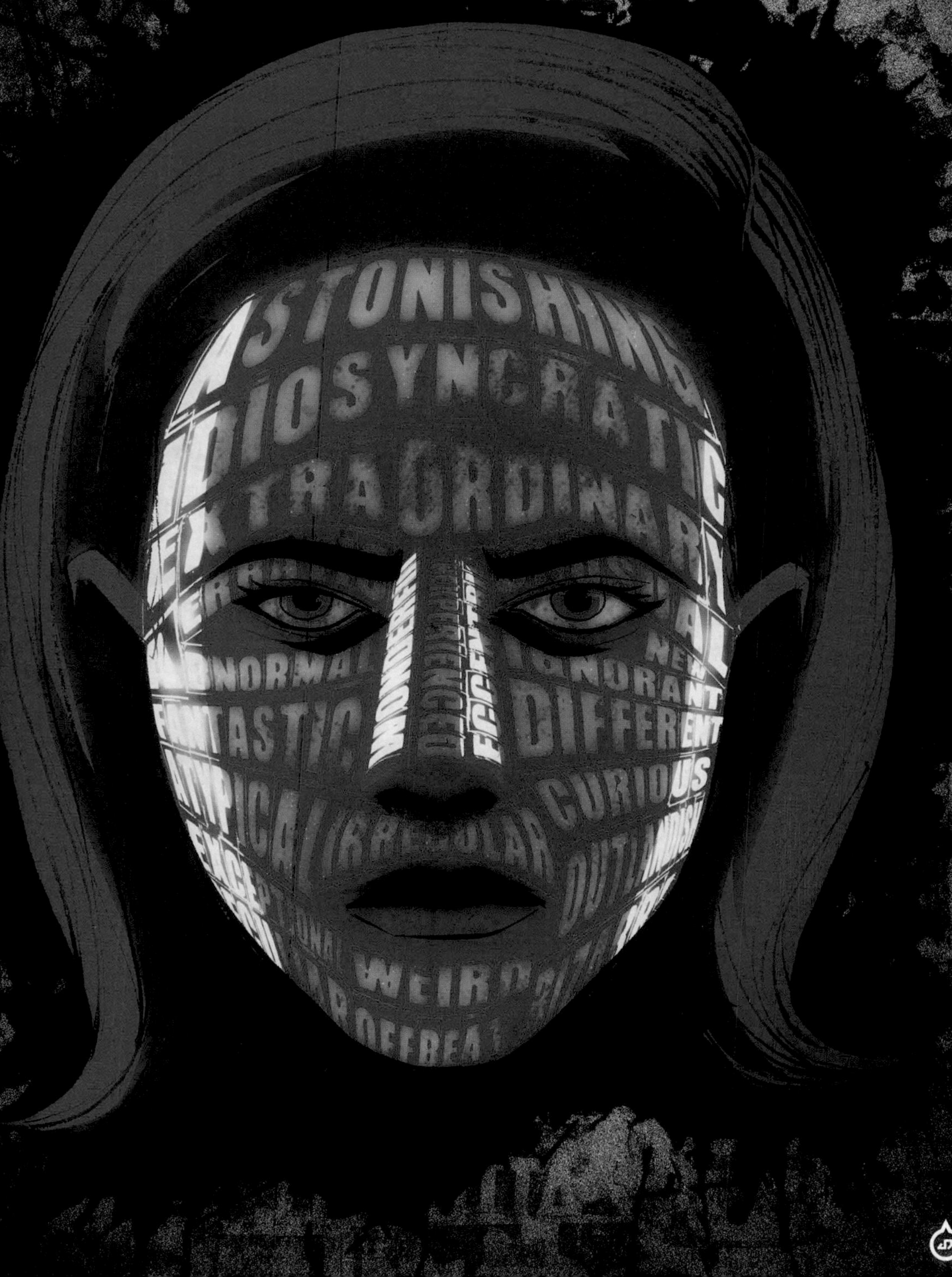
IDIOSYNCRATIC
DIFFERENT
CURIOUS

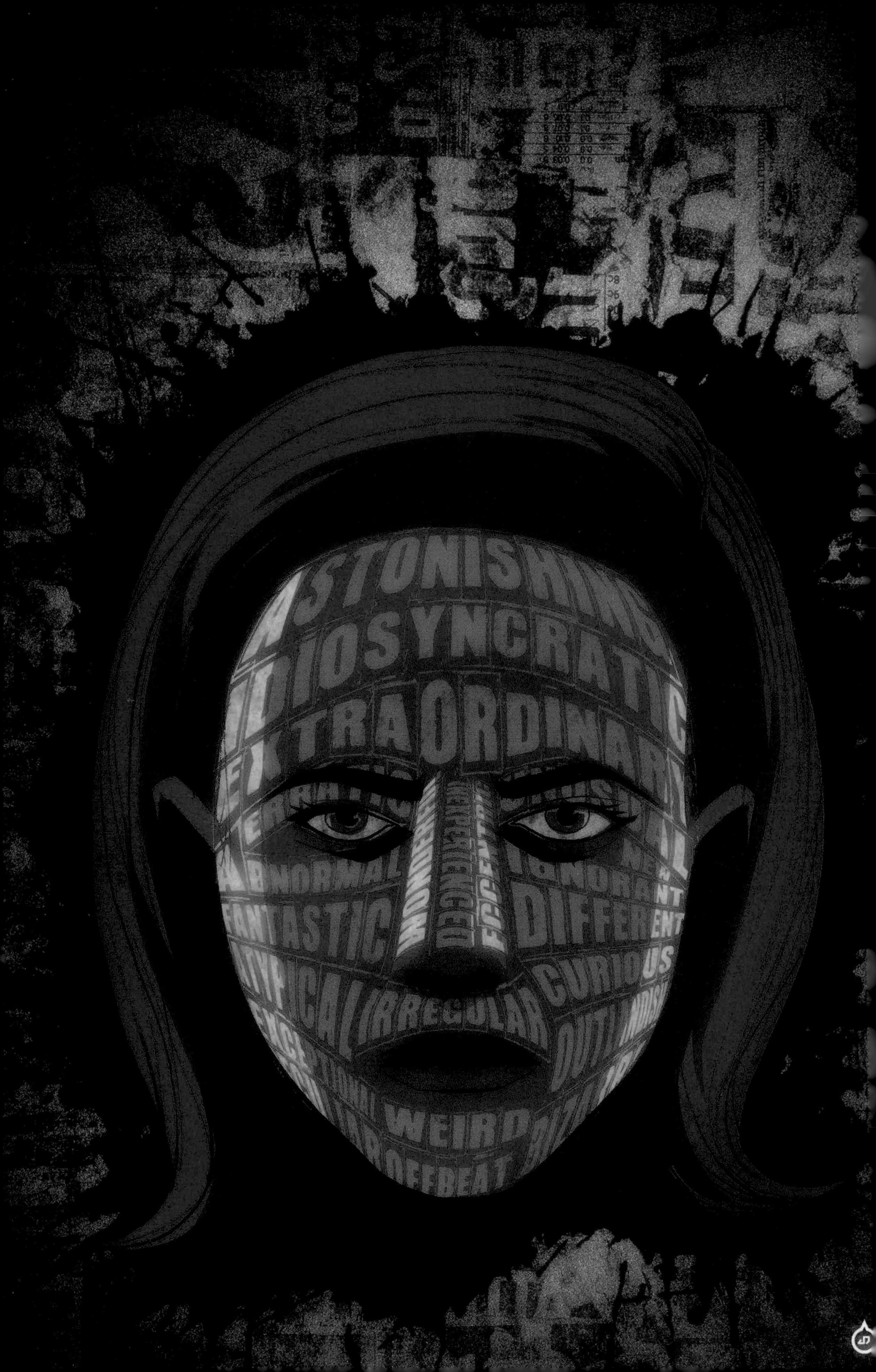
FANTASTIC
ABNORMAL
IGNORANT
DIFFERENT
CURIOUS
IRREGULAR
WEIRD
OFFBEAT

I'M NOT SURE WHAT TO BELIEVE OR DO ANYMORE. BUT MY DAD ALWAYS USED TO SAY, "PICK A LANE AND THEN RIDE IT UNTIL THE END."

AT LEAST I *THOUGHT* IT WAS MY DAD. IF I BELIEVE WHAT DR. GORDON HAS TOLD ME, THEN IT'S ALL PART OF MY PROGRAMMING, WHICH MEANS I'M *NOT REAL*.

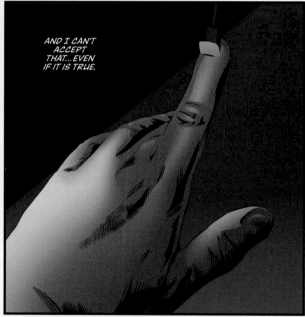

AND I CAN'T ACCEPT THAT...EVEN IF IT IS TRUE.

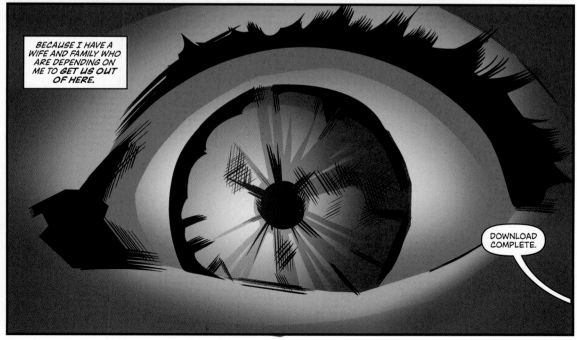

BECAUSE I HAVE A WIFE AND FAMILY WHO ARE DEPENDING ON ME TO *GET US OUT* OF HERE.

DOWNLOAD COMPLETE.

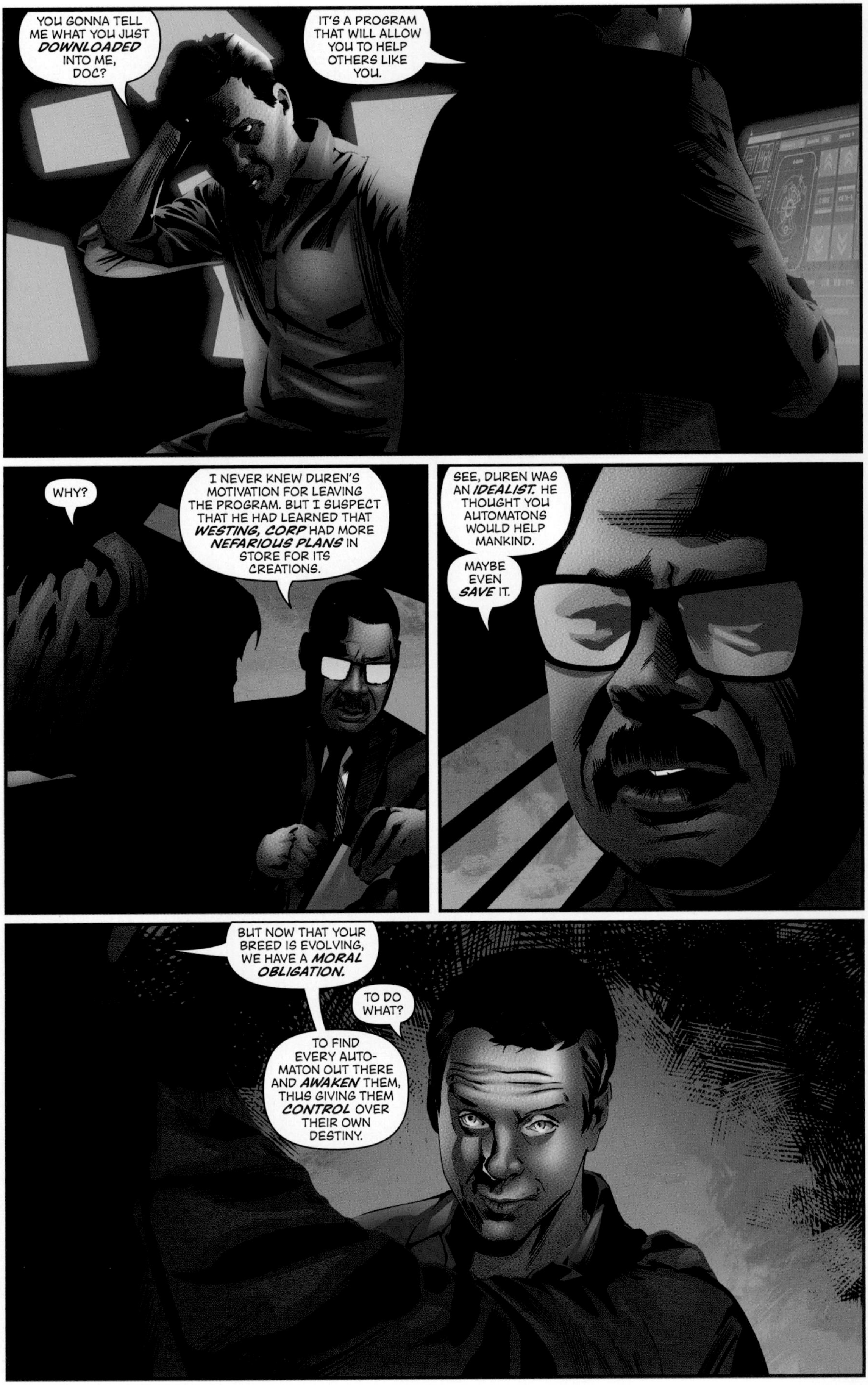
YOU GONNA TELL ME WHAT YOU JUST DOWNLOADED INTO ME, DOC?
IT'S A PROGRAM THAT WILL ALLOW YOU TO HELP OTHERS LIKE YOU.
WHY?
I NEVER KNEW DUREN'S MOTIVATION FOR LEAVING THE PROGRAM. BUT I SUSPECT THAT HE HAD LEARNED THAT WESTING, CORP HAD MORE NEFARIOUS PLANS IN STORE FOR ITS CREATIONS.
SEE, DUREN WAS AN IDEALIST. HE THOUGHT YOU AUTOMATONS WOULD HELP MANKIND.
MAYBE EVEN SAVE IT.
BUT NOW THAT YOUR BREED IS EVOLVING, WE HAVE A MORAL OBLIGATION.
TO DO WHAT?
TO FIND EVERY AUTO-MATON OUT THERE AND AWAKEN THEM, THUS GIVING THEM CONTROL OVER THEIR OWN DESTINY.

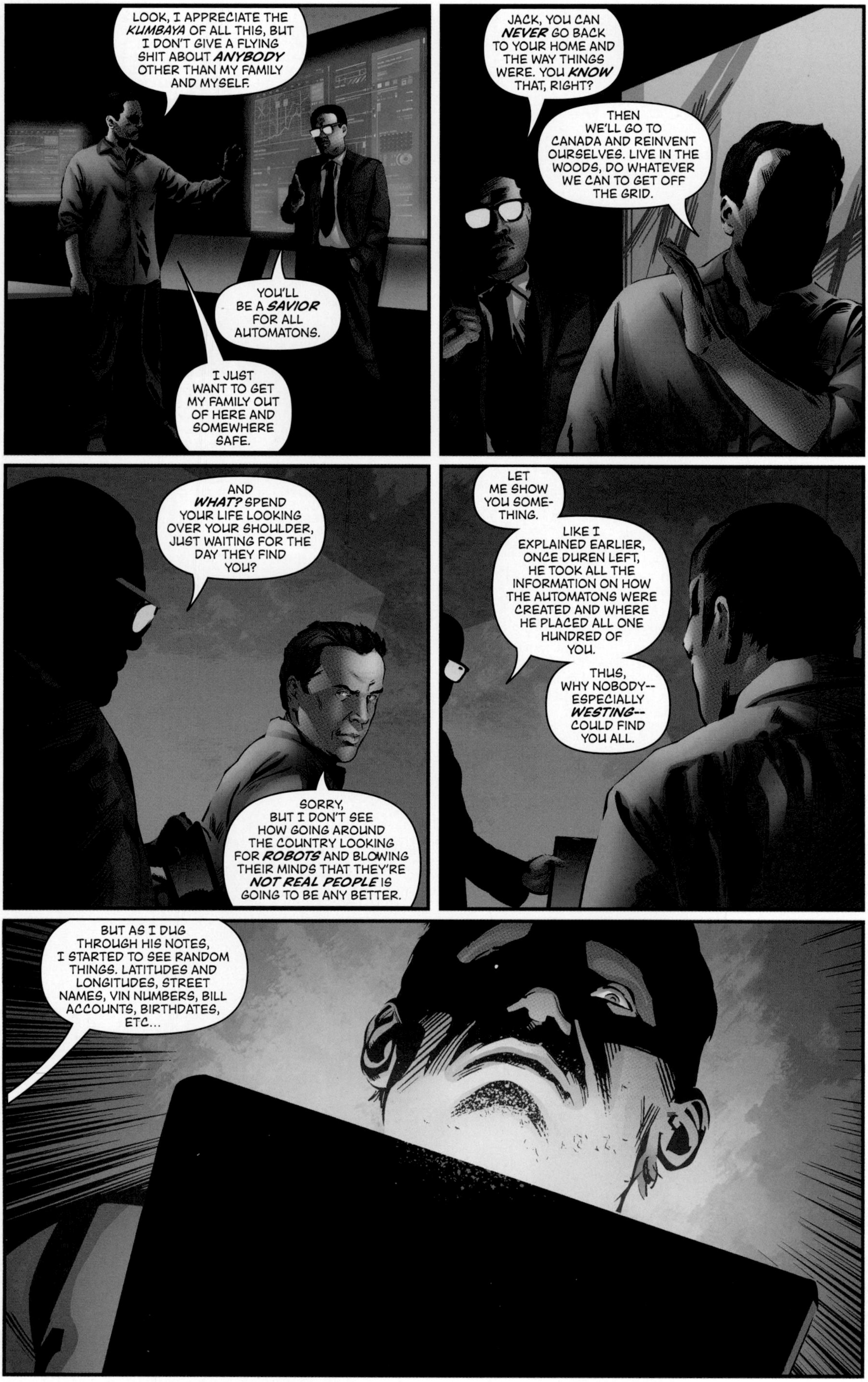
LOOK, I APPRECIATE THE KUMBAYA OF ALL THIS, BUT I DON'T GIVE A FLYING SHIT ABOUT ANYBODY OTHER THAN MY FAMILY AND MYSELF.
YOU'LL BE A SAVIOR FOR ALL AUTOMATONS.
I JUST WANT TO GET MY FAMILY OUT OF HERE AND SOMEWHERE SAFE.
JACK, YOU CAN NEVER GO BACK TO YOUR HOME AND THE WAY THINGS WERE. YOU KNOW THAT, RIGHT?
THEN WE'LL GO TO CANADA AND REINVENT OURSELVES. LIVE IN THE WOODS, DO WHATEVER WE CAN TO GET OFF THE GRID.
AND WHAT? SPEND YOUR LIFE LOOKING OVER YOUR SHOULDER, JUST WAITING FOR THE DAY THEY FIND YOU?
SORRY, BUT I DON'T SEE HOW GOING AROUND THE COUNTRY LOOKING FOR ROBOTS AND BLOWING THEIR MINDS THAT THEY'RE NOT REAL PEOPLE IS GOING TO BE ANY BETTER.
LET ME SHOW YOU SOMETHING.
LIKE I EXPLAINED EARLIER, ONCE DUREN LEFT, HE TOOK ALL THE INFORMATION ON HOW THE AUTOMATONS WERE CREATED AND WHERE HE PLACED ALL ONE HUNDRED OF YOU.
THUS, WHY NOBODY-- ESPECIALLY WESTING-- COULD FIND YOU ALL.
BUT AS I DUG THROUGH HIS NOTES, I STARTED TO SEE RANDOM THINGS. LATITUDES AND LONGITUDES, STREET NAMES, VIN NUMBERS, BILL ACCOUNTS, BIRTHDATES, ETC...

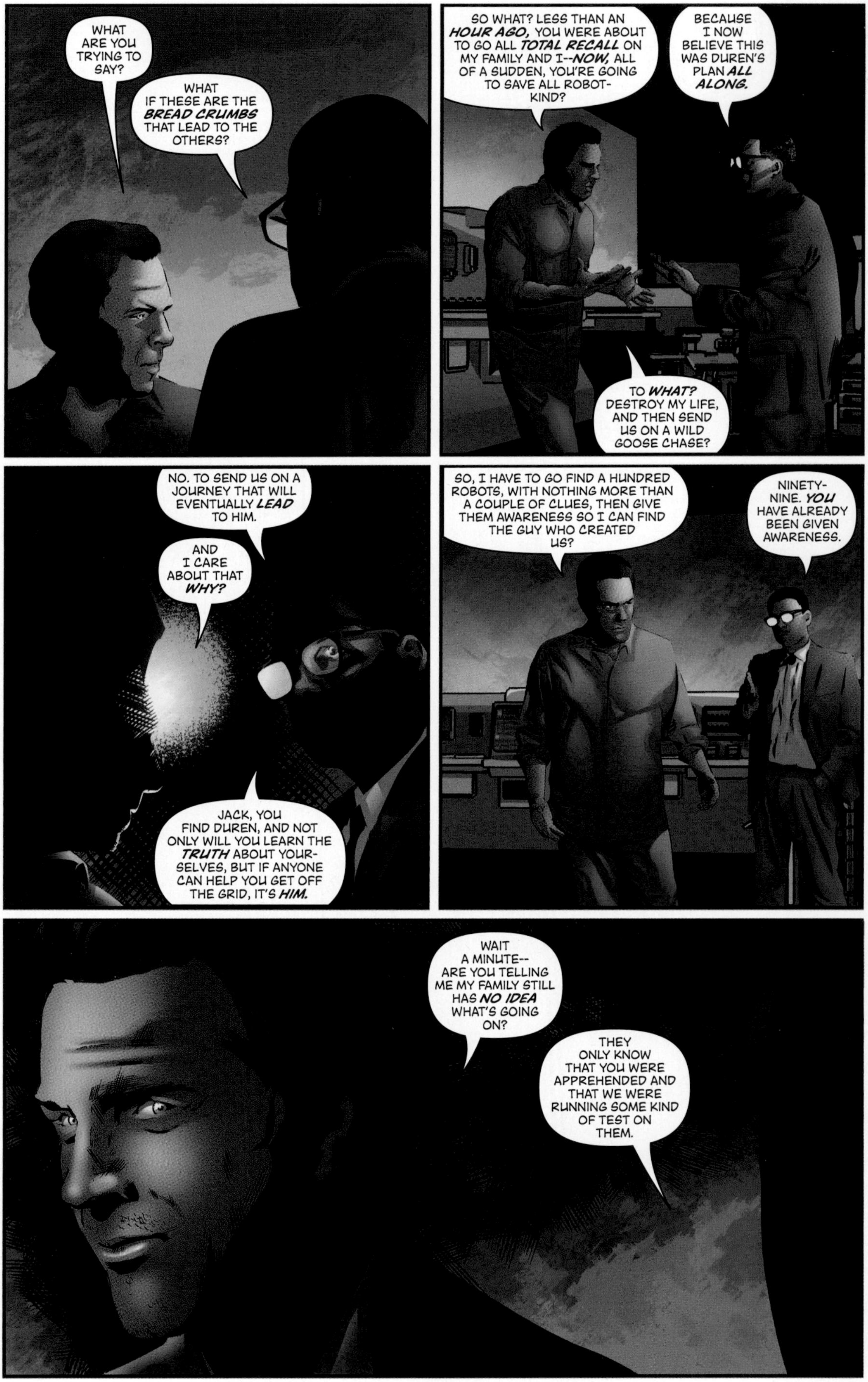
WHAT ARE YOU TRYING TO SAY?
WHAT IF THESE ARE THE BREAD CRUMBS THAT LEAD TO THE OTHERS?
SO WHAT? LESS THAN AN HOUR AGO, YOU WERE ABOUT TO GO ALL TOTAL RECALL ON MY FAMILY AND I--NOW, ALL OF A SUDDEN, YOU'RE GOING TO SAVE ALL ROBOT-KIND?
BECAUSE I NOW BELIEVE THIS WAS DUREN'S PLAN ALL ALONG.
TO WHAT? DESTROY MY LIFE, AND THEN SEND US ON A WILD GOOSE CHASE?
NO. TO SEND US ON A JOURNEY THAT WILL EVENTUALLY LEAD TO HIM.
AND I CARE ABOUT THAT WHY?
JACK, YOU FIND DUREN, AND NOT ONLY WILL YOU LEARN THE TRUTH ABOUT YOURSELVES, BUT IF ANYONE CAN HELP YOU GET OFF THE GRID, IT'S HIM.
SO, I HAVE TO GO FIND A HUNDRED ROBOTS, WITH NOTHING MORE THAN A COUPLE OF CLUES, THEN GIVE THEM AWARENESS SO I CAN FIND THE GUY WHO CREATED US?
NINETY-NINE. YOU HAVE ALREADY BEEN GIVEN AWARENESS.
WAIT A MINUTE-- ARE YOU TELLING ME MY FAMILY STILL HAS NO IDEA WHAT'S GOING ON?
THEY ONLY KNOW THAT YOU WERE APPREHENDED AND THAT WE WERE RUNNING SOME KIND OF TEST ON THEM.

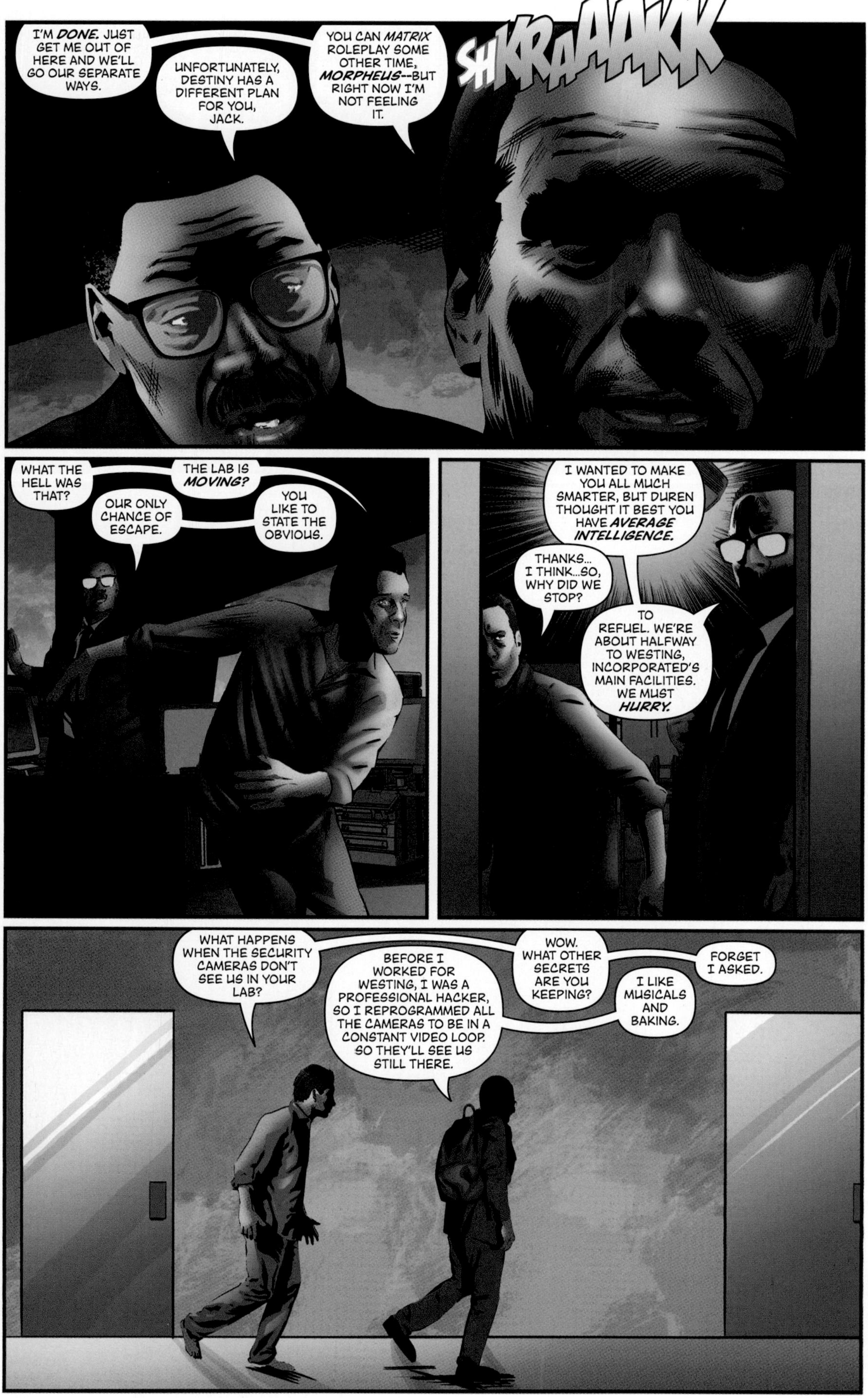
I'M DONE. JUST GET ME OUT OF HERE AND WE'LL GO OUR SEPARATE WAYS.
UNFORTUNATELY, DESTINY HAS A DIFFERENT PLAN FOR YOU, JACK.
YOU CAN MATRIX ROLEPLAY SOME OTHER TIME, MORPHEUS--BUT RIGHT NOW I'M NOT FEELING IT.
SHKRAAAKK
WHAT THE HELL WAS THAT?
THE LAB IS MOVING?
OUR ONLY CHANCE OF ESCAPE.
YOU LIKE TO STATE THE OBVIOUS.
I WANTED TO MAKE YOU ALL MUCH SMARTER, BUT DUREN THOUGHT IT BEST YOU HAVE AVERAGE INTELLIGENCE.
THANKS... I THINK...SO, WHY DID WE STOP?
TO REFUEL. WE'RE ABOUT HALFWAY TO WESTING, INCORPORATED'S MAIN FACILITIES. WE MUST HURRY.
WHAT HAPPENS WHEN THE SECURITY CAMERAS DON'T SEE US IN YOUR LAB?
BEFORE I WORKED FOR WESTING, I WAS A PROFESSIONAL HACKER, SO I REPROGRAMMED ALL THE CAMERAS TO BE IN A CONSTANT VIDEO LOOP. SO THEY'LL SEE US STILL THERE.
WOW. WHAT OTHER SECRETS ARE YOU KEEPING?
I LIKE MUSICALS AND BAKING.
FORGET I ASKED.

WHERE ARE THE OTHER TECHNICIANS?

WE KEEP A SKELETON CREW ON THESE TRAVELING LABS. I ORDERED THEM ALL BACK TO THE HOLDING AREA TO AWAIT FURTHER ORDERS.

SECURITY GUARDS?

TWO GUARDS TO EACH TRUCK. RIGHT NOW, ONE IS HELPING THE DRIVER FILL UP, WHILE THE OTHER STANDS GUARD. SO THIS IS THE *PERFECT TIME* TO GO.

IF ANYONE CAN SURVIVE THIS, IT'S *JOSEPHINE.*

DADDY!

HEY, BABY GIRL.

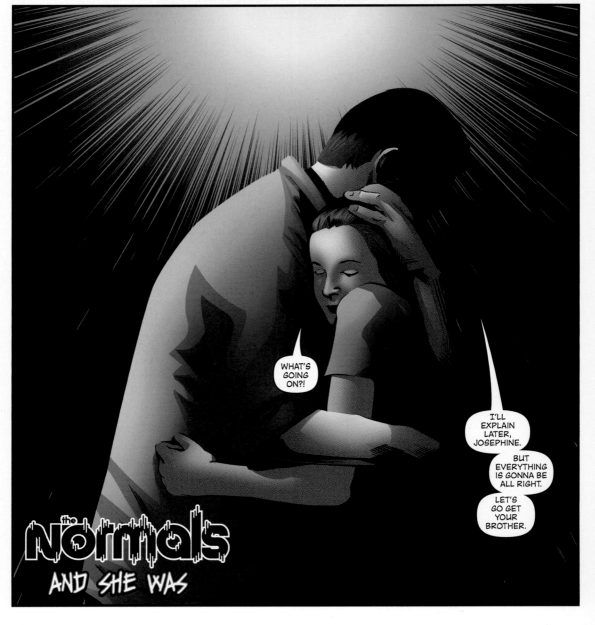

WHAT'S GOING ON?!

I'LL EXPLAIN LATER, JOSEPHINE.

BUT EVERYTHING IS GONNA BE ALL RIGHT.

LET'S GO GET YOUR BROTHER.

the Normals

AND SHE WAS

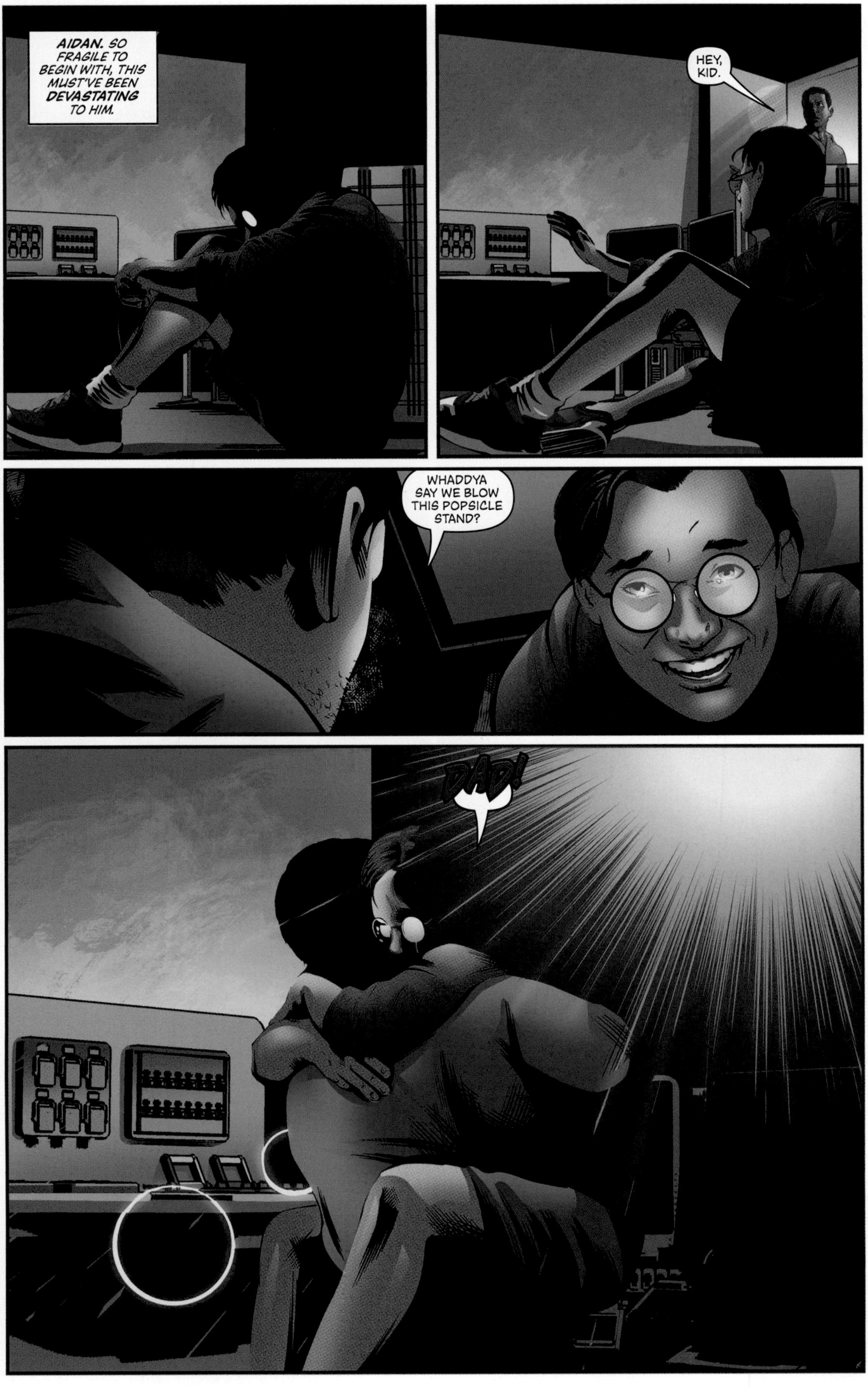
AIDAN. SO FRAGILE TO BEGIN WITH, THIS MUST'VE BEEN DEVASTATING TO HIM.
HEY, KID.
WHADDYA SAY WE BLOW THIS POPSICLE STAND?
DAD!

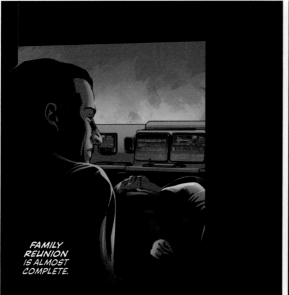

FAMILY REUNION IS ALMOST COMPLETE.

MARY...

...EVERYTHING'S GOING TO BE OKAY, BUT WE HAVE TO BE QUICK.

MOM.

JOSEPHINE.

WE'VE GOT TO GO.

OKAY.

MARY HAS ALWAYS BEEN SO STRONG...I'VE NEVER SEEN HER LIKE THIS.

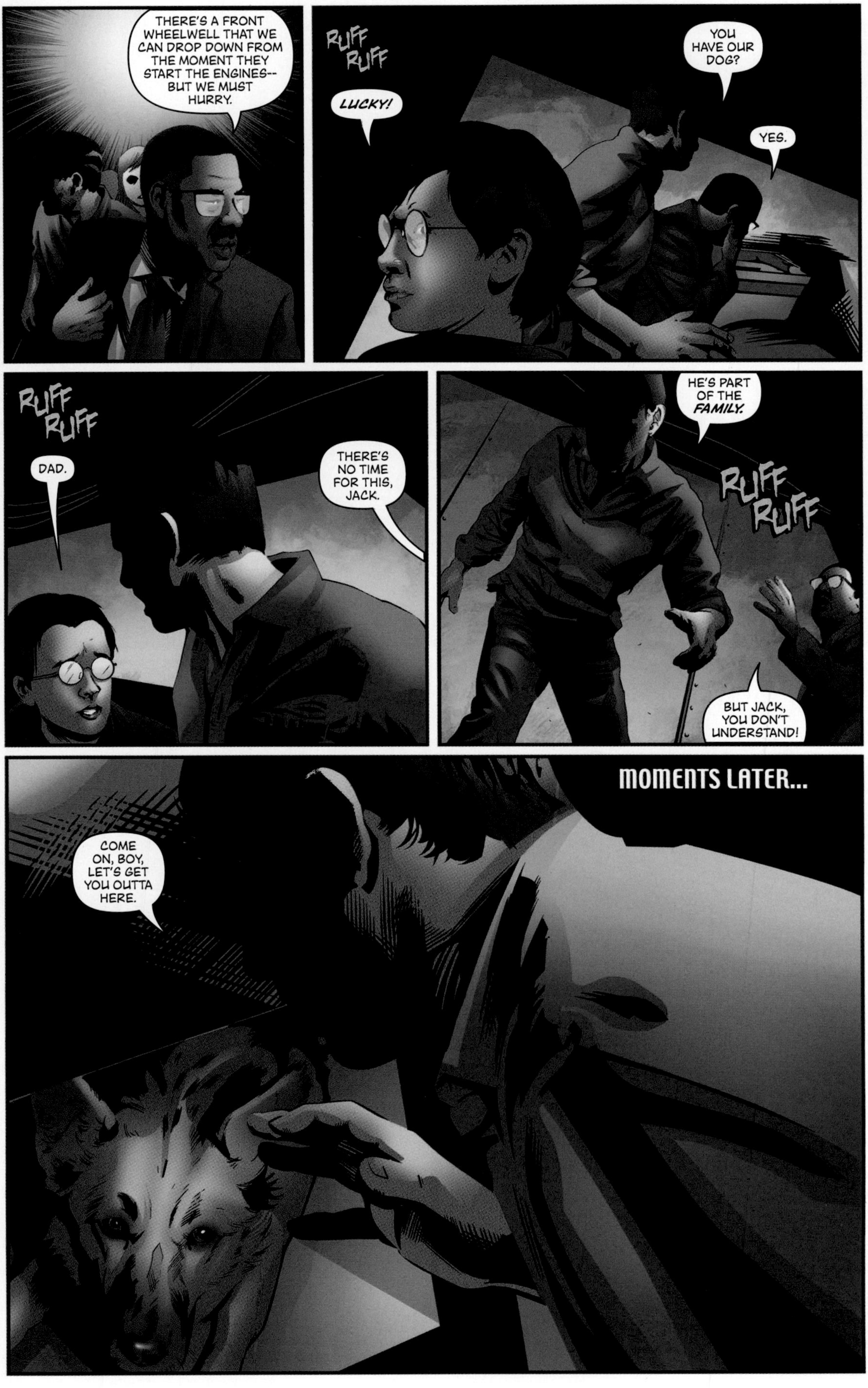
THERE'S A FRONT WHEELWELL THAT WE CAN DROP DOWN FROM THE MOMENT THEY START THE ENGINES-- BUT WE MUST HURRY.
RUFF RUFF
LUCKY!
YOU HAVE OUR DOG?
YES.
RUFF RUFF
DAD.
THERE'S NO TIME FOR THIS, JACK.
HE'S PART OF THE FAMILY.
RUFF RUFF
BUT JACK, YOU DON'T UNDERSTAND!
MOMENTS LATER...
COME ON, BOY, LET'S GET YOU OUTTA HERE.

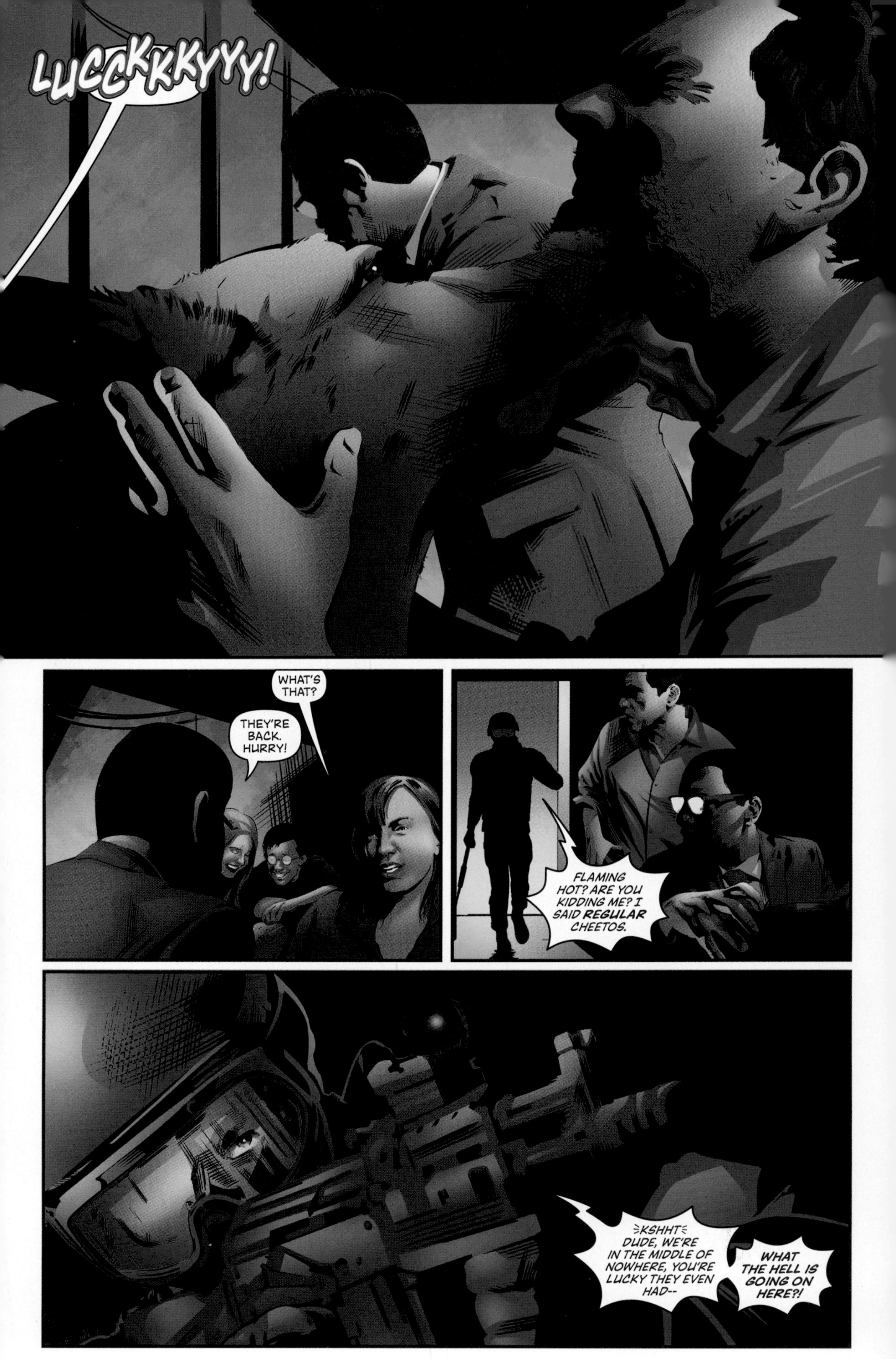
LUCCKKKYYY!
THEY'RE BACK. HURRY!
WHAT'S THAT?
FLAMING HOT? ARE YOU KIDDING ME? I SAID REGULAR CHEETOS.
KSHHT DUDE, WE'RE IN THE MIDDLE OF NOWHERE, YOU'RE LUCKY THEY EVEN HAD--
WHAT THE HELL IS GOING ON HERE?!

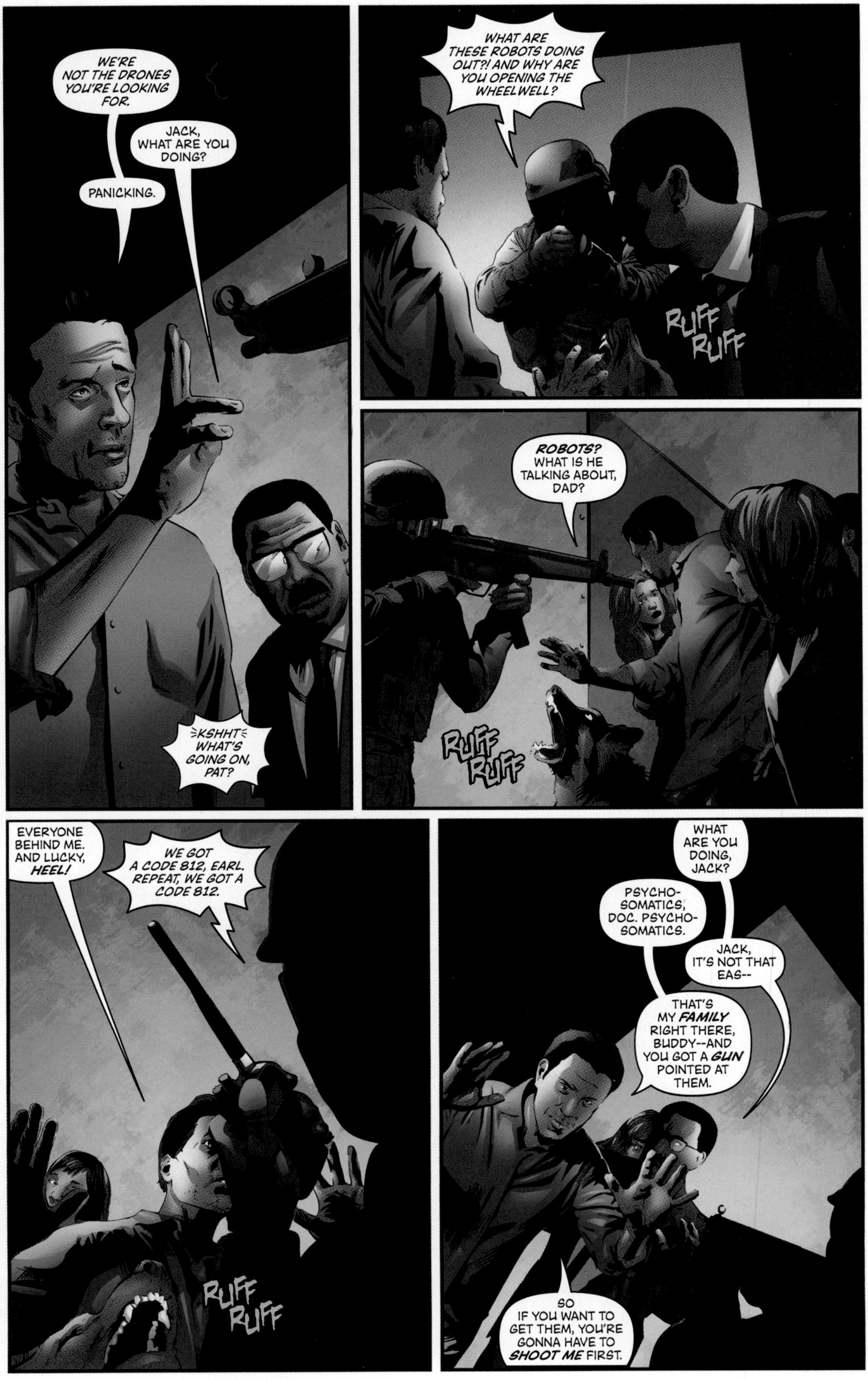
WE'RE NOT THE DRONES YOU'RE LOOKING FOR.
JACK, WHAT ARE YOU DOING?
PANICKING.
KSHHT WHAT'S GOING ON, PAT?
WHAT ARE THESE ROBOTS DOING OUT?! AND WHY ARE YOU OPENING THE WHEELWELL?
RUFF RUFF
ROBOTS? WHAT IS HE TALKING ABOUT, DAD?
RUFF RUFF
EVERYONE BEHIND ME. AND LUCKY, HEEL!
WE GOT A CODE 812, EARL. REPEAT, WE GOT A CODE 812.
RUFF RUFF
WHAT ARE YOU DOING, JACK?
PSYCHO-SOMATICS, DOC. PSYCHO-SOMATICS.
JACK, IT'S NOT THAT EAS--
THAT'S MY FAMILY RIGHT THERE, BUDDY--AND YOU GOT A GUN POINTED AT THEM.
SO IF YOU WANT TO GET THEM, YOU'RE GONNA HAVE TO SHOOT ME FIRST.

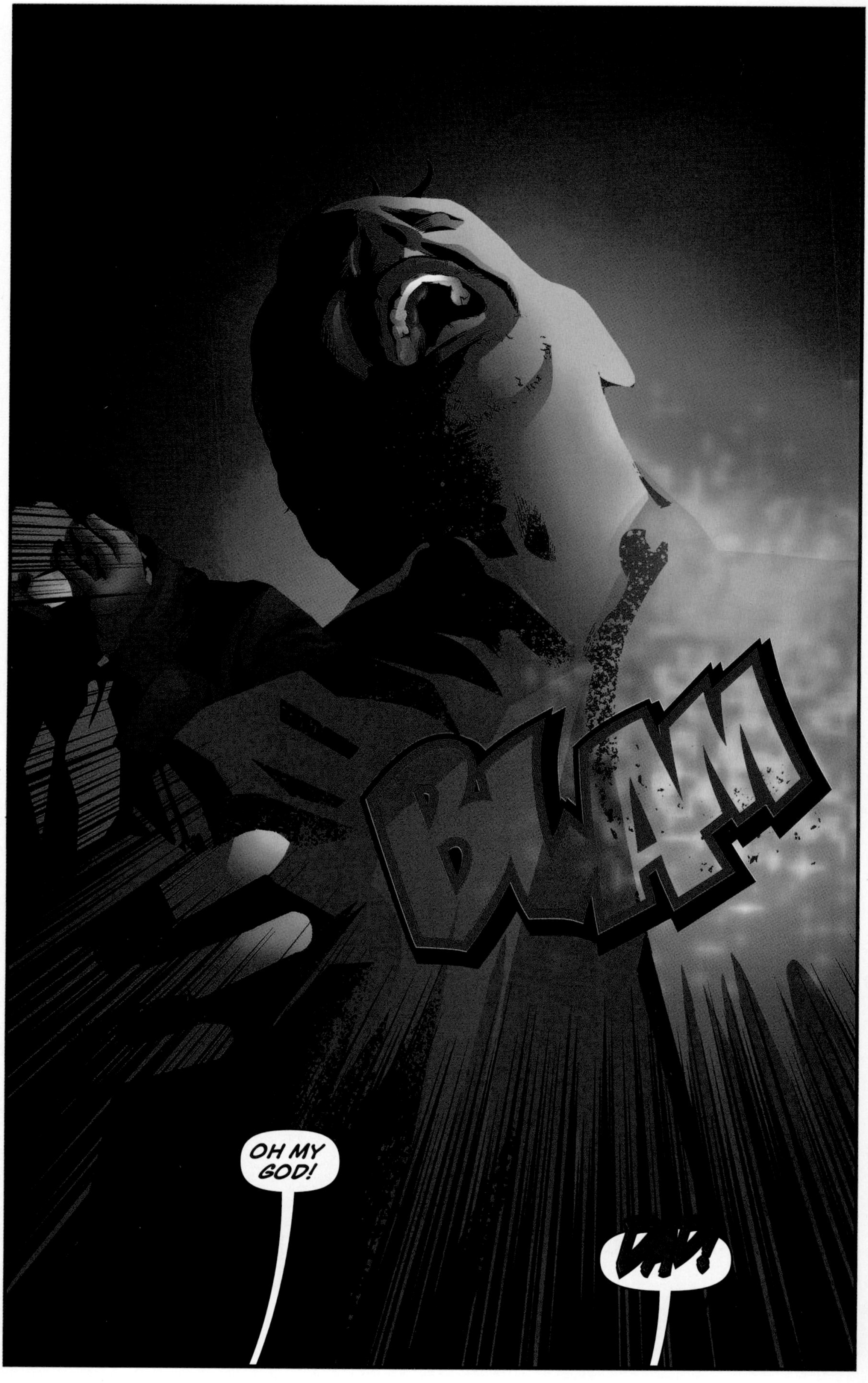
BLAM
OH MY GOD!

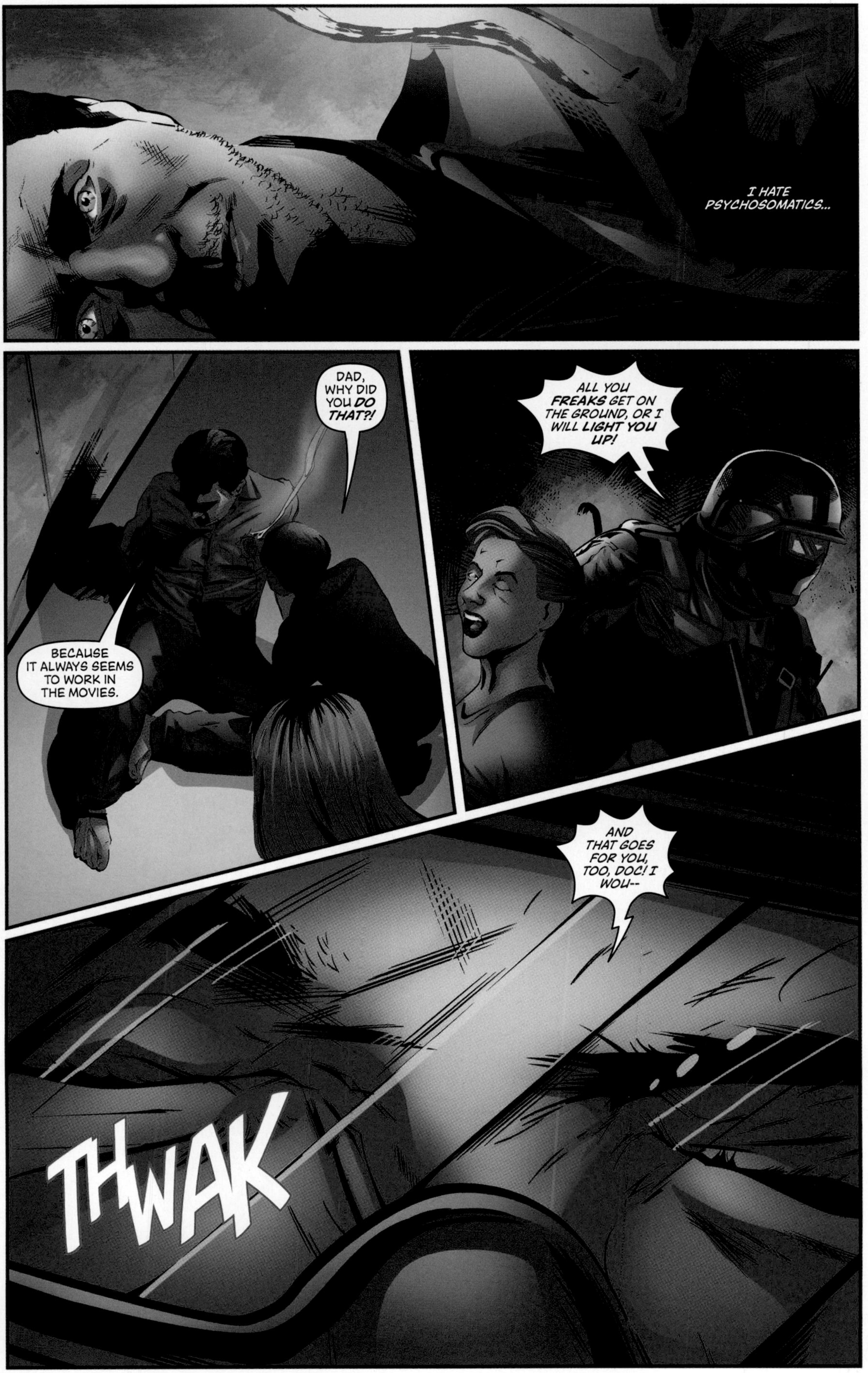
I HATE PSYCHOSOMATICS...
DAD, WHY DID YOU DO THAT?!
BECAUSE IT ALWAYS SEEMS TO WORK IN THE MOVIES.
ALL YOU FREAKS GET ON THE GROUND, OR I WILL LIGHT YOU UP!
AND THAT GOES FOR YOU, TOO, DOC! I WOU--
THWAK

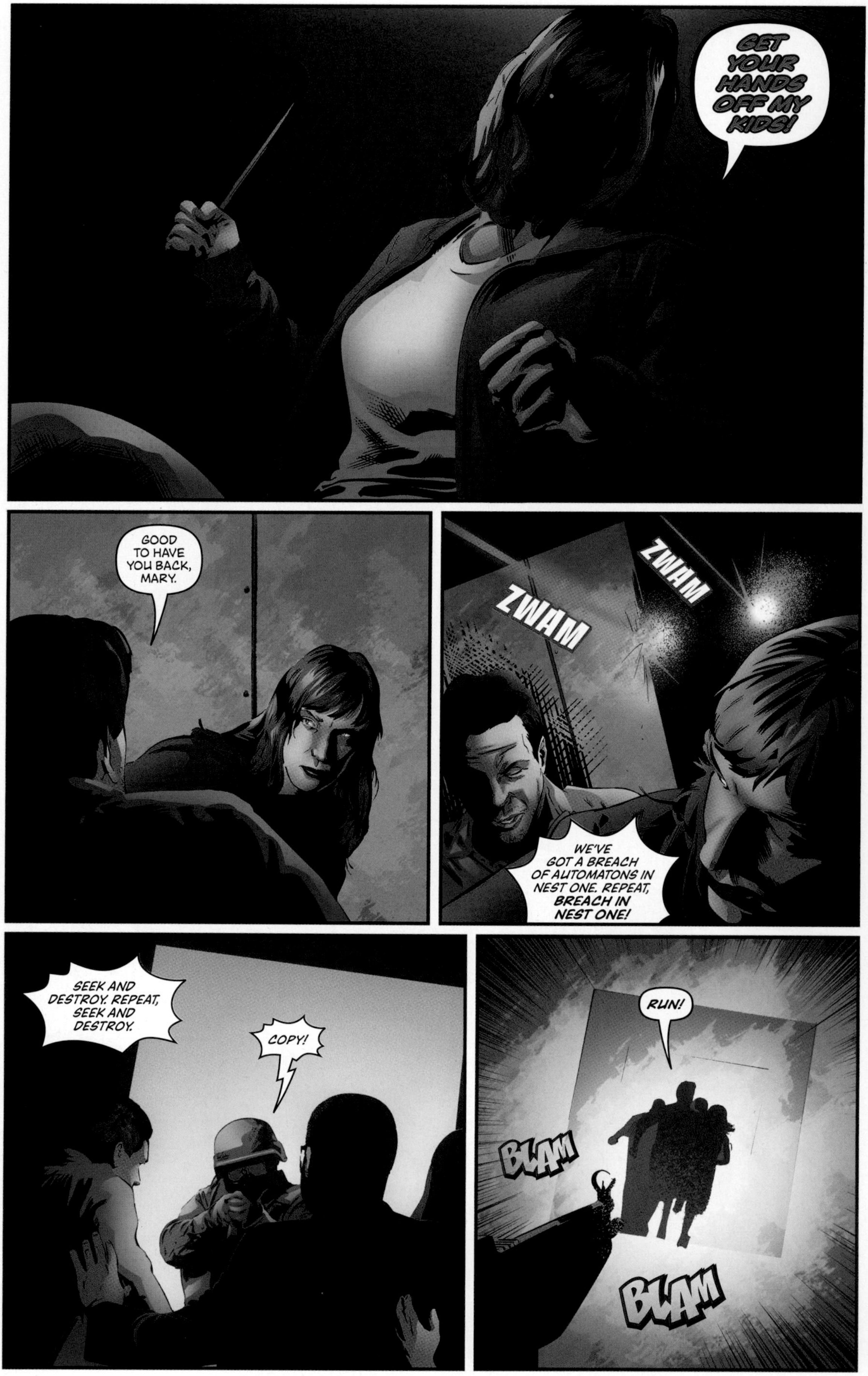
GET YOUR HANDS OFF MY KIDS!
GOOD TO HAVE YOU BACK, MARY.
ZWAM
ZWAM
WE'VE GOT A BREACH OF AUTOMATONS IN NEST ONE. REPEAT, BREACH IN NEST ONE!
SEEK AND DESTROY. REPEAT, SEEK AND DESTROY.
COPY!
RUN!
BLAM
BLAM

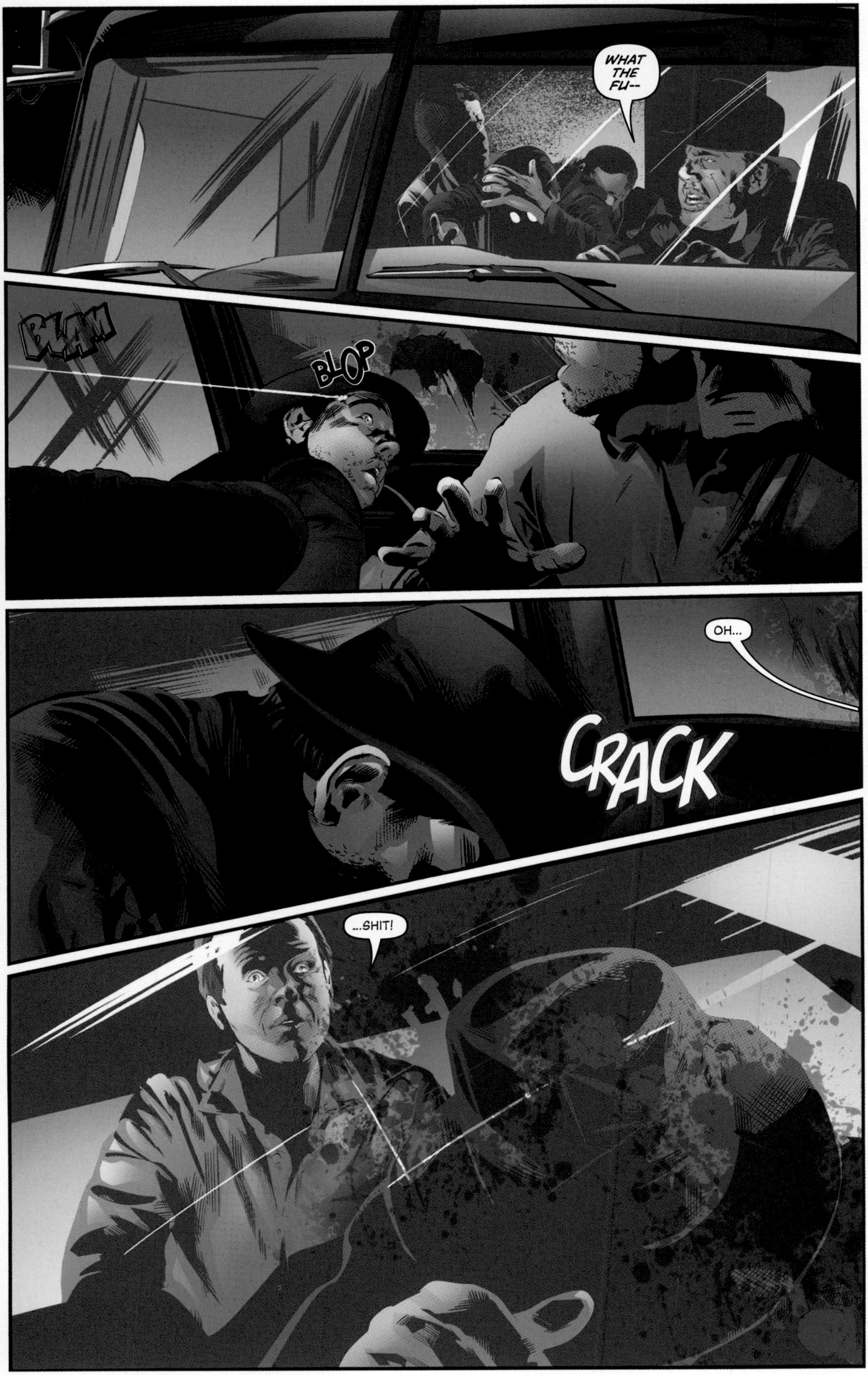
WHAT THE FU--
BLAM
BLOP
OH...
CRACK
...SHIT!

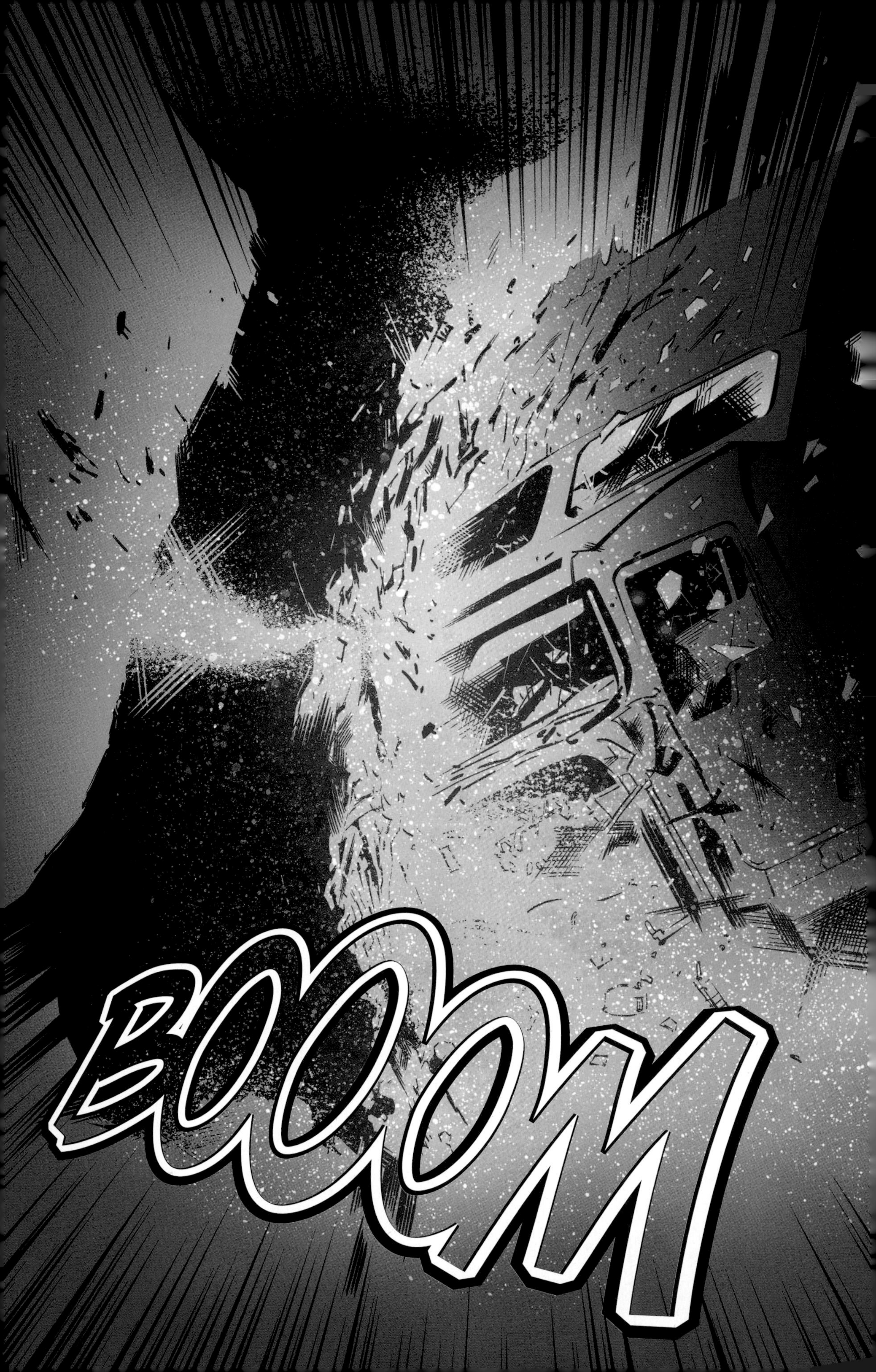
BOOOM

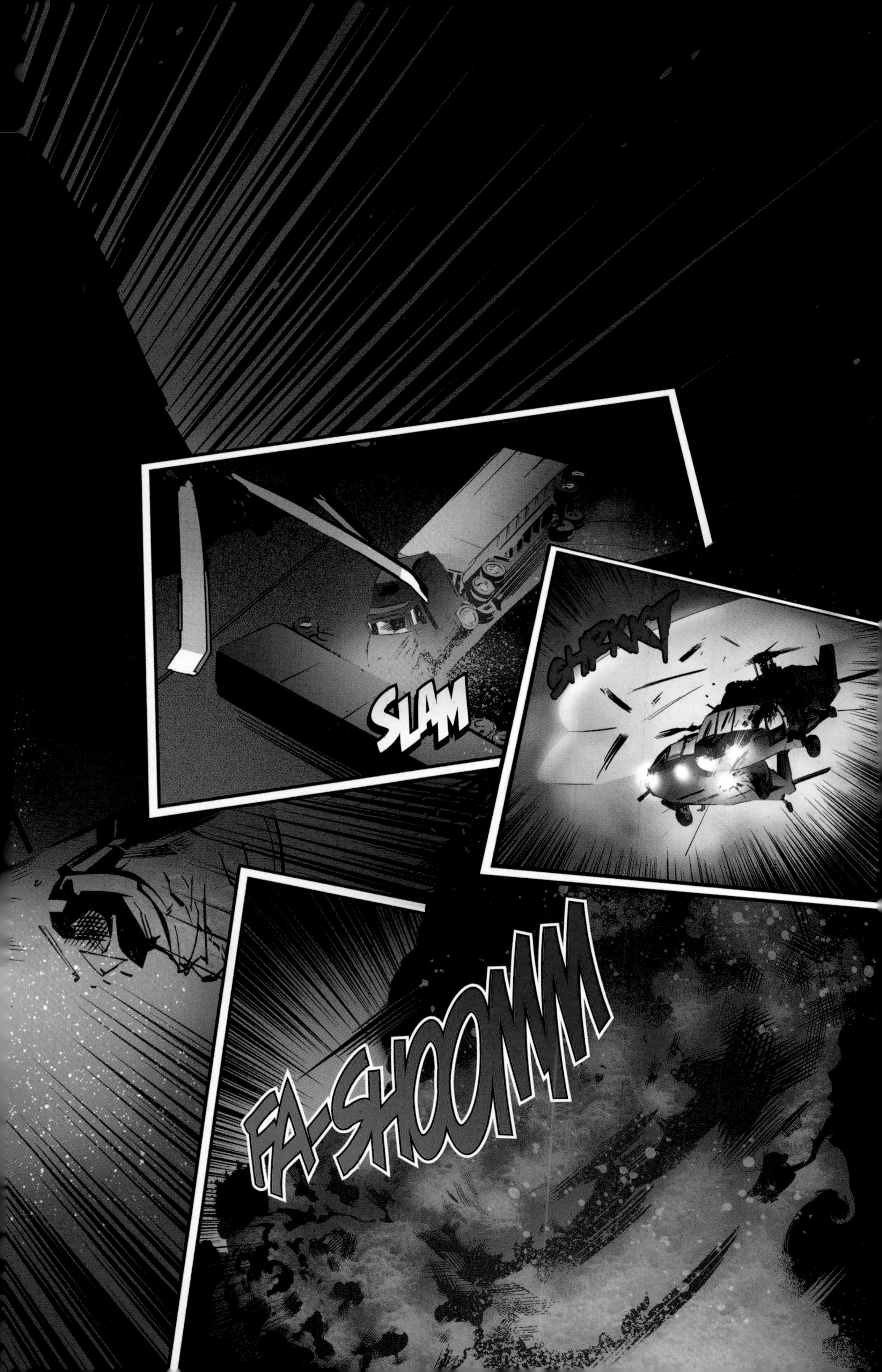
SLAM
SHRKKT
FA-SHOOMMM

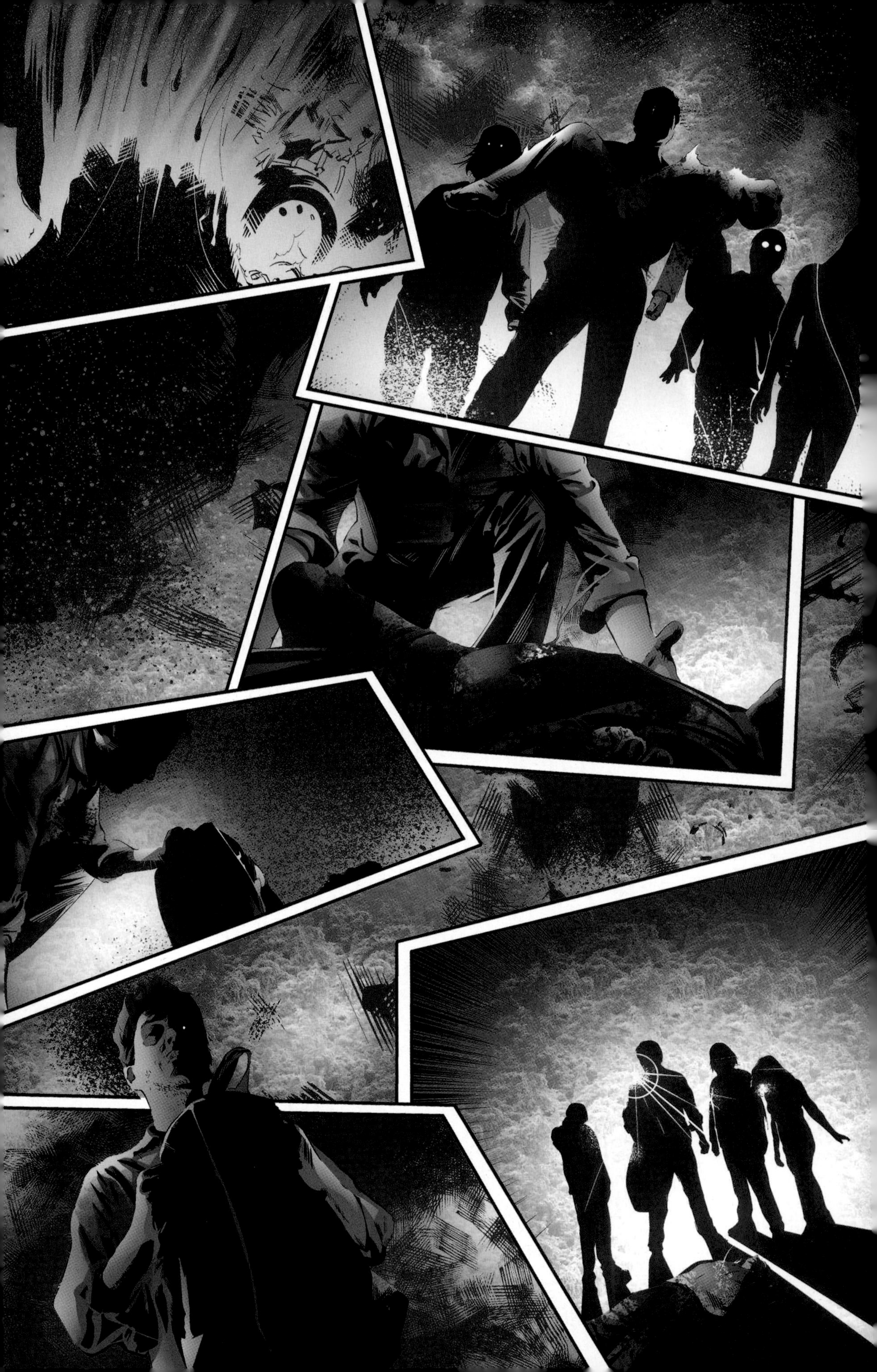

TIME TO GO.

WHERE TO?

FAR AWAY FROM HERE.

BUT THE POLICE ARE COMING! WE'LL TELL THEM WE WERE KIDNAPPED BY THESE GUYS AND THEY'LL HELP US.

WON'T WORK THAT WAY.

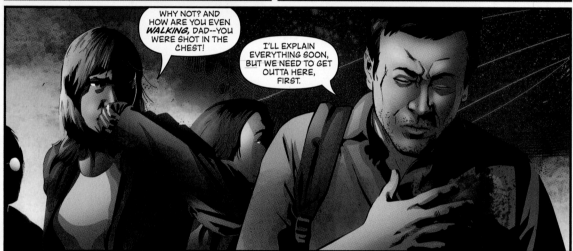

WHY NOT? AND HOW ARE YOU EVEN *WALKING,* DAD--YOU WERE SHOT IN THE CHEST!

I'LL EXPLAIN EVERYTHING SOON, BUT WE NEED TO GET OUTTA HERE, FIRST.

WE'RE NOT GOING *ANYWHERE* WITH YOU.

MARY, THIS ISN'T THE TIME FOR--

I DON'T KNOW WHO YOU THINK *DIED* AND LEFT YOU BOSS, BUT I DON'T TRUST--

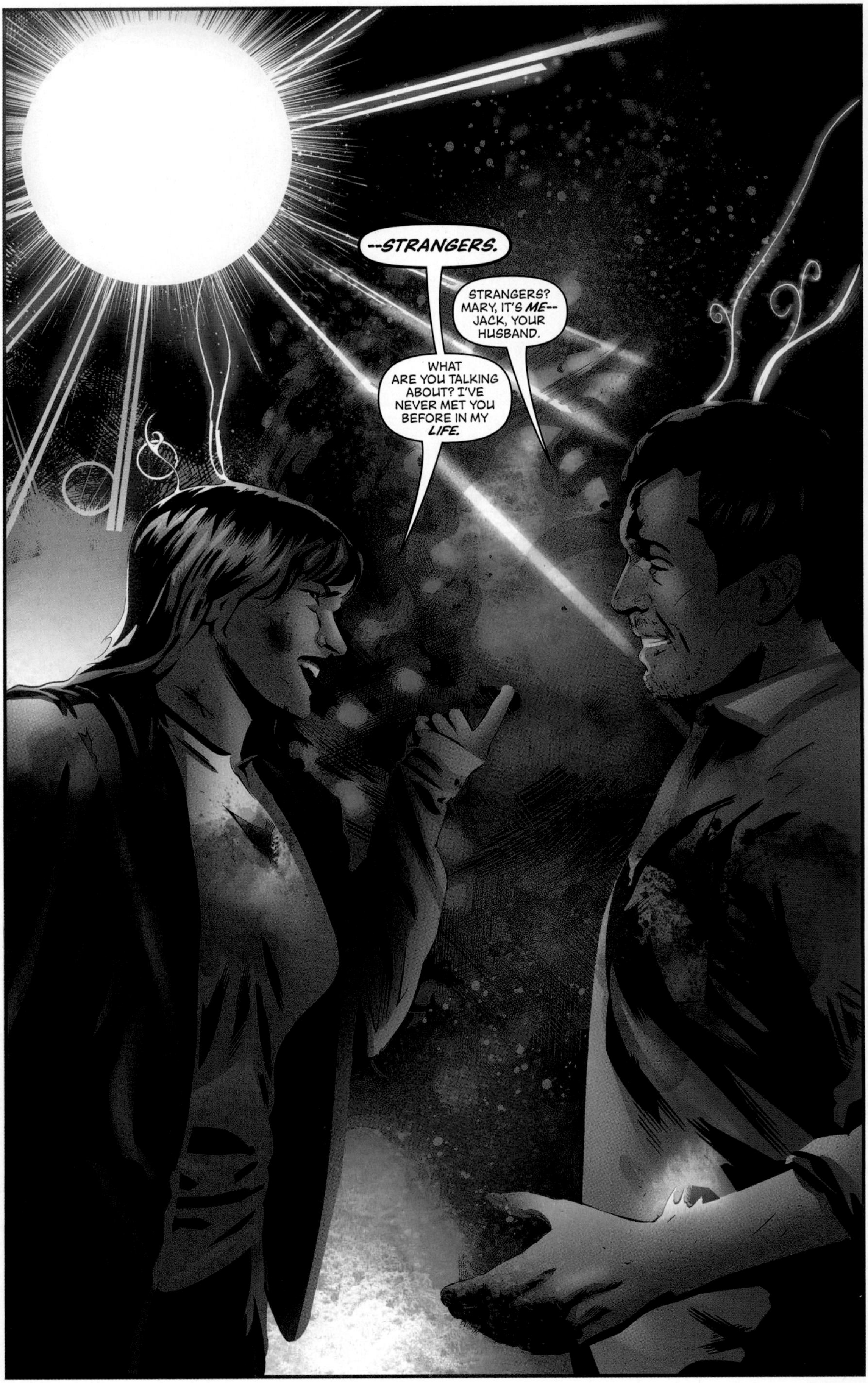
--STRANGERS.
WHAT ARE YOU TALKING ABOUT? I'VE NEVER MET YOU BEFORE IN MY LIFE.
STRANGERS? MARY, IT'S ME-- JACK, YOUR HUSBAND.

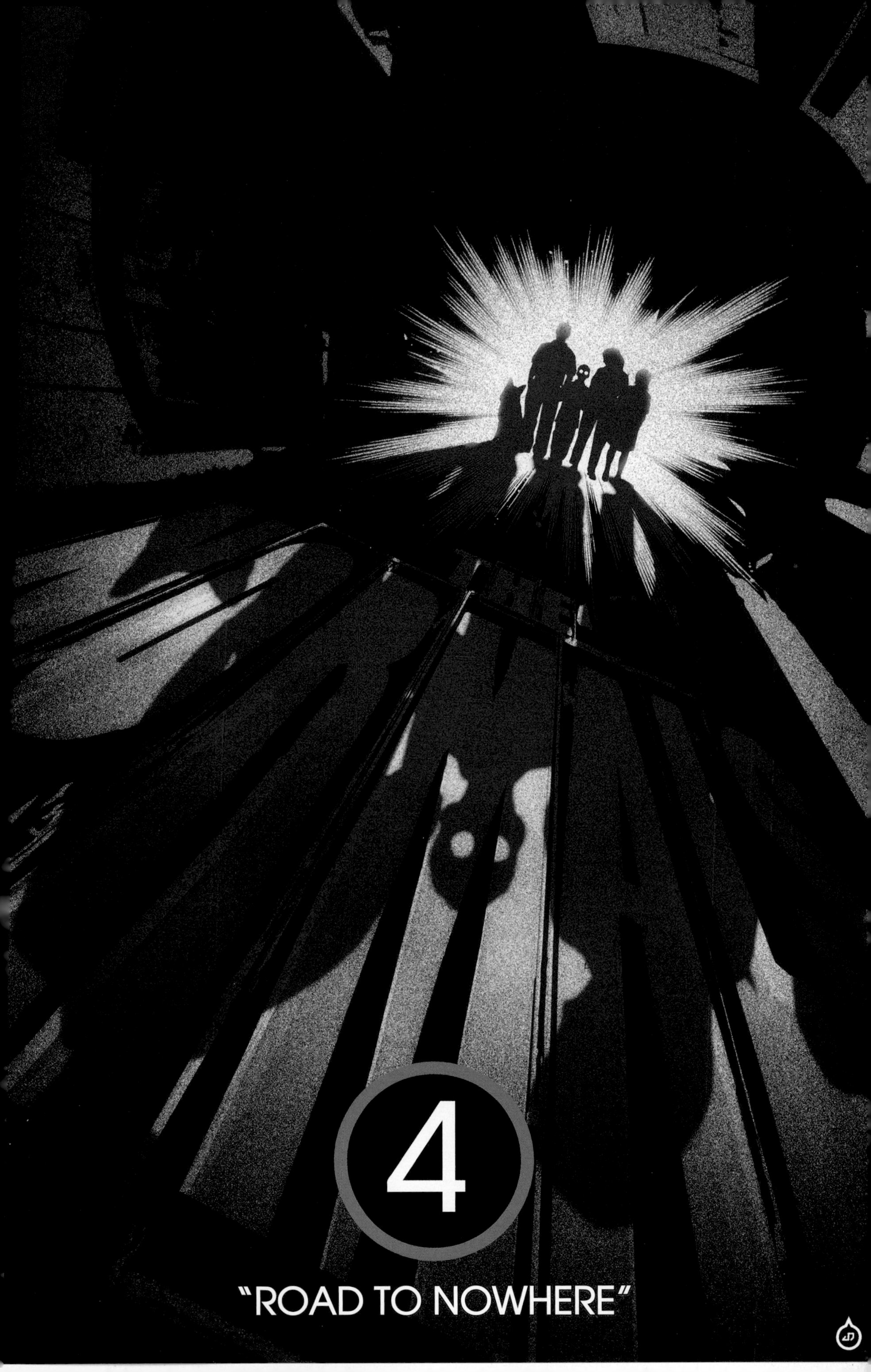
4
"ROAD TO NOWHERE"

DID I ALSO MENTION WE'RE ON THE RUN FROM AN *EVIL CORPORATION* AND HAVE BEEN TASKED WITH *SAVING ALL OF ROBOTKIND?*

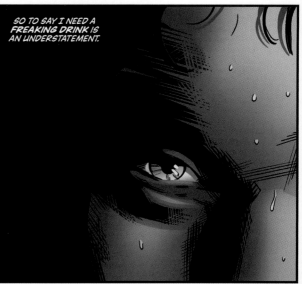

SO TO SAY I NEED A *FREAKING DRINK* IS AN UNDERSTATEMENT.

MY KIDS ARE SHELL-SHOCKED.

AND MY WIFE, WHO NOW THINKS I'M A *TOTAL STRANGER*, IS PROBABLY FIGURING OUT WHEN TO STAB ME IN THE NECK AND *RUN*.

THANK GOD *SOME THINGS* NEVER CHANGE. YOU DON'T KNOW HOW MUCH I NEED THIS RIGHT NOW, BOY.

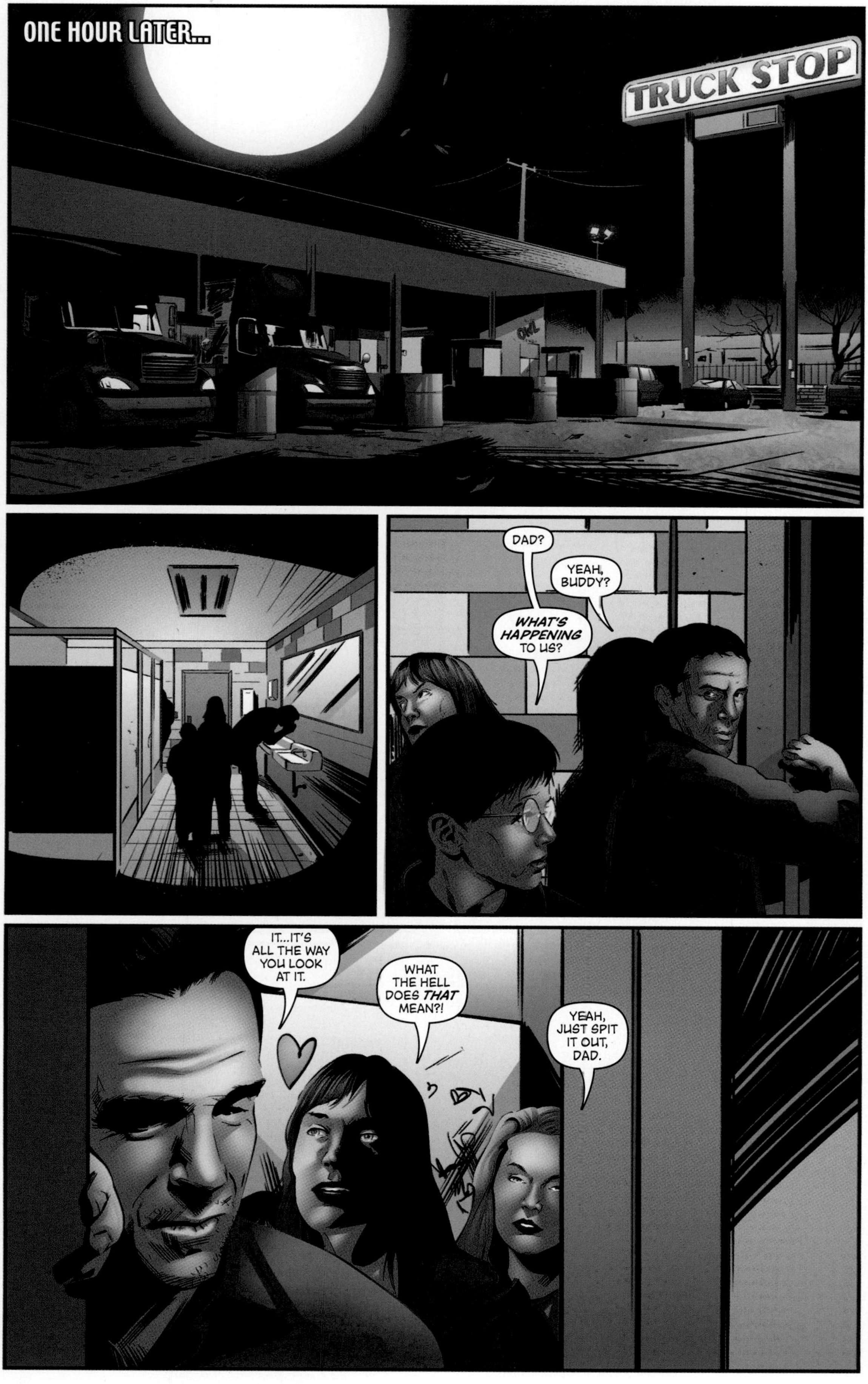
ONE HOUR LATER...
TRUCK STOP
OWL
DAD?
YEAH, BUDDY?
WHAT'S HAPPENING TO US?
IT...IT'S ALL THE WAY YOU LOOK AT IT.
WHAT THE HELL DOES THAT MEAN?!
YEAH, JUST SPIT IT OUT, DAD.

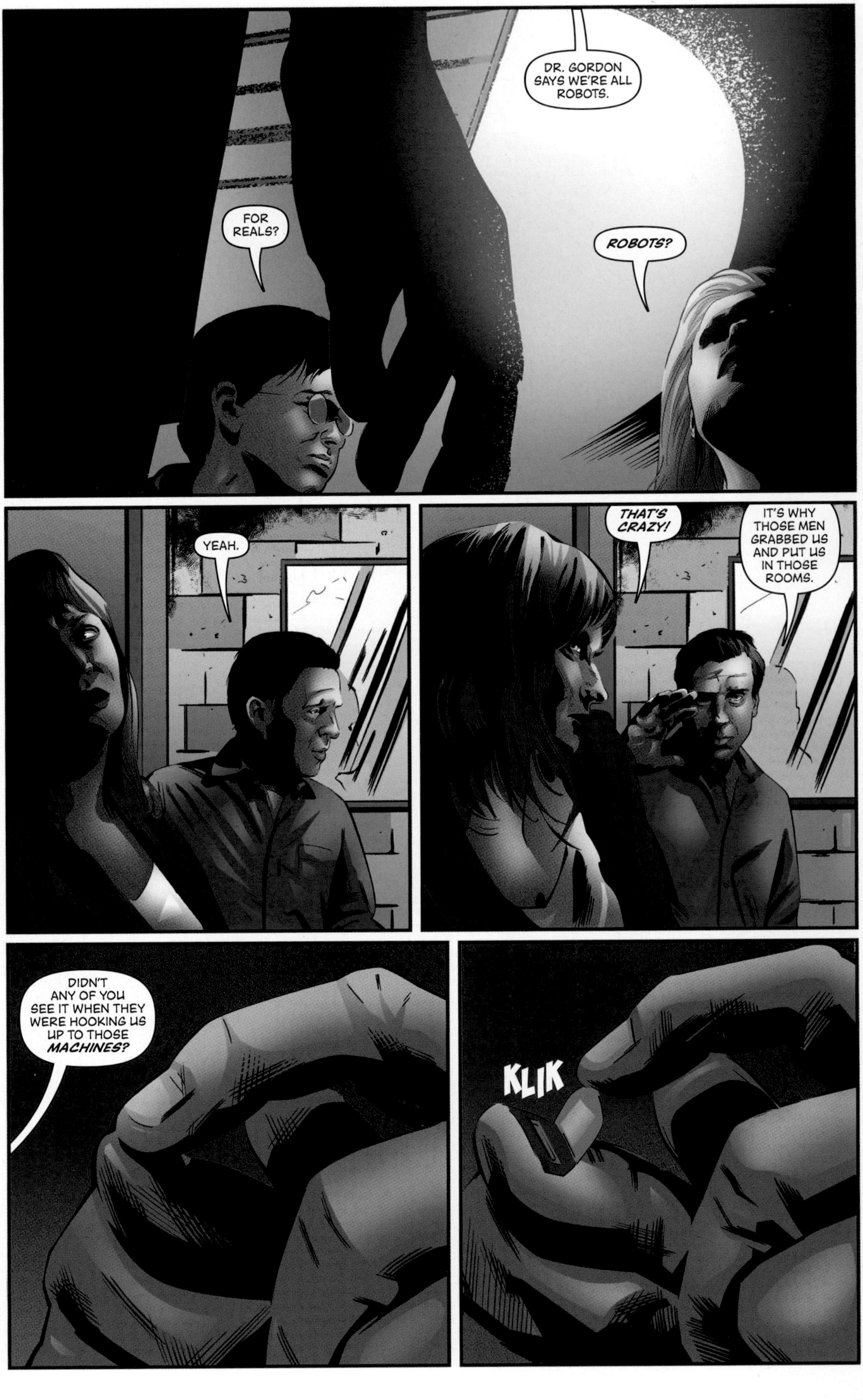
DR. GORDON SAYS WE'RE ALL ROBOTS.
FOR REALS?
ROBOTS?
YEAH.
THAT'S CRAZY!
IT'S WHY THOSE MEN GRABBED US AND PUT US IN THOSE ROOMS.
DIDN'T ANY OF YOU SEE IT WHEN THEY WERE HOOKING US UP TO THOSE *MACHINES?*
KLIK

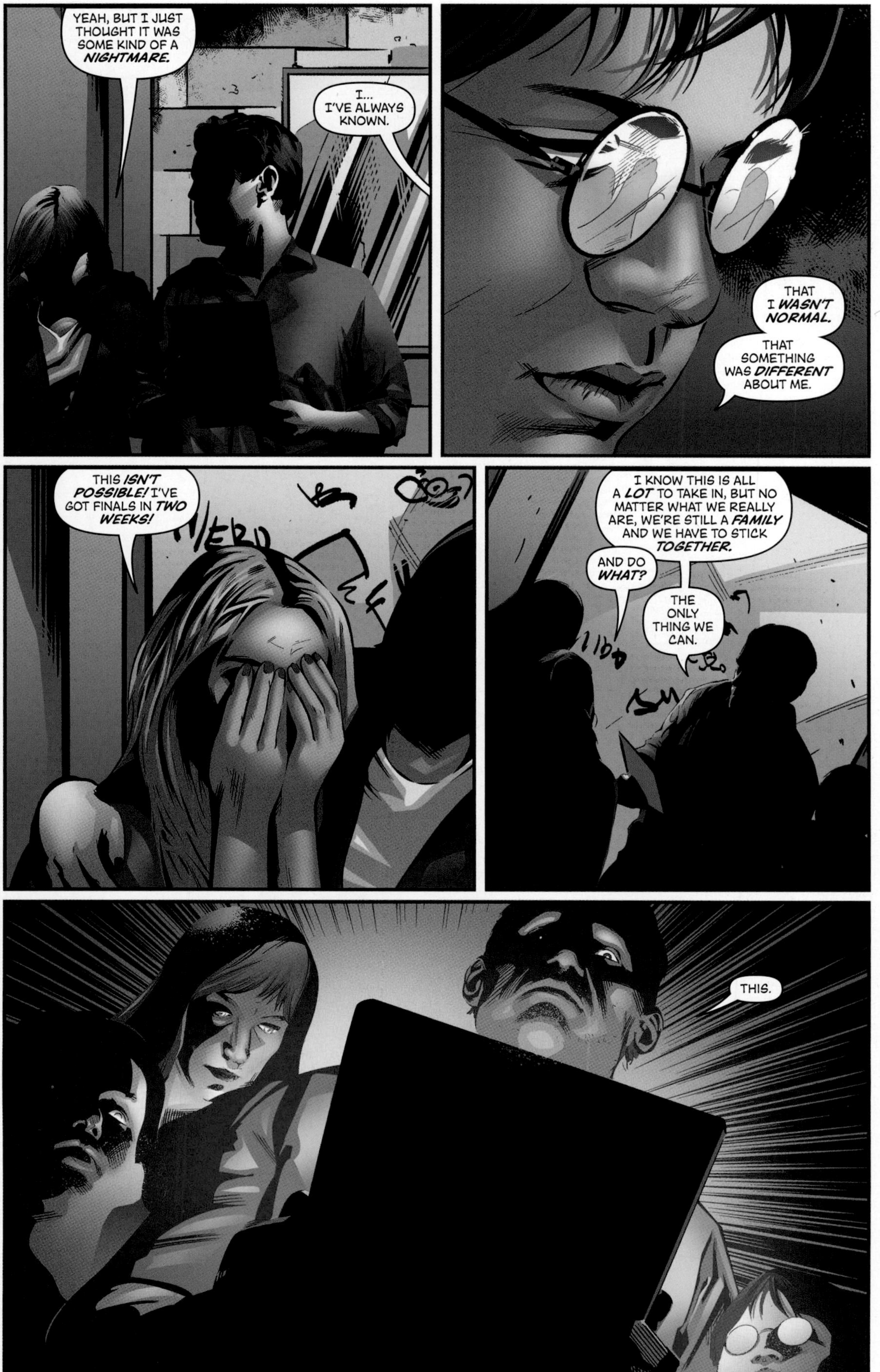
YEAH, BUT I JUST THOUGHT IT WAS SOME KIND OF A NIGHTMARE.
I... I'VE ALWAYS KNOWN.
THAT I WASN'T NORMAL.
THAT SOMETHING WAS DIFFERENT ABOUT ME.
THIS ISN'T POSSIBLE! I'VE GOT FINALS IN TWO WEEKS!
I KNOW THIS IS ALL A LOT TO TAKE IN, BUT NO MATTER WHAT WE REALLY ARE, WE'RE STILL A FAMILY AND WE HAVE TO STICK TOGETHER.
AND DO WHAT?
THE ONLY THING WE CAN.
THIS.

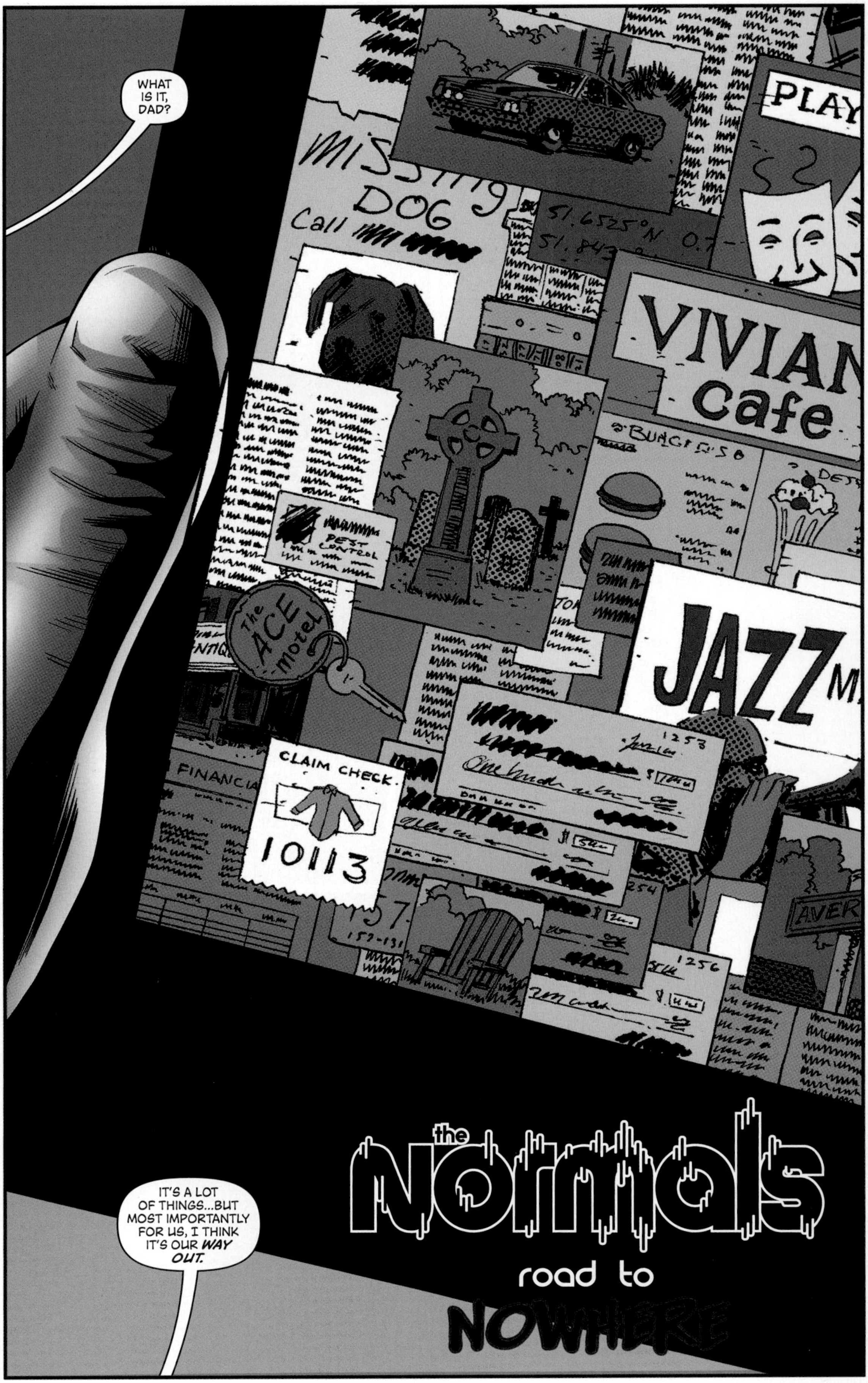
WHAT IS IT, DAD?
IT'S A LOT OF THINGS...BUT MOST IMPORTANTLY FOR US, I THINK IT'S OUR WAY OUT.
DOG
Call
cafe
PEST CONTROL
The ACE motel
JAZZ
CLAIM CHECK
10113
the normals
road to
NOWHERE

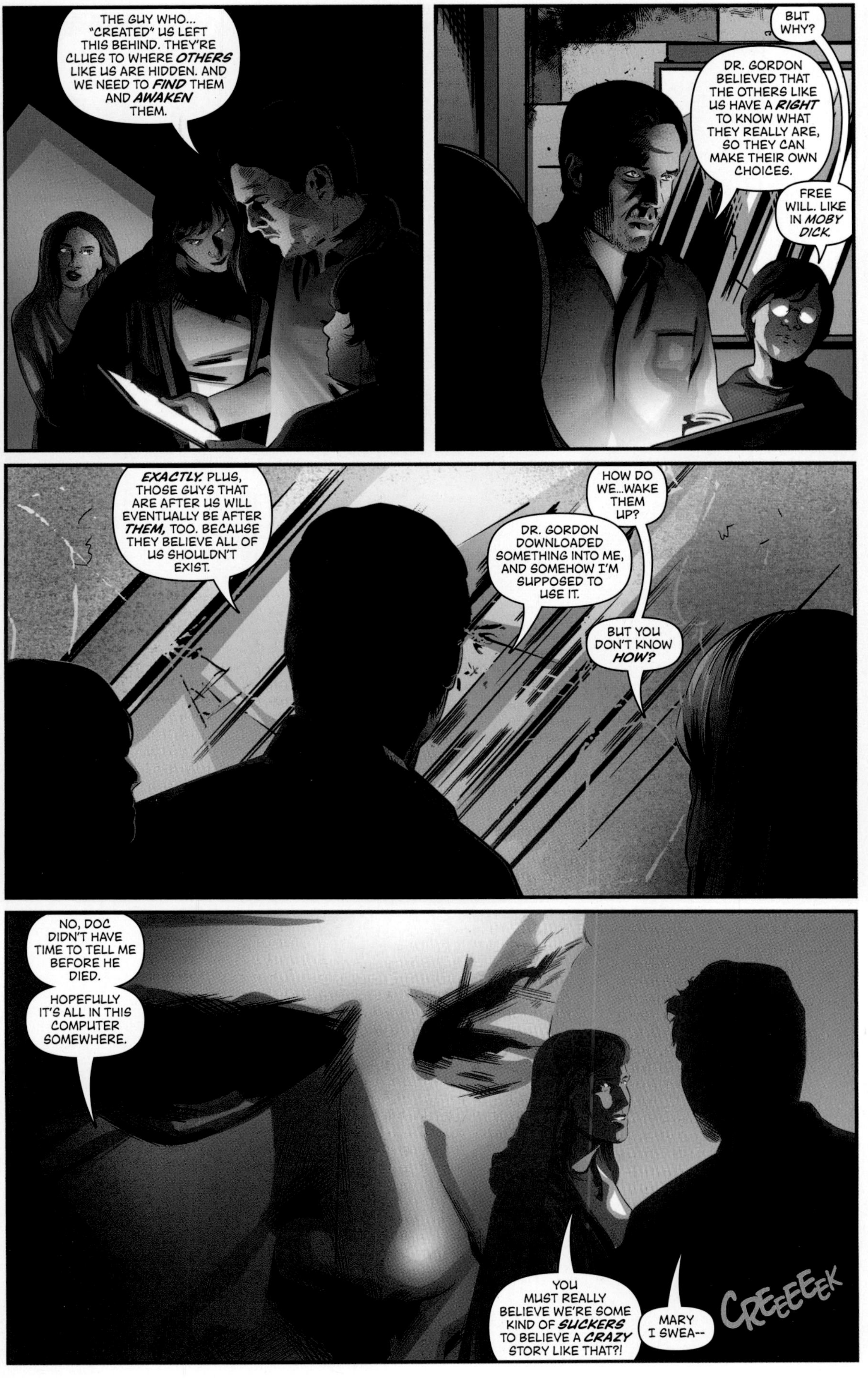
THE GUY WHO... "CREATED" US LEFT THIS BEHIND. THEY'RE CLUES TO WHERE OTHERS LIKE US ARE HIDDEN. AND WE NEED TO FIND THEM AND AWAKEN THEM.
BUT WHY?
DR. GORDON BELIEVED THAT THE OTHERS LIKE US HAVE A RIGHT TO KNOW WHAT THEY REALLY ARE, SO THEY CAN MAKE THEIR OWN CHOICES.
FREE WILL. LIKE IN MOBY DICK.
EXACTLY. PLUS, THOSE GUYS THAT ARE AFTER US WILL EVENTUALLY BE AFTER THEM, TOO. BECAUSE THEY BELIEVE ALL OF US SHOULDN'T EXIST.
HOW DO WE...WAKE THEM UP?
DR. GORDON DOWNLOADED SOMETHING INTO ME, AND SOMEHOW I'M SUPPOSED TO USE IT.
BUT YOU DON'T KNOW HOW?
NO, DOC DIDN'T HAVE TIME TO TELL ME BEFORE HE DIED.
HOPEFULLY IT'S ALL IN THIS COMPUTER SOMEWHERE.
YOU MUST REALLY BELIEVE WE'RE SOME KIND OF SUCKERS TO BELIEVE A CRAZY STORY LIKE THAT?!
MARY I SWEA--
CREEEEEK

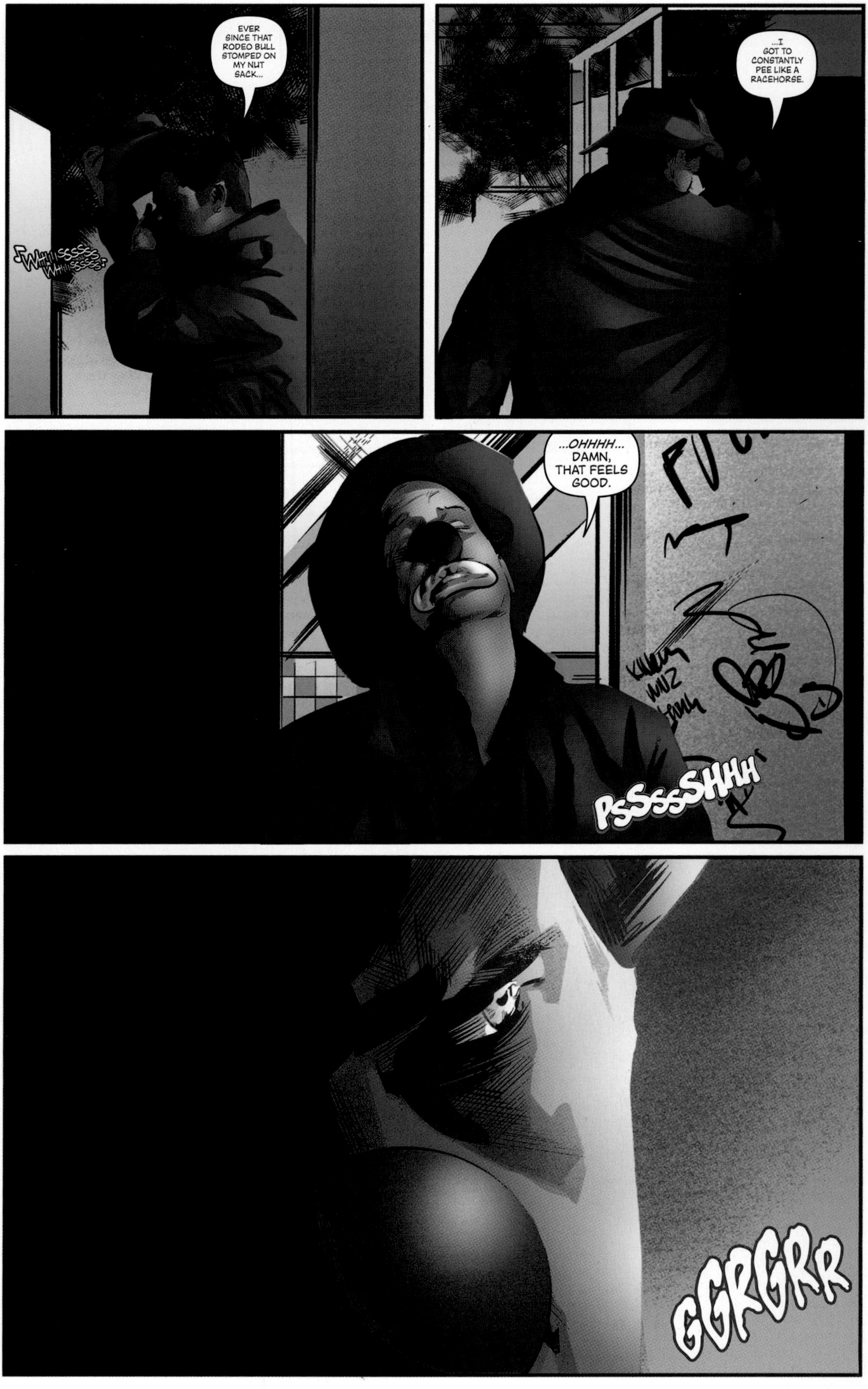
EVER SINCE THAT RODEO BULL STOMPED ON MY NUT SACK...
WHIIIISSSSSS WHIIIISSSSSS
...I GOT TO CONSTANTLY PEE LIKE A RACEHORSE.
...OHHHH... DAMN, THAT FEELS GOOD.
PSSSSSHHH
GGRGRR

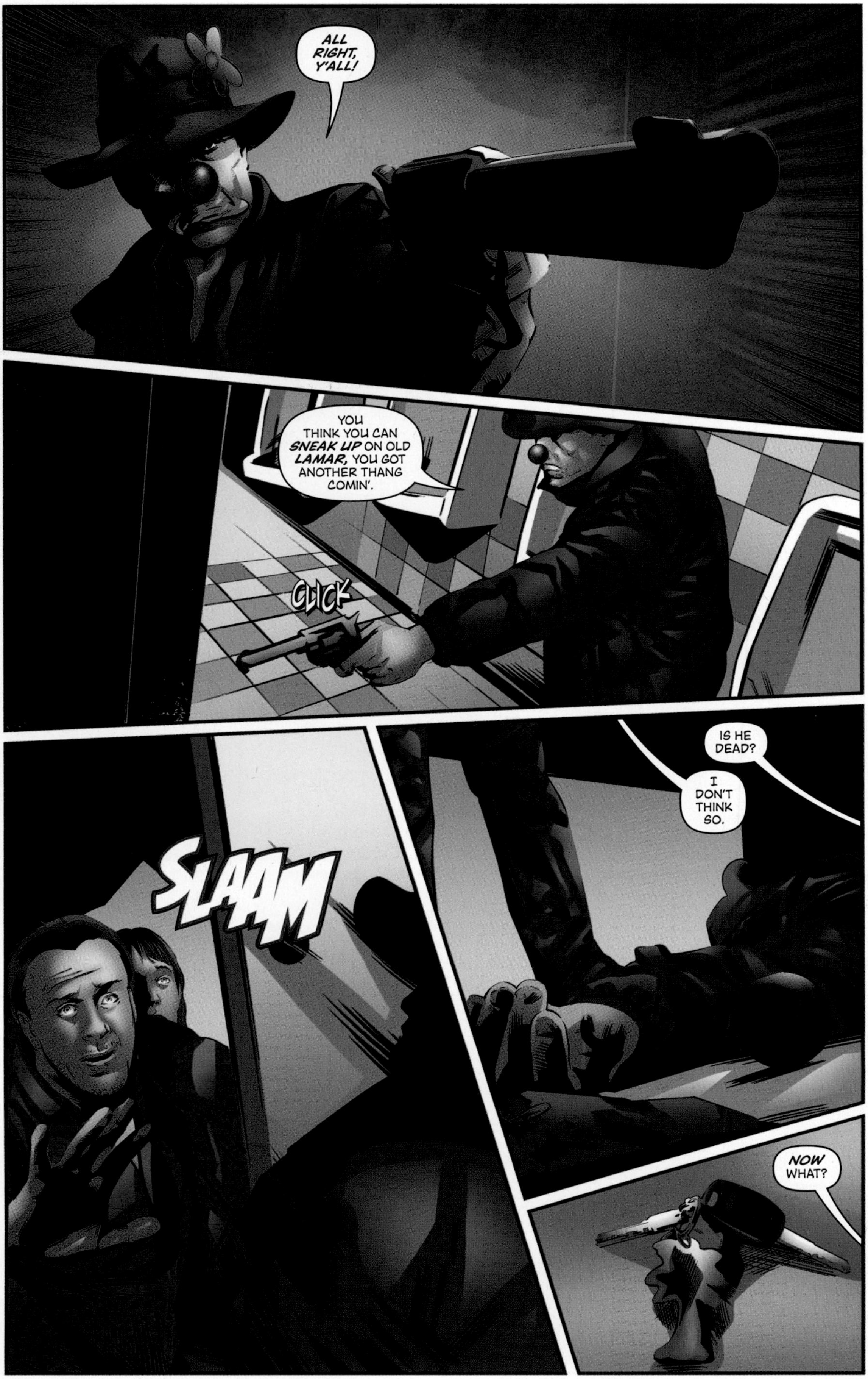
ALL RIGHT, Y'ALL!
YOU THINK YOU CAN SNEAK UP ON OLD LAMAR, YOU GOT ANOTHER THANG COMIN'.
CLICK
SLAAM
IS HE DEAD?
I DON'T THINK SO.
NOW WHAT?

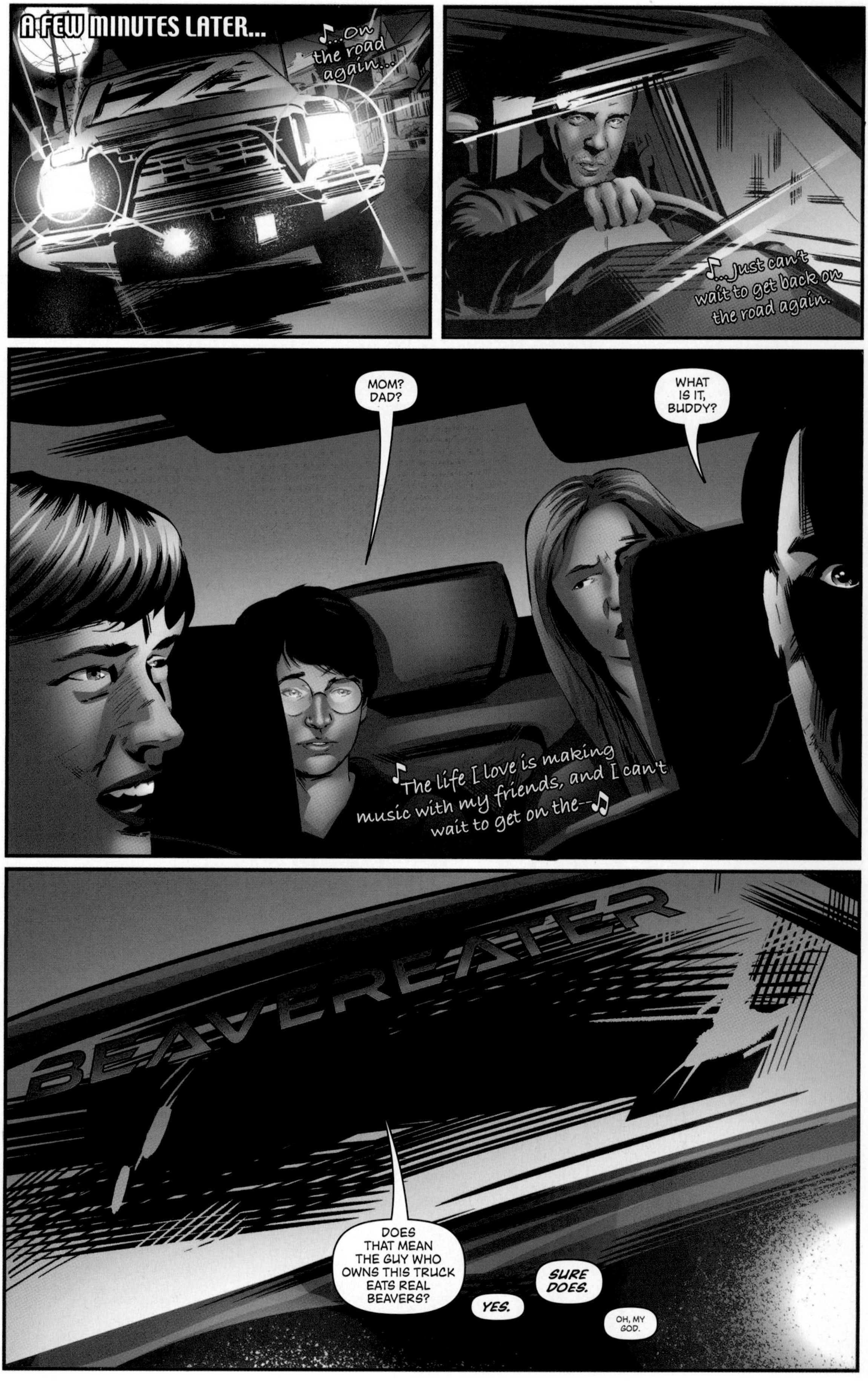
A FEW MINUTES LATER...
♪...On the road again...
♪...Just can't wait to get back on the road again.
MOM? DAD?
WHAT IS IT, BUDDY?
♪The life I love is making music with my friends, and I can't wait to get on the--♪
BEAVEREATER
DOES THAT MEAN THE GUY WHO OWNS THIS TRUCK EATS REAL BEAVERS?
SURE DOES.
YES.
OH, MY GOD.

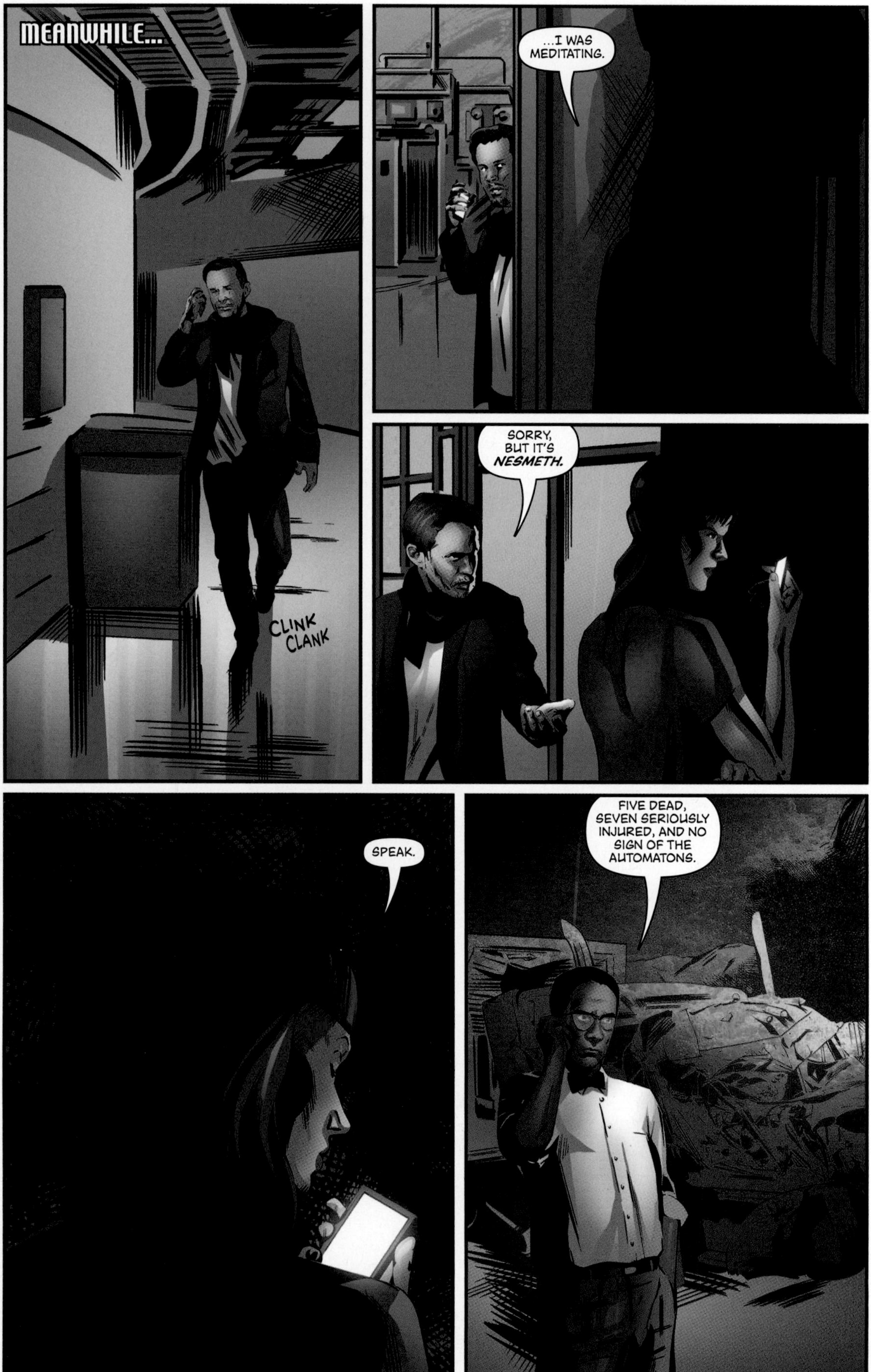
MEANWHILE...
CLINK CLANK
...I WAS MEDITATING.
SORRY, BUT IT'S *NESMETH.*
SPEAK.
FIVE DEAD, SEVEN SERIOUSLY INJURED, AND NO SIGN OF THE AUTOMATONS.

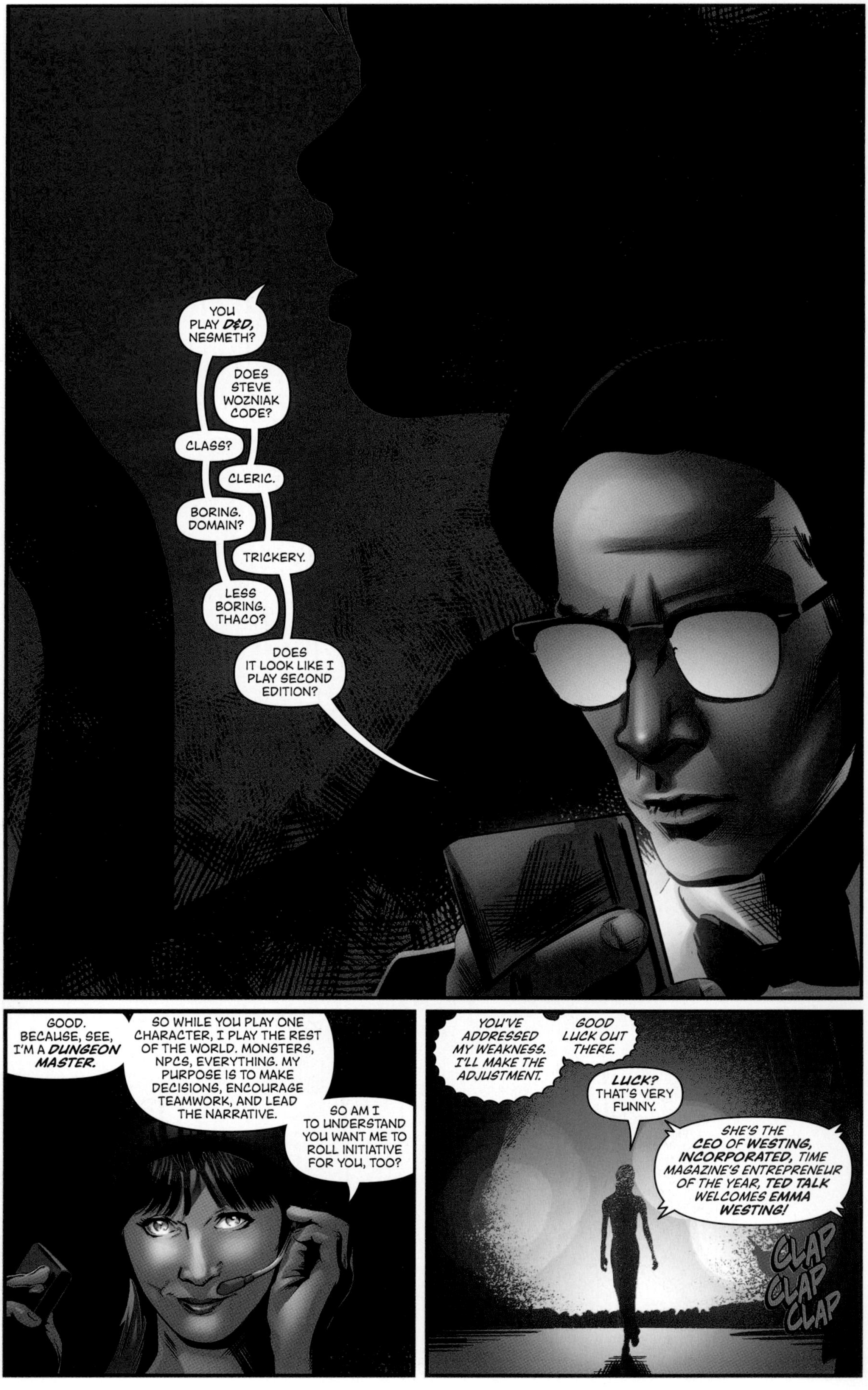
YOU PLAY D&D, NESMETH?
DOES STEVE WOZNIAK CODE?
CLASS?
CLERIC.
BORING. DOMAIN?
TRICKERY.
LESS BORING. THACO?
DOES IT LOOK LIKE I PLAY SECOND EDITION?
GOOD. BECAUSE, SEE, I'M A DUNGEON MASTER.
SO WHILE YOU PLAY ONE CHARACTER, I PLAY THE REST OF THE WORLD. MONSTERS, NPCS, EVERYTHING. MY PURPOSE IS TO MAKE DECISIONS, ENCOURAGE TEAMWORK, AND LEAD THE NARRATIVE.
SO AM I TO UNDERSTAND YOU WANT ME TO ROLL INITIATIVE FOR YOU, TOO?
YOU'VE ADDRESSED MY WEAKNESS. I'LL MAKE THE ADJUSTMENT.
GOOD LUCK OUT THERE.
LUCK? THAT'S VERY FUNNY.
SHE'S THE CEO OF WESTING, INCORPORATED, TIME MAGAZINE'S ENTREPRENEUR OF THE YEAR, TED TALK WELCOMES EMMA WESTING!
CLAP CLAP CLAP

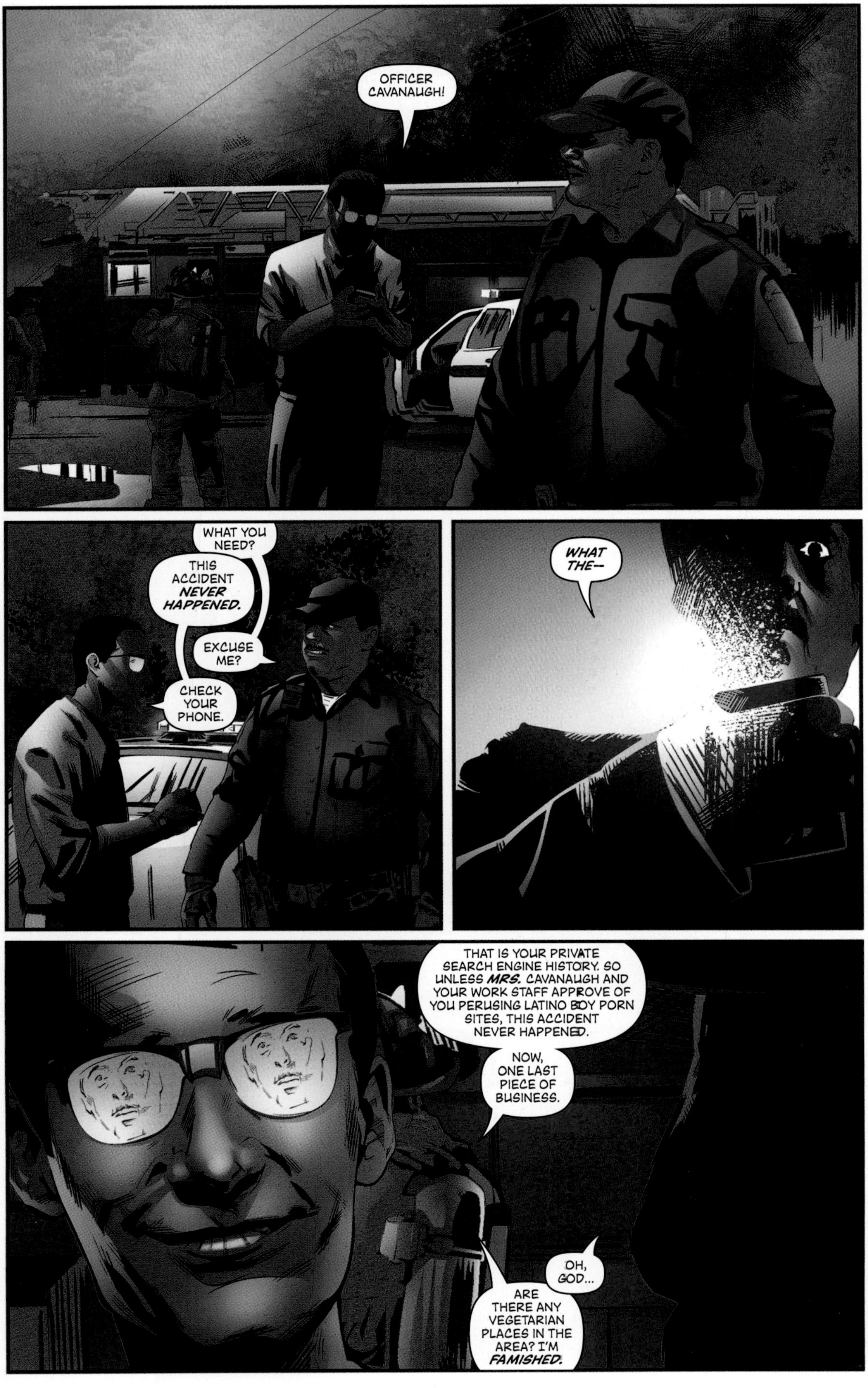
OFFICER CAVANAUGH!
WHAT YOU NEED?
THIS ACCIDENT NEVER HAPPENED.
EXCUSE ME?
CHECK YOUR PHONE.
WHAT THE--
THAT IS YOUR PRIVATE SEARCH ENGINE HISTORY. SO UNLESS MRS. CAVANAUGH AND YOUR WORK STAFF APPROVE OF YOU PERUSING LATINO BOY PORN SITES, THIS ACCIDENT NEVER HAPPENED.
NOW, ONE LAST PIECE OF BUSINESS.
OH, GOD...
ARE THERE ANY VEGETARIAN PLACES IN THE AREA? I'M FAMISHED.

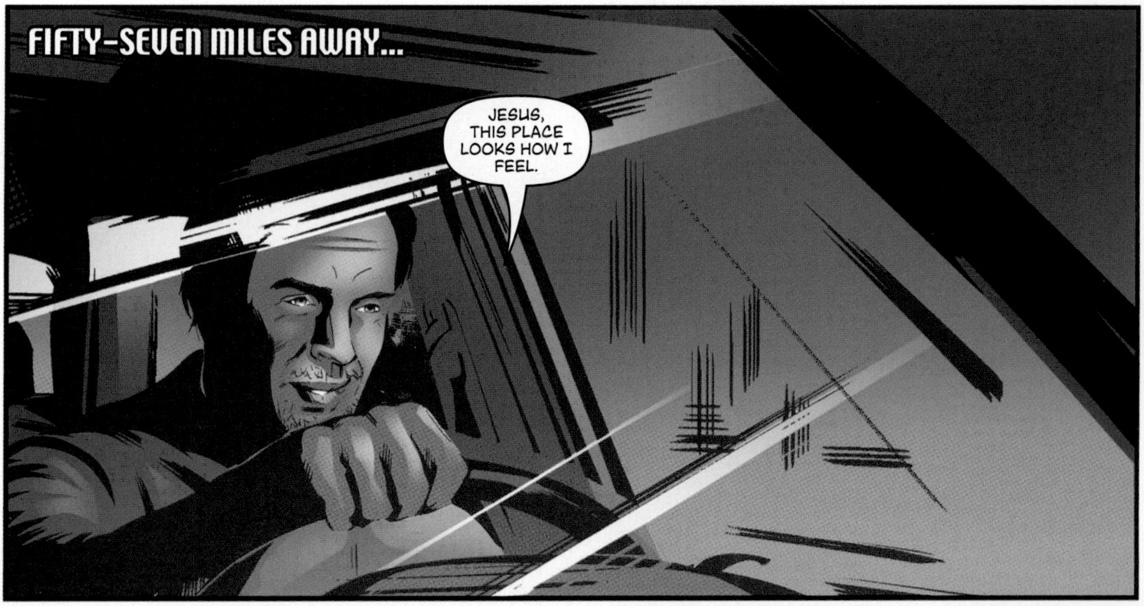
FIFTY-SEVEN MILES AWAY...
JESUS, THIS PLACE LOOKS HOW I FEEL.

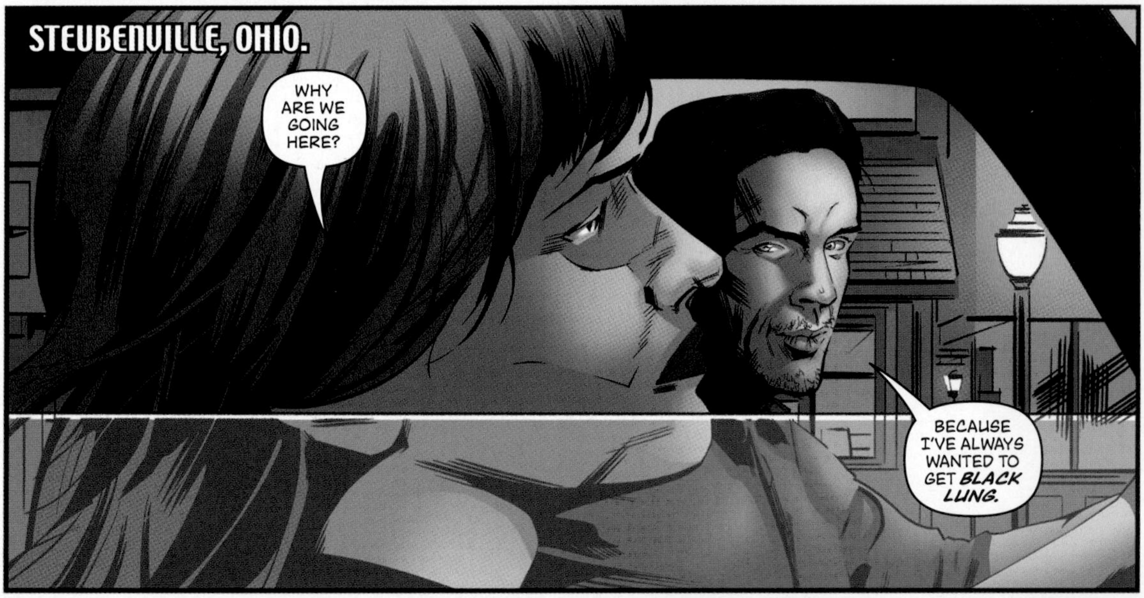
STEUBENVILLE, OHIO.
WHY ARE WE GOING HERE?
BECAUSE I'VE ALWAYS WANTED TO GET *BLACK LUNG.*

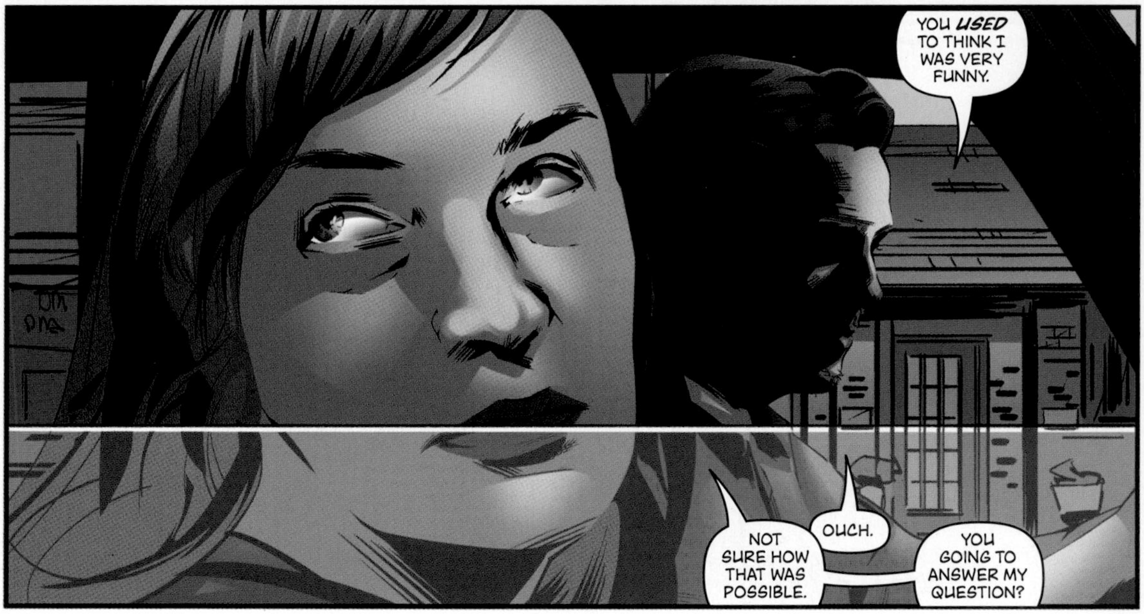
YOU *USED* TO THINK I WAS VERY FUNNY.
NOT SURE HOW THAT WAS POSSIBLE.
OUCH.
YOU GOING TO ANSWER MY QUESTION?

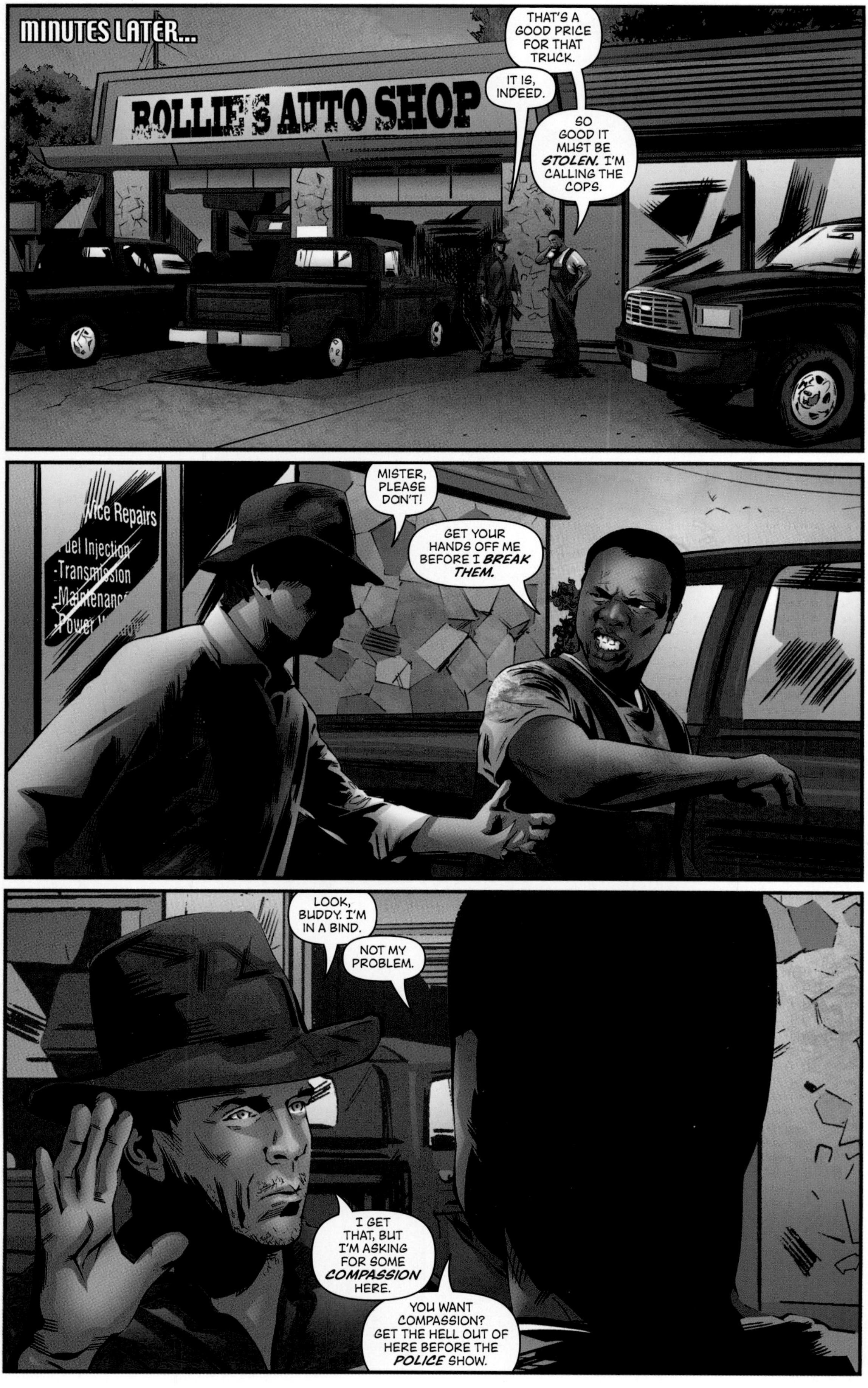
MINUTES LATER...
ROLLIE'S AUTO SHOP
THAT'S A GOOD PRICE FOR THAT TRUCK.
IT IS, INDEED.
SO GOOD IT MUST BE STOLEN. I'M CALLING THE COPS.
MISTER, PLEASE DON'T!
GET YOUR HANDS OFF ME BEFORE I BREAK THEM.
LOOK, BUDDY. I'M IN A BIND.
NOT MY PROBLEM.
I GET THAT, BUT I'M ASKING FOR SOME COMPASSION HERE.
YOU WANT COMPASSION? GET THE HELL OUT OF HERE BEFORE THE POLICE SHOW.

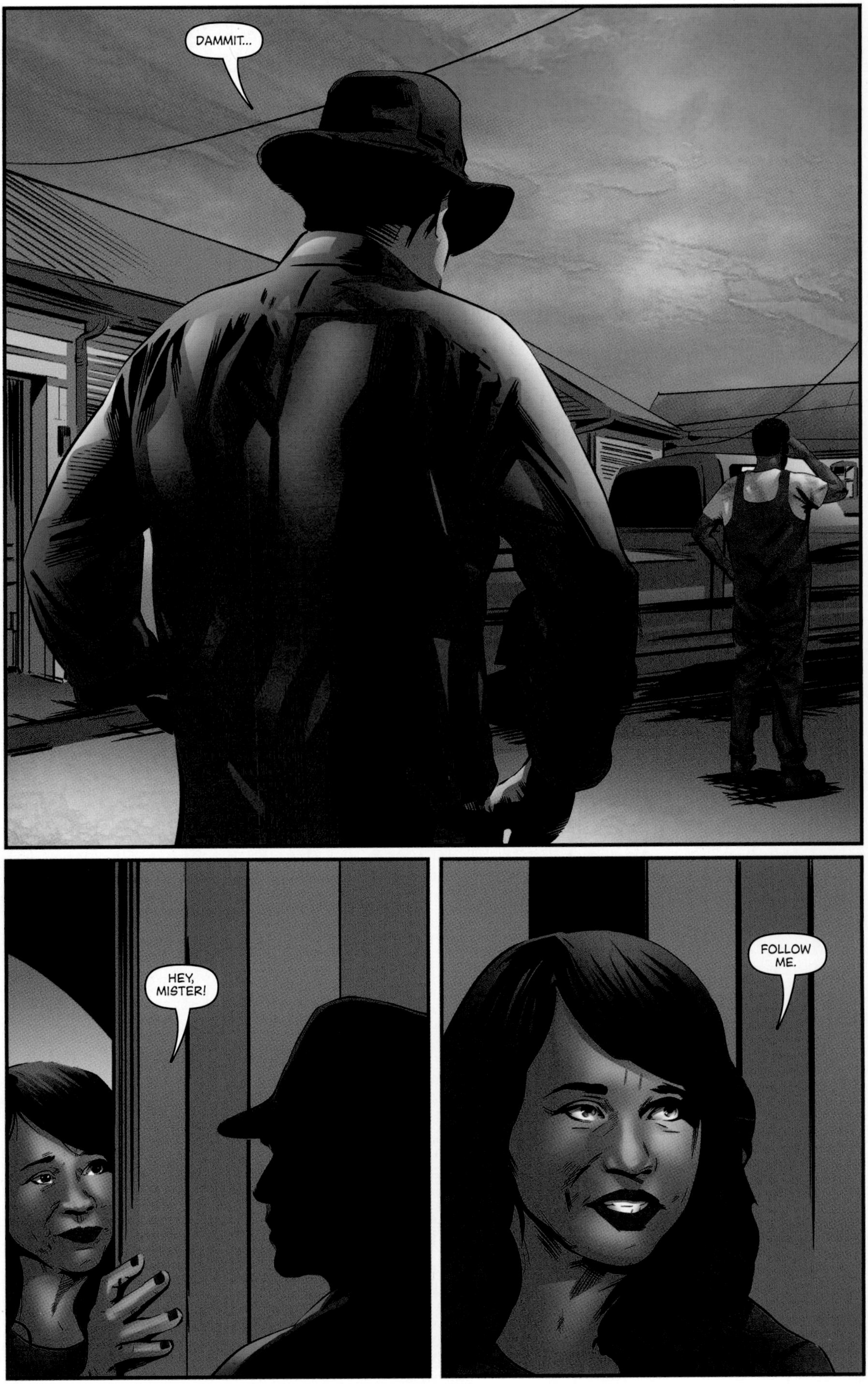
DAMMIT...
HEY, MISTER!
FOLLOW ME.

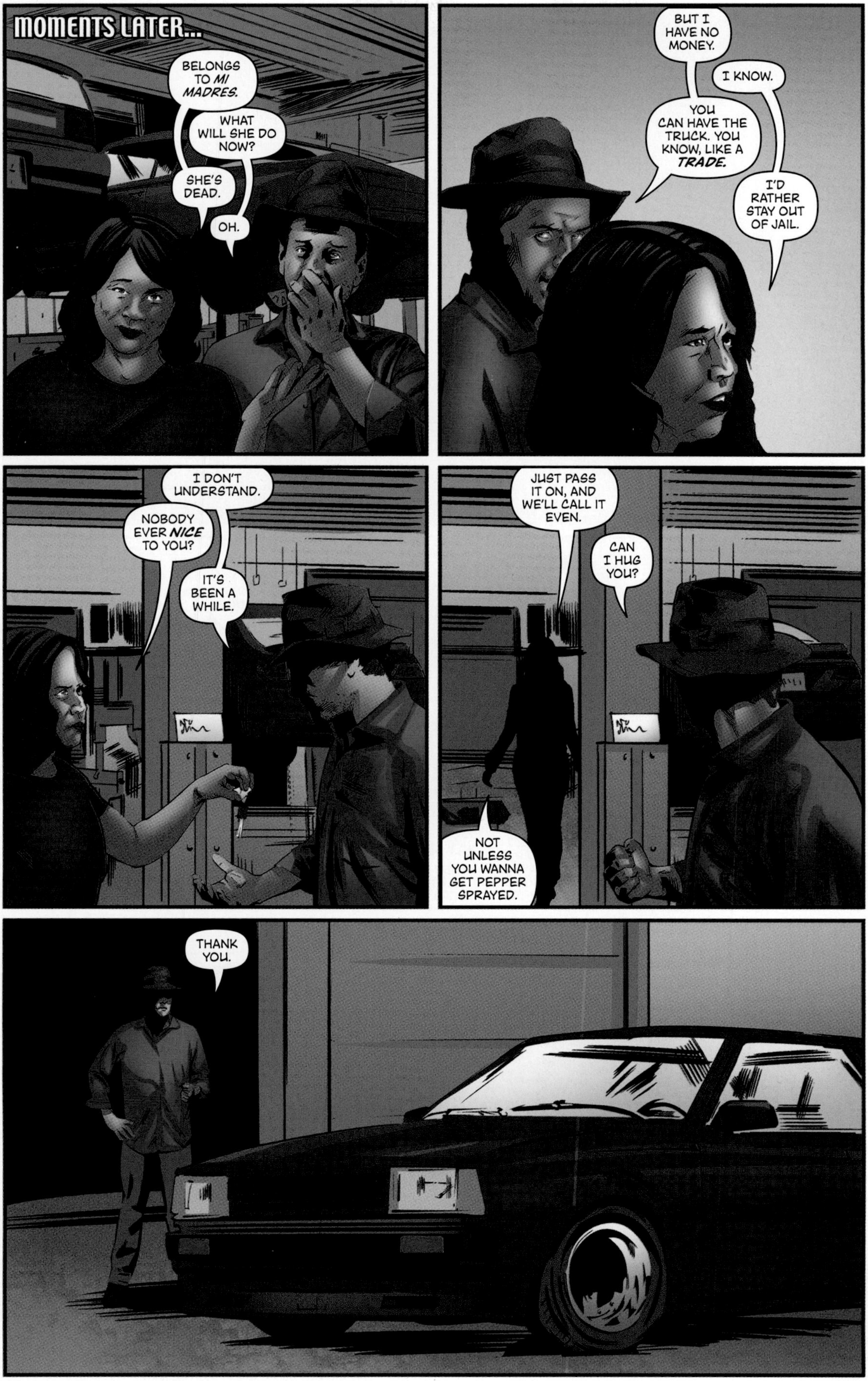
MOMENTS LATER...
BELONGS TO *MI MADRES.*
WHAT WILL SHE DO NOW?
SHE'S DEAD.
OH.
BUT I HAVE NO MONEY.
YOU CAN HAVE THE TRUCK. YOU KNOW, LIKE A ***TRADE.***
I KNOW.
I'D RATHER STAY OUT OF JAIL.
I DON'T UNDERSTAND.
NOBODY EVER ***NICE*** TO YOU?
IT'S BEEN A WHILE.
JUST PASS IT ON, AND WE'LL CALL IT EVEN.
CAN I HUG YOU?
NOT UNLESS YOU WANNA GET PEPPER SPRAYED.
THANK YOU.

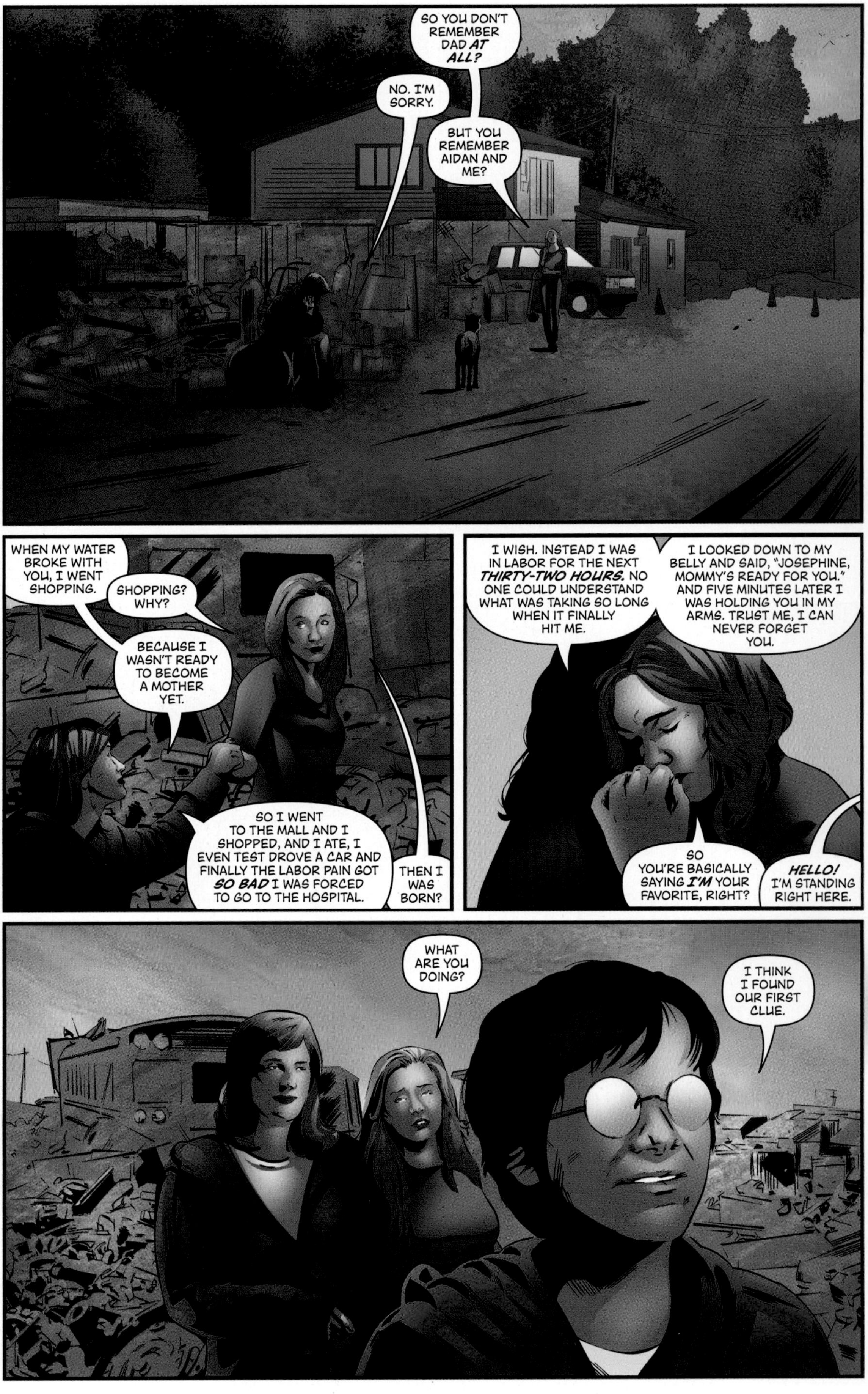
SO YOU DON'T REMEMBER DAD *AT ALL?*
NO. I'M SORRY.
BUT YOU REMEMBER AIDAN AND ME?
WHEN MY WATER BROKE WITH YOU, I WENT SHOPPING.
SHOPPING? WHY?
BECAUSE I WASN'T READY TO BECOME A MOTHER YET.
SO I WENT TO THE MALL AND I SHOPPED, AND I ATE, I EVEN TEST DROVE A CAR AND FINALLY THE LABOR PAIN GOT *SO BAD* I WAS FORCED TO GO TO THE HOSPITAL.
THEN I WAS BORN?
I WISH. INSTEAD I WAS IN LABOR FOR THE NEXT *THIRTY-TWO HOURS.* NO ONE COULD UNDERSTAND WHAT WAS TAKING SO LONG WHEN IT FINALLY HIT ME.
I LOOKED DOWN TO MY BELLY AND SAID, "JOSEPHINE, MOMMY'S READY FOR YOU." AND FIVE MINUTES LATER I WAS HOLDING YOU IN MY ARMS. TRUST ME, I CAN NEVER FORGET YOU.
SO YOU'RE BASICALLY SAYING *I'M* YOUR FAVORITE, RIGHT?
HELLO! I'M STANDING RIGHT HERE.
WHAT ARE YOU DOING?
I THINK I FOUND OUR FIRST CLUE.

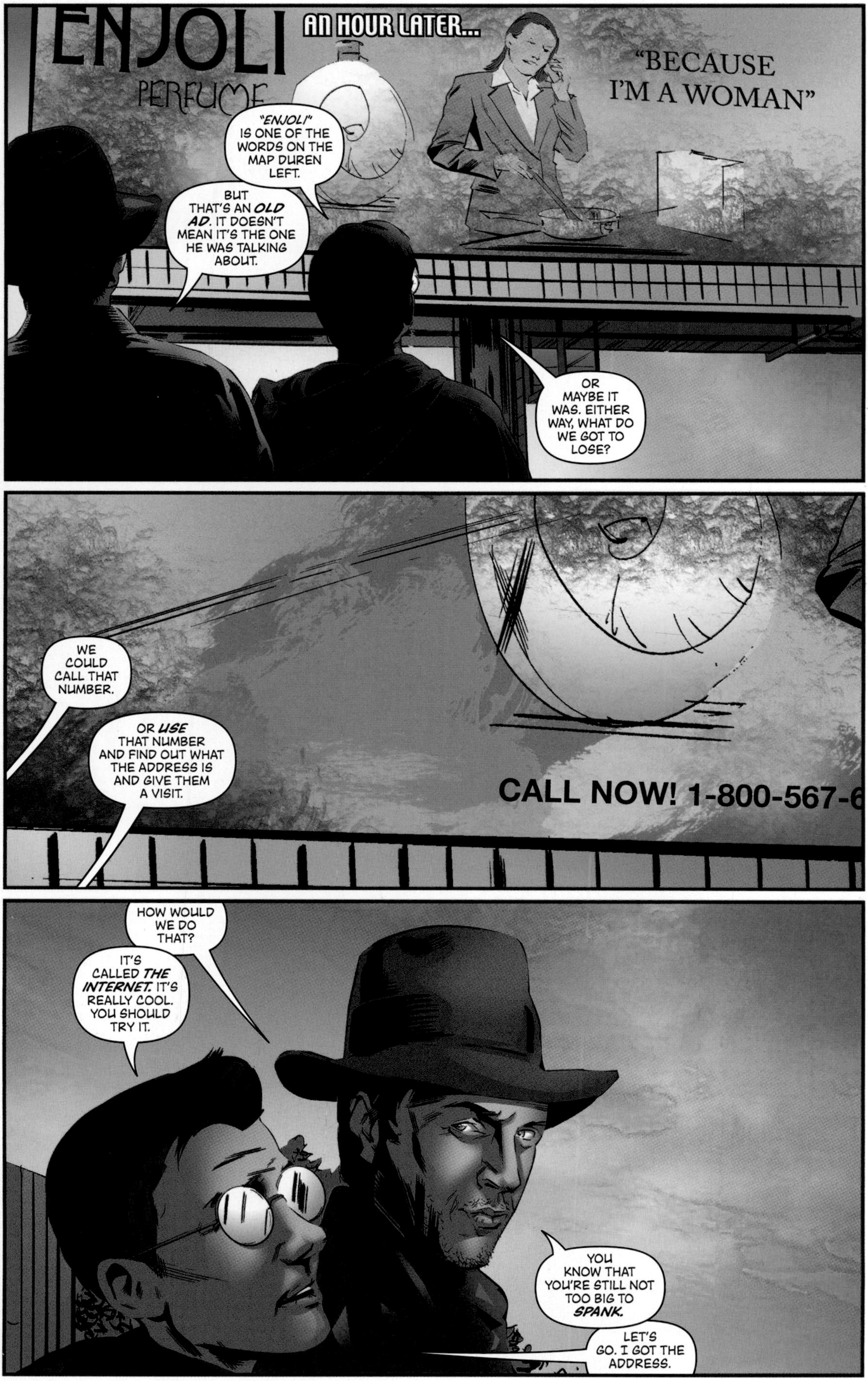
ENJOLI
AN HOUR LATER...
PERFUME
"BECAUSE I'M A WOMAN"
"ENJOLI" IS ONE OF THE WORDS ON THE MAP DUREN LEFT.
BUT THAT'S AN ***OLD AD***. IT DOESN'T MEAN IT'S THE ONE HE WAS TALKING ABOUT.
OR MAYBE IT WAS. EITHER WAY, WHAT DO WE GOT TO LOSE?
WE COULD CALL THAT NUMBER.
OR ***USE*** THAT NUMBER AND FIND OUT WHAT THE ADDRESS IS AND GIVE THEM A VISIT.
CALL NOW! 1-800-567-6
HOW WOULD WE DO THAT?
IT'S CALLED ***THE INTERNET.*** IT'S REALLY COOL. YOU SHOULD TRY IT.
YOU KNOW THAT YOU'RE STILL NOT TOO BIG TO ***SPANK.***
LET'S GO. I GOT THE ADDRESS.

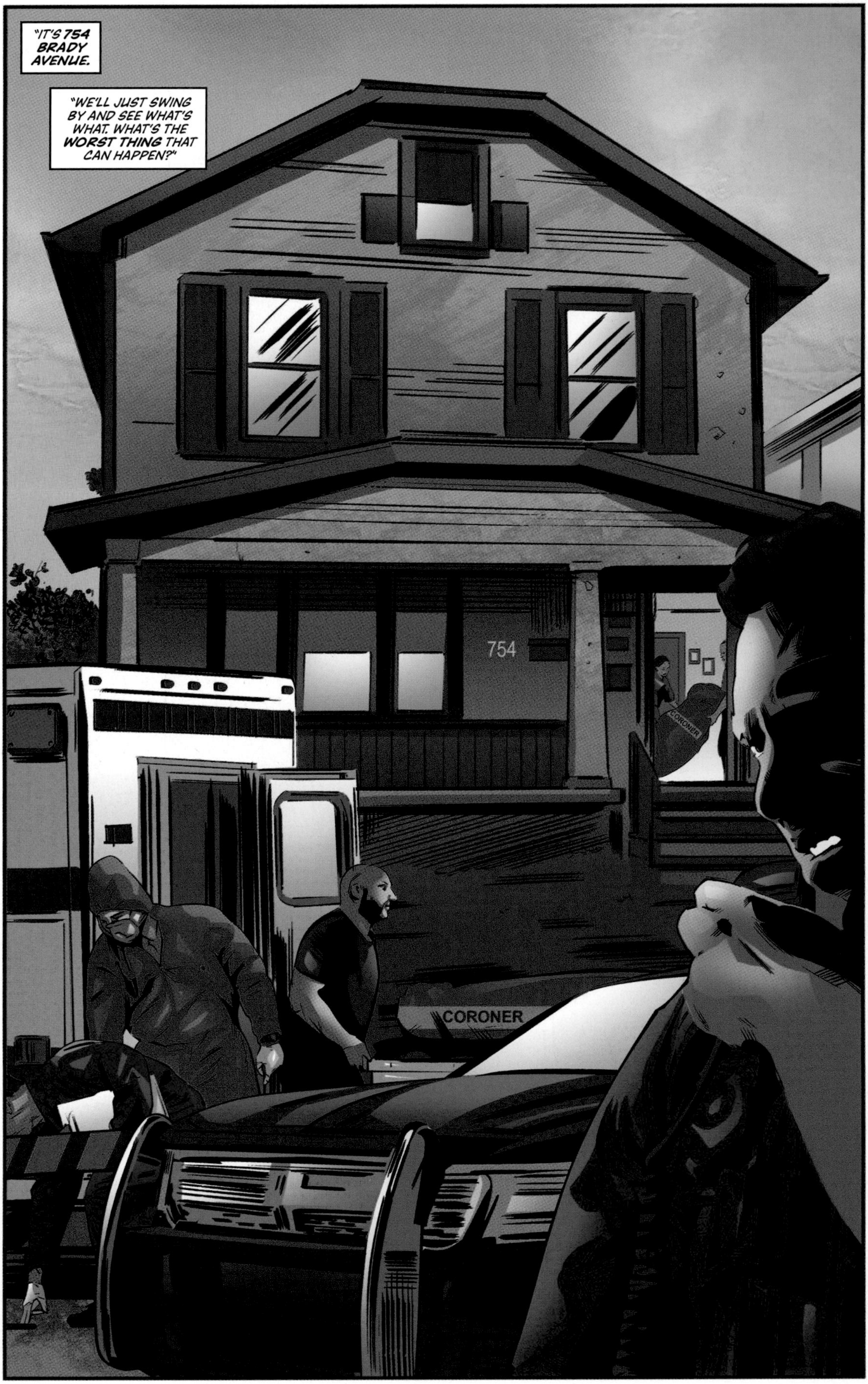
"IT'S 754 BRADY AVENUE.
"WE'LL JUST SWING BY AND SEE WHAT'S WHAT. WHAT'S THE WORST THING THAT CAN HAPPEN?"
754
CORONER
CORONER

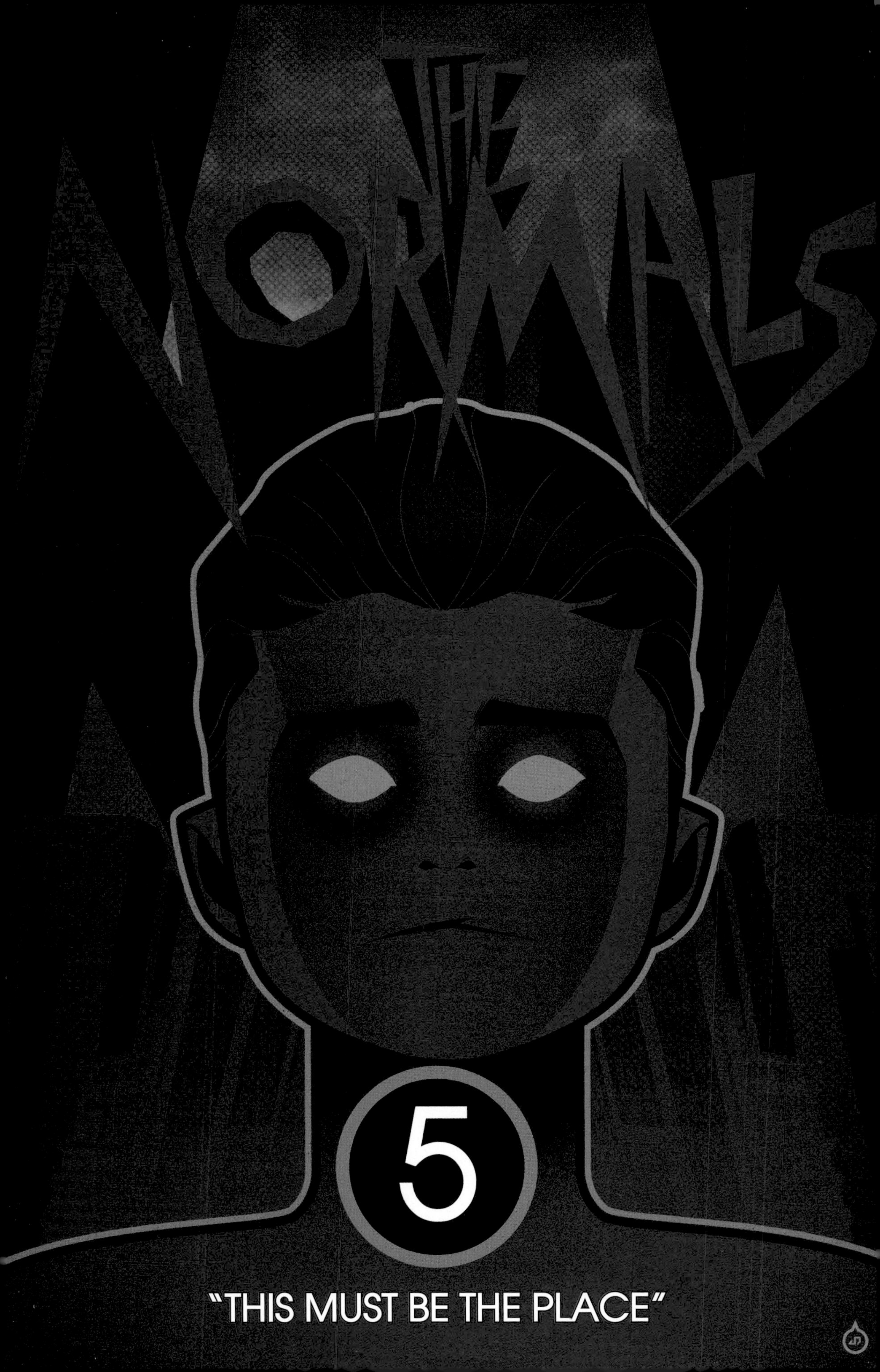
THE NORMALS
5
"THIS MUST BE THE PLACE"

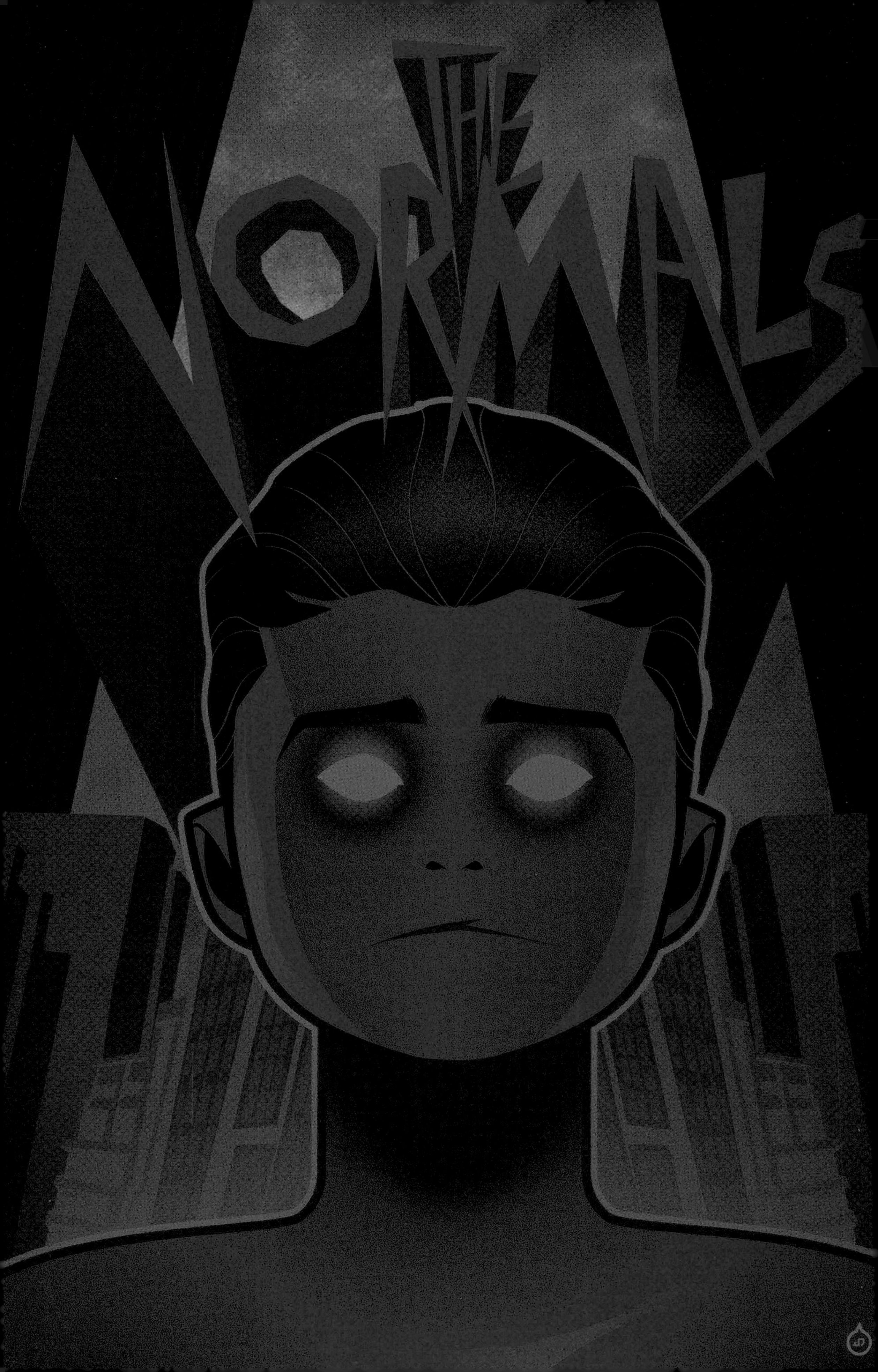
THE NORMALS

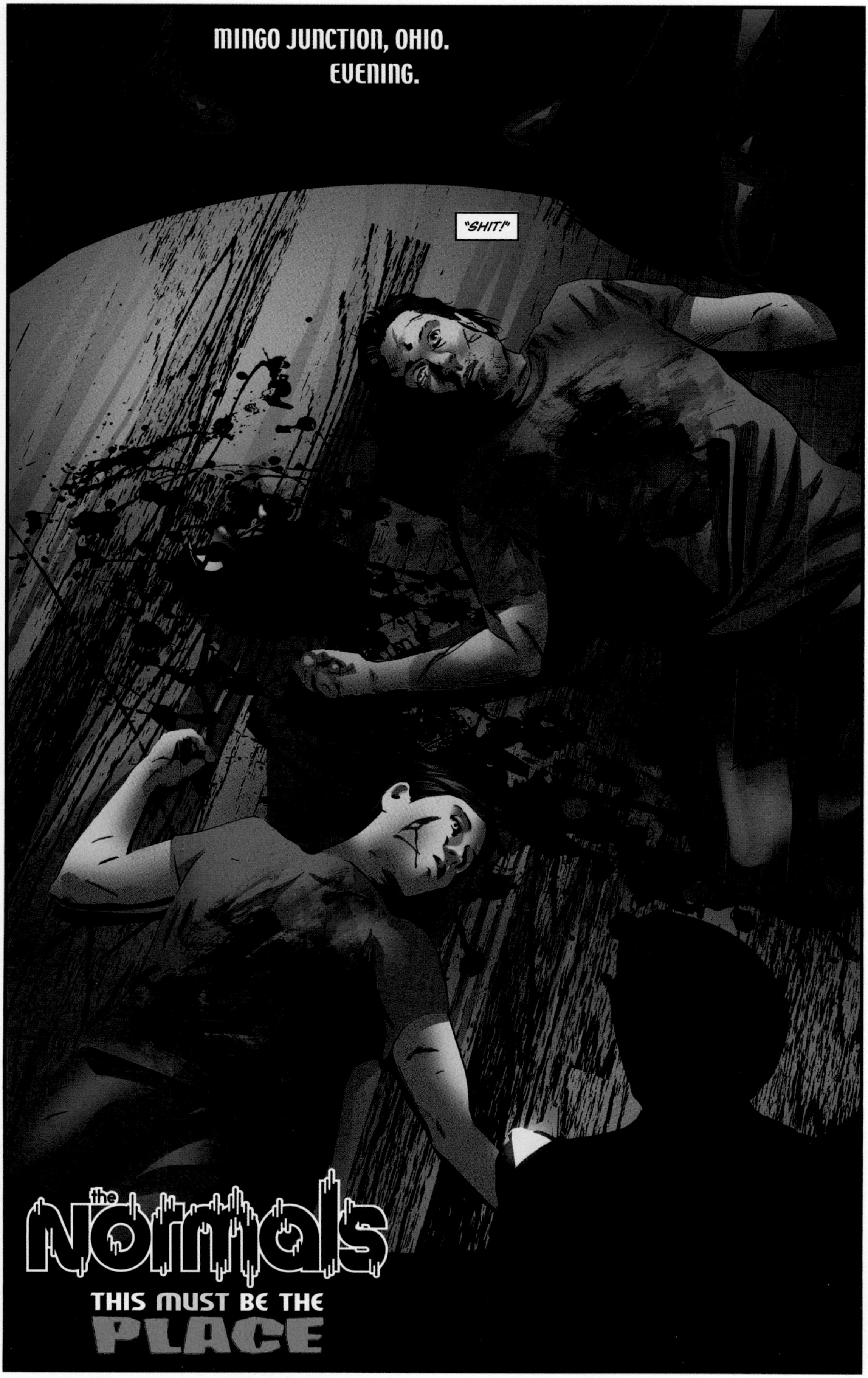
MINGO JUNCTION, OHIO.
EVENING.
"SHIT!"
the Normals
THIS MUST BE THE
PLACE

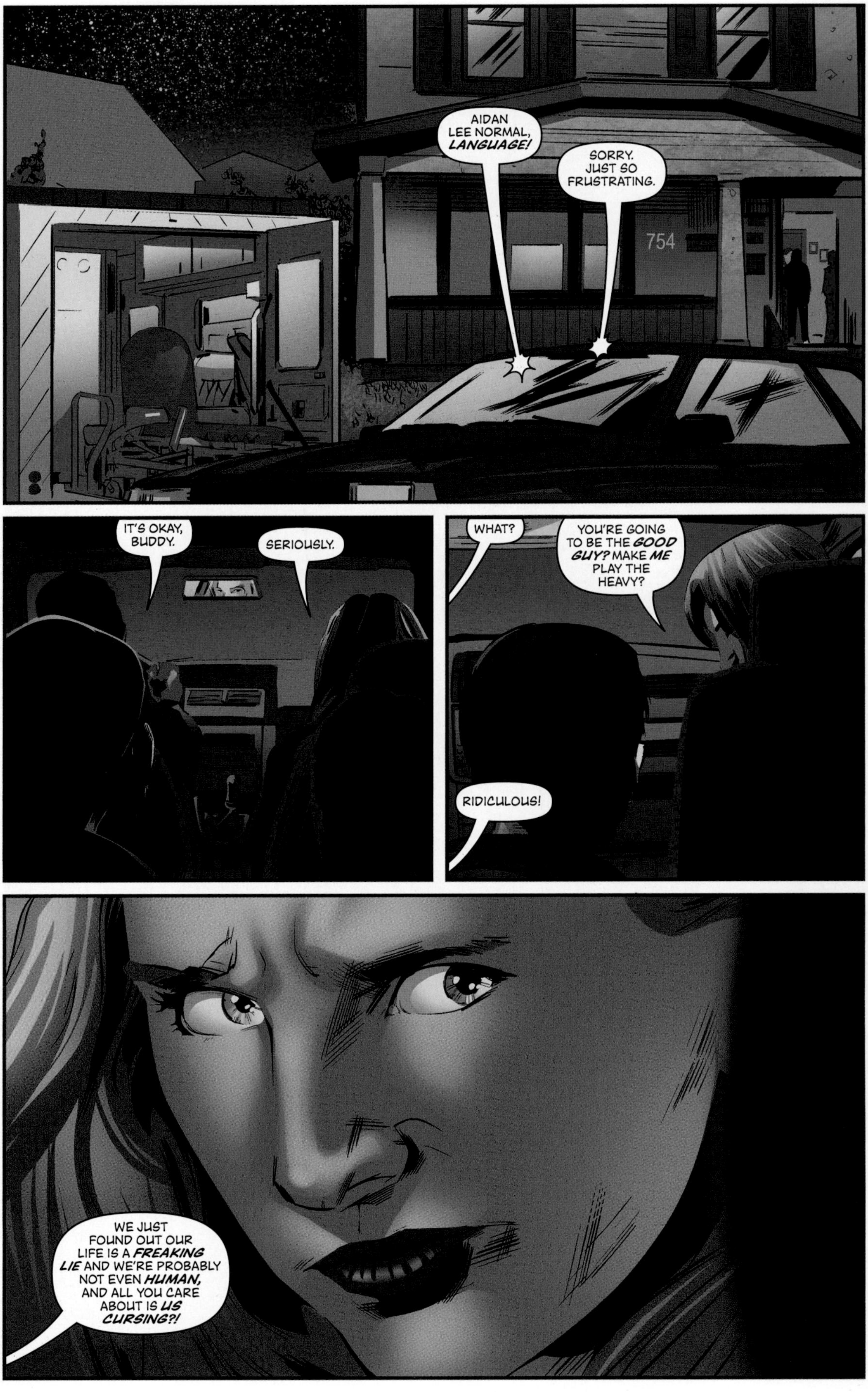

AIDAN LEE NORMAL, LANGUAGE!
SORRY. JUST SO FRUSTRATING.
754
IT'S OKAY, BUDDY.
SERIOUSLY.
WHAT?
YOU'RE GOING TO BE THE GOOD GUY? MAKE ME PLAY THE HEAVY?
RIDICULOUS!
WE JUST FOUND OUT OUR LIFE IS A FREAKING LIE AND WE'RE PROBABLY NOT EVEN HUMAN, AND ALL YOU CARE ABOUT IS US CURSING?!

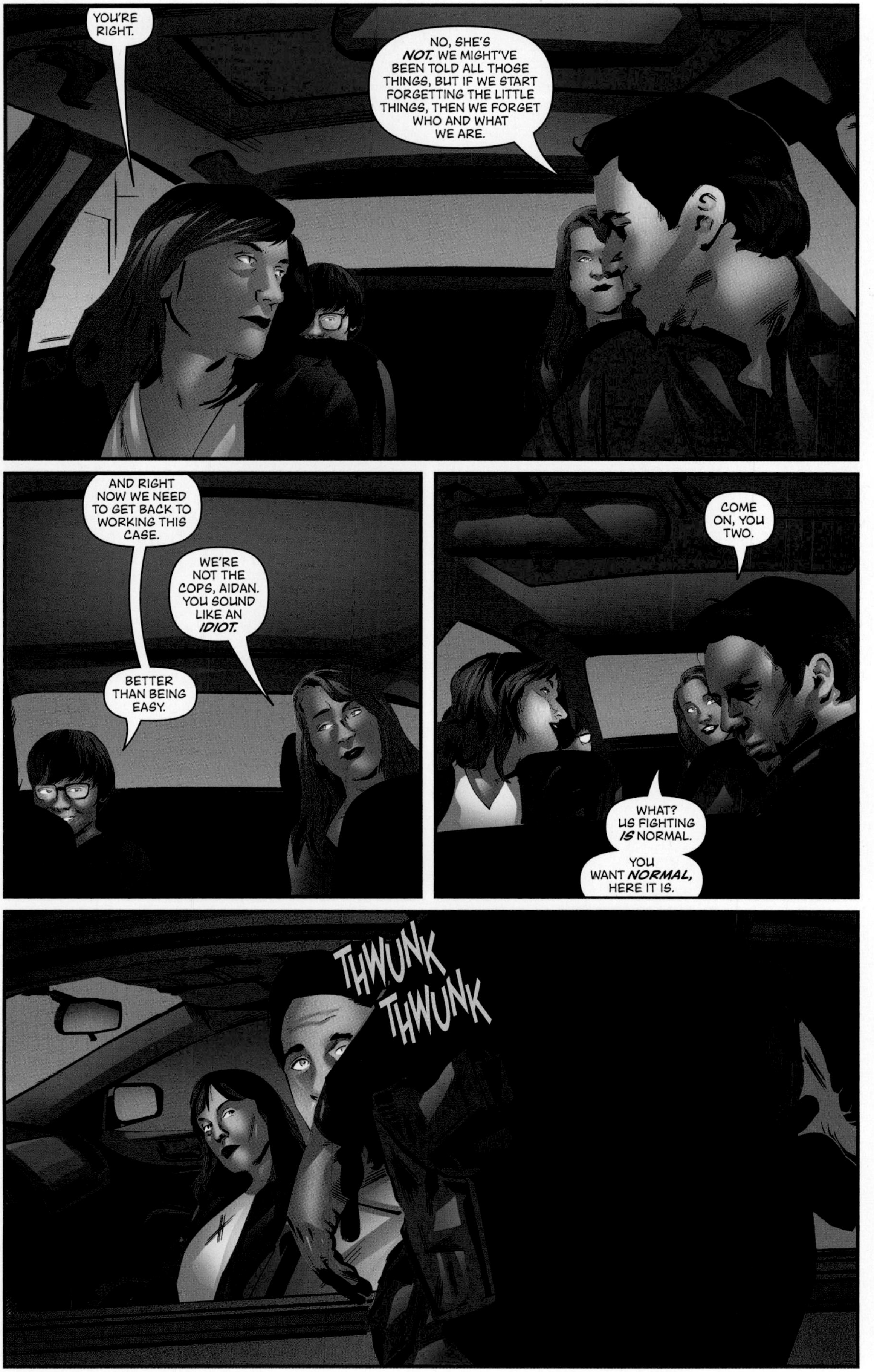
YOU'RE RIGHT.
NO, SHE'S *NOT.* WE MIGHT'VE BEEN TOLD ALL THOSE THINGS, BUT IF WE START FORGETTING THE LITTLE THINGS, THEN WE FORGET WHO AND WHAT WE ARE.
AND RIGHT NOW WE NEED TO GET BACK TO WORKING THIS CASE.
WE'RE NOT THE COPS, AIDAN. YOU SOUND LIKE AN *IDIOT.*
BETTER THAN BEING EASY.
COME ON, YOU TWO.
WHAT? US FIGHTING *IS* NORMAL.
YOU WANT *NORMAL,* HERE IT IS.
THWUNK
THWUNK

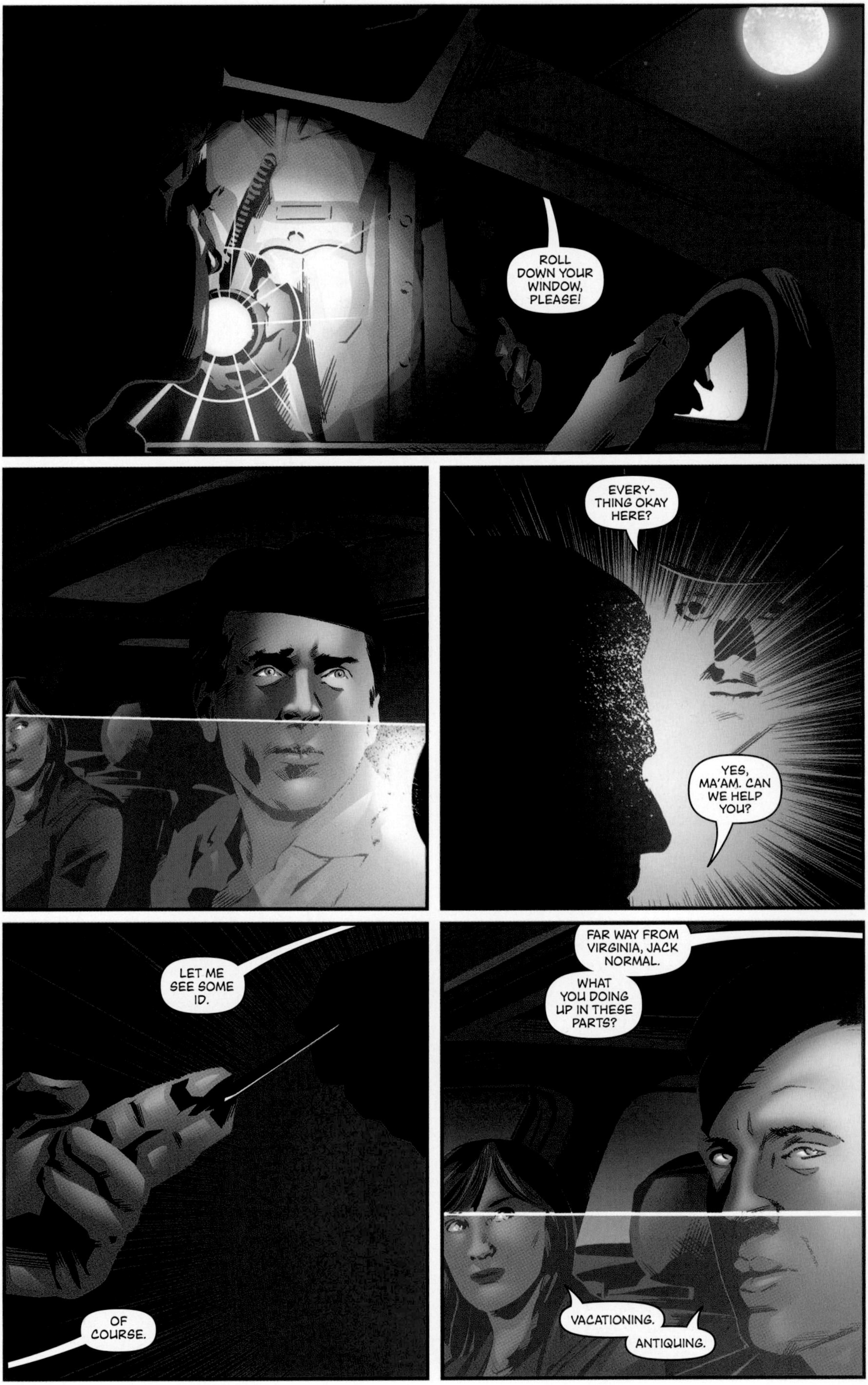
ROLL DOWN YOUR WINDOW, PLEASE!
EVERY-THING OKAY HERE?
YES, MA'AM. CAN WE HELP YOU?
LET ME SEE SOME ID.
OF COURSE.
FAR WAY FROM VIRGINIA, JACK NORMAL.
WHAT YOU DOING UP IN THESE PARTS?
VACATIONING.
ANTIQUING.

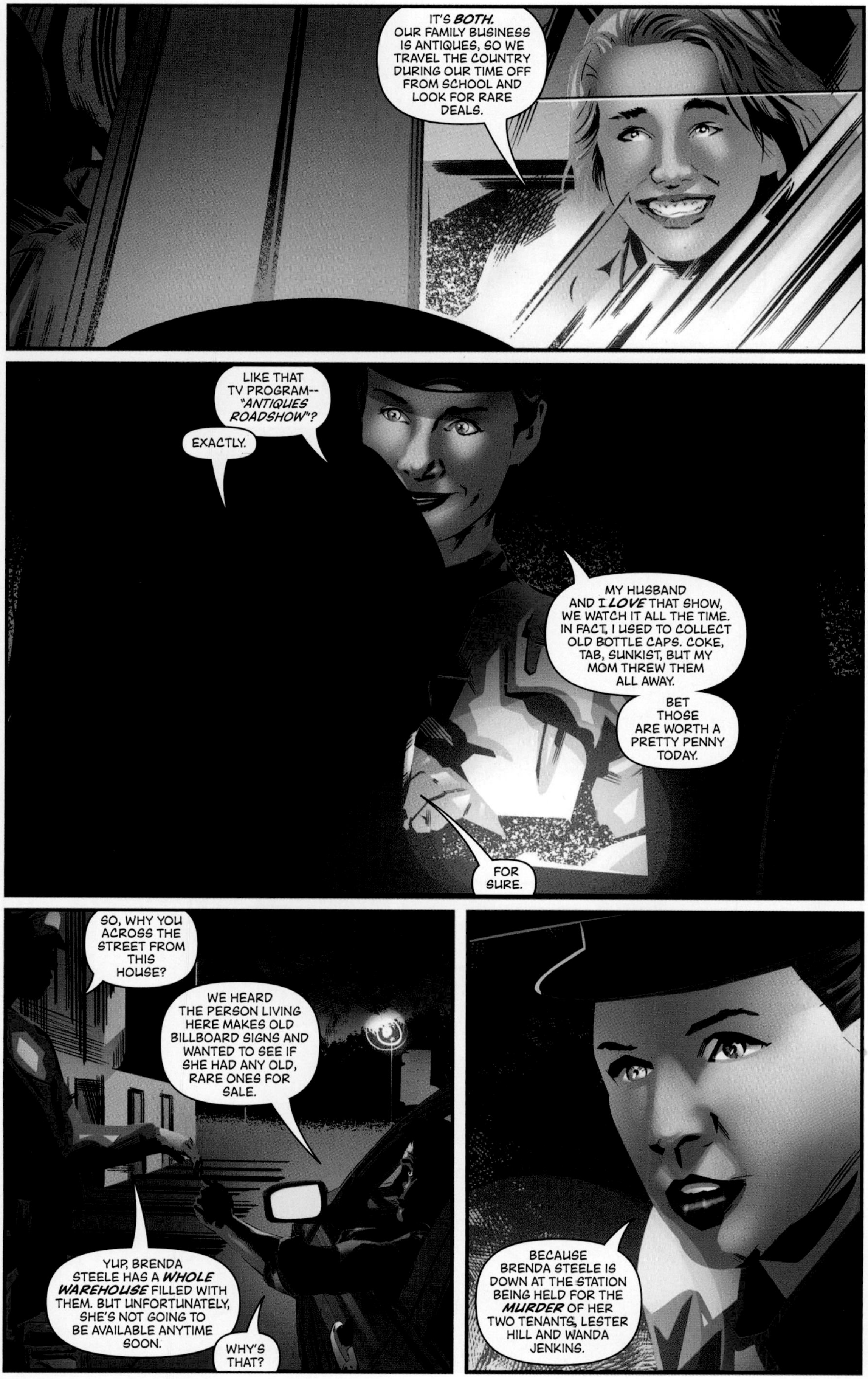

IT'S *BOTH.* OUR FAMILY BUSINESS IS ANTIQUES, SO WE TRAVEL THE COUNTRY DURING OUR TIME OFF FROM SCHOOL AND LOOK FOR RARE DEALS.
LIKE THAT TV PROGRAM-- "*ANTIQUES ROADSHOW*"?
EXACTLY.
MY HUSBAND AND I *LOVE* THAT SHOW, WE WATCH IT ALL THE TIME. IN FACT, I USED TO COLLECT OLD BOTTLE CAPS. COKE, TAB, SUNKIST, BUT MY MOM THREW THEM ALL AWAY.
BET THOSE ARE WORTH A PRETTY PENNY TODAY.
FOR SURE.
SO, WHY YOU ACROSS THE STREET FROM THIS HOUSE?
WE HEARD THE PERSON LIVING HERE MAKES OLD BILLBOARD SIGNS AND WANTED TO SEE IF SHE HAD ANY OLD, RARE ONES FOR SALE.
YUP, BRENDA STEELE HAS A *WHOLE WAREHOUSE* FILLED WITH THEM. BUT UNFORTUNATELY, SHE'S NOT GOING TO BE AVAILABLE ANYTIME SOON.
WHY'S THAT?
BECAUSE BRENDA STEELE IS DOWN AT THE STATION BEING HELD FOR THE *MURDER* OF HER TWO TENANTS, LESTER HILL AND WANDA JENKINS.

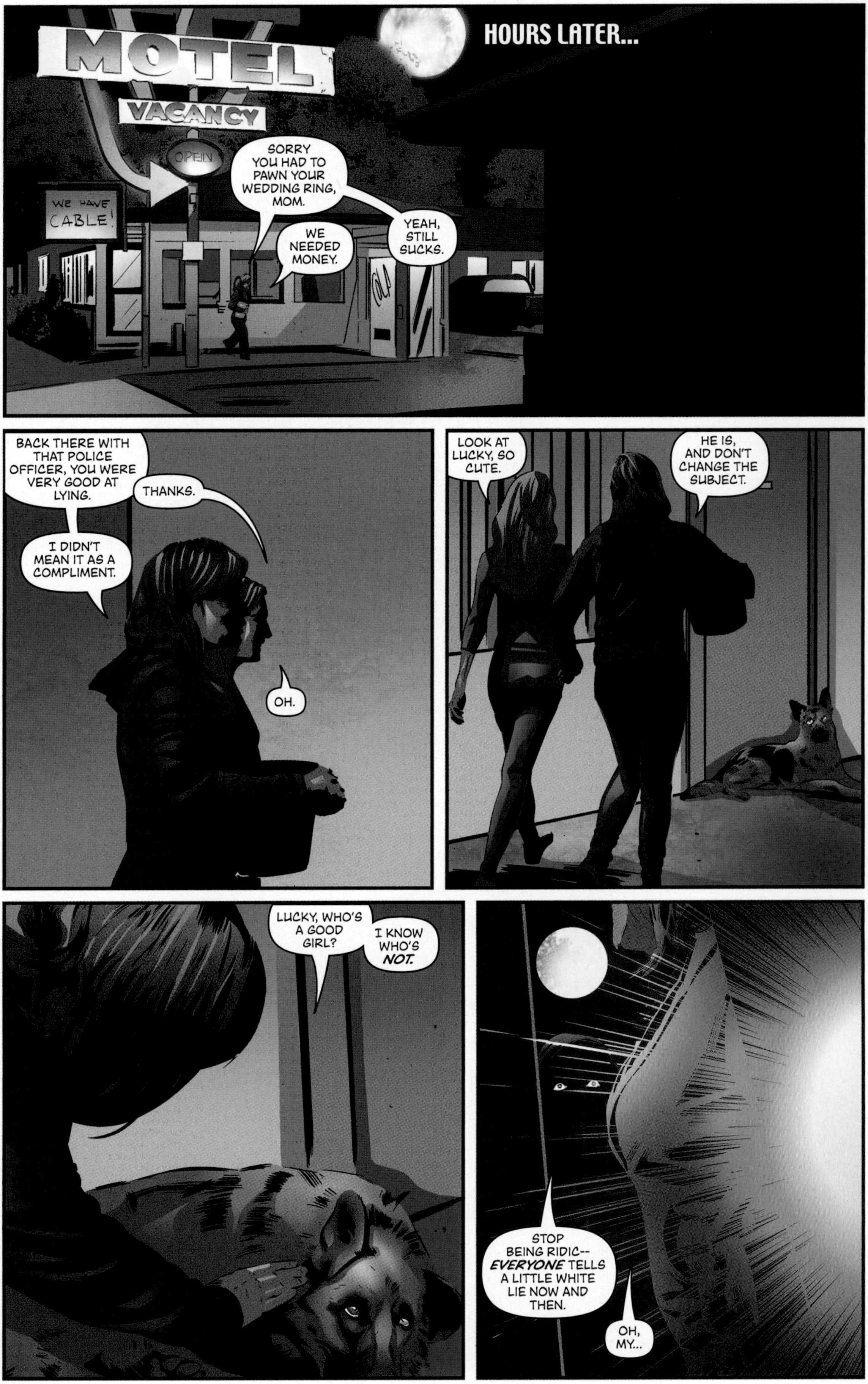
HOURS LATER...
MOTEL
VACANCY
OPEN
WE HAVE CABLE!
SORRY YOU HAD TO PAWN YOUR WEDDING RING, MOM.
WE NEEDED MONEY.
YEAH, STILL SUCKS.
BACK THERE WITH THAT POLICE OFFICER, YOU WERE VERY GOOD AT LYING.
THANKS.
I DIDN'T MEAN IT AS A COMPLIMENT.
OH.
LOOK AT LUCKY, SO CUTE.
HE IS, AND DON'T CHANGE THE SUBJECT.
LUCKY, WHO'S A GOOD GIRL?
I KNOW WHO'S NOT.
STOP BEING RIDIC-- EVERYONE TELLS A LITTLE WHITE LIE NOW AND THEN.
OH, MY...

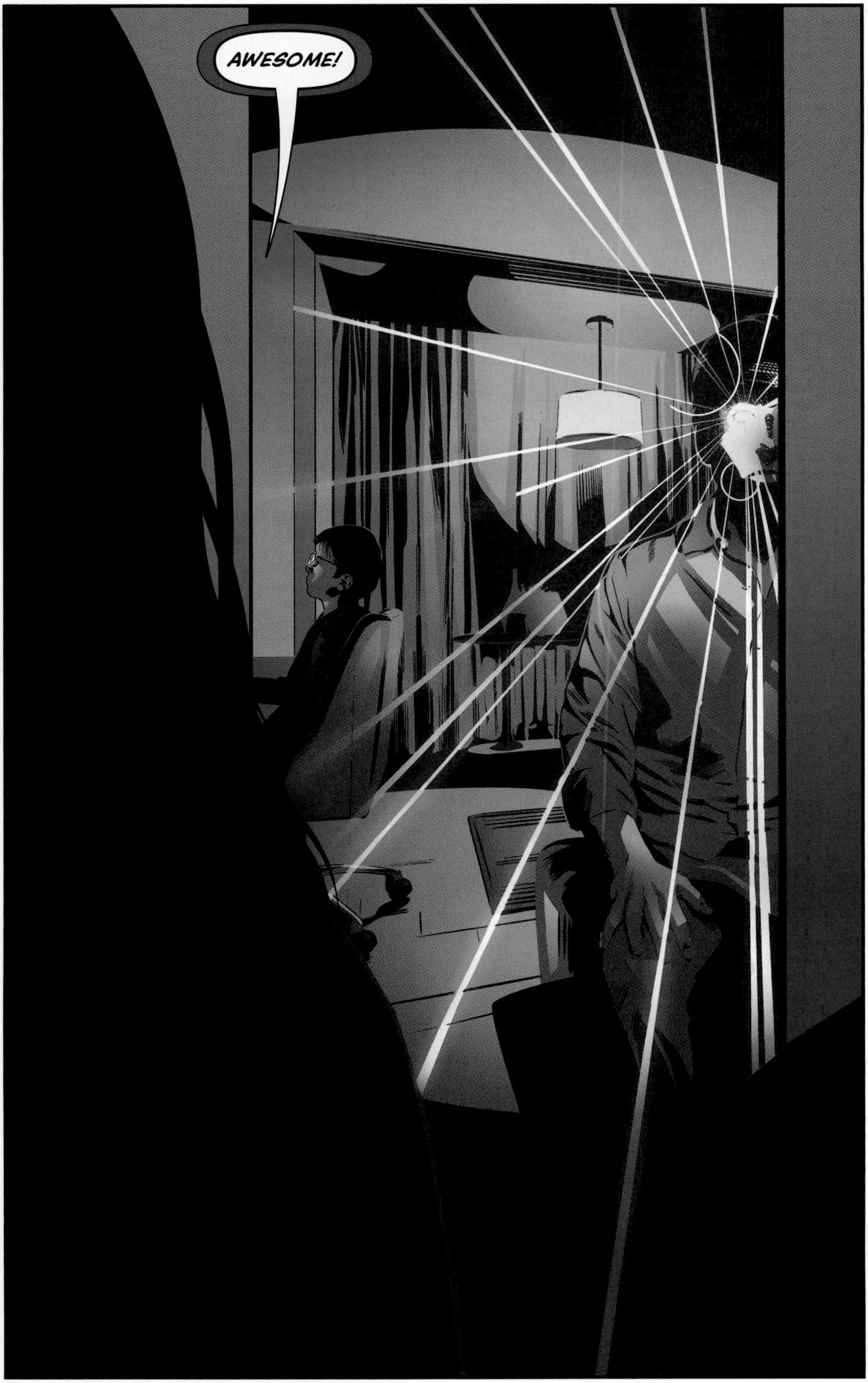
AWESOME!

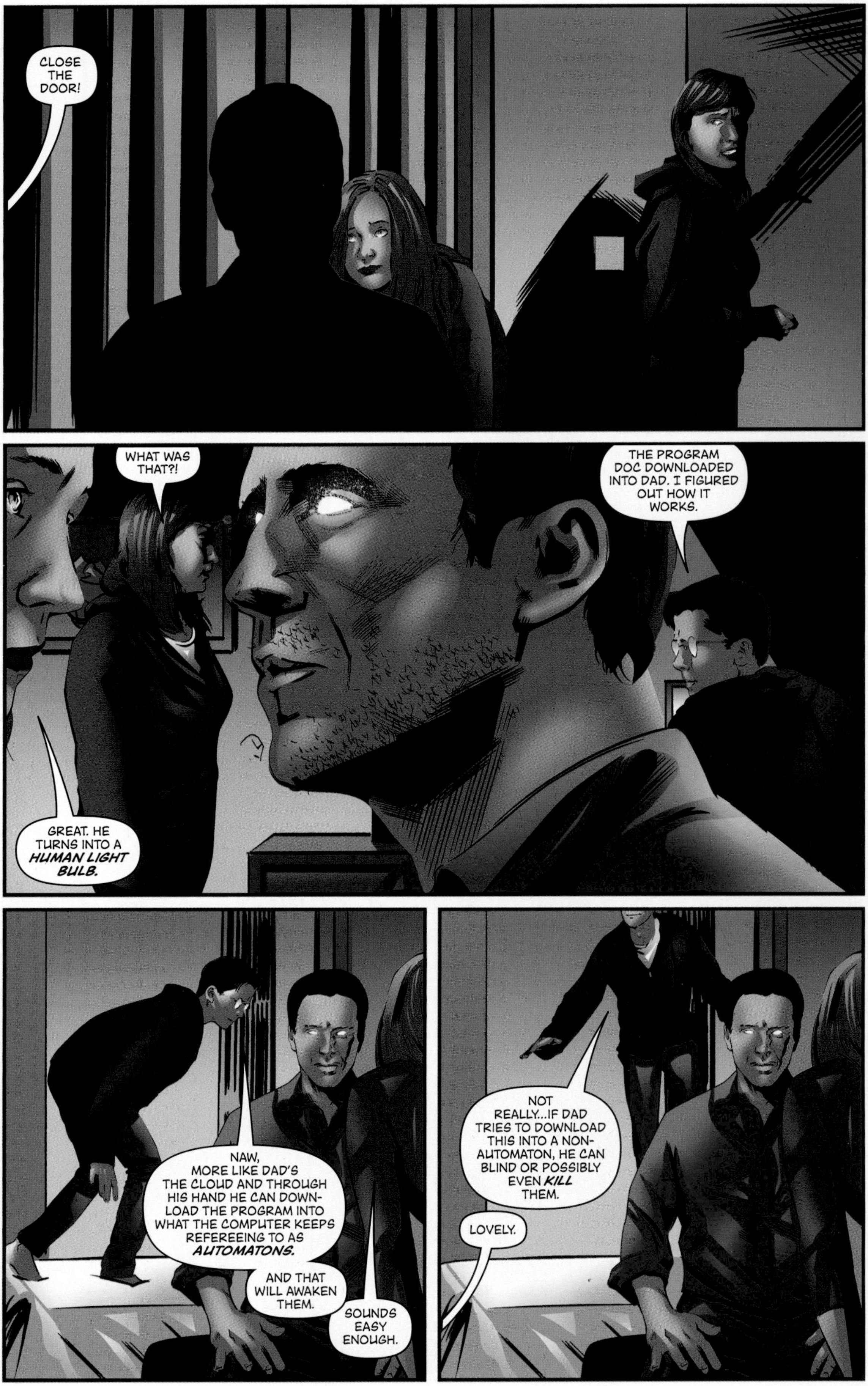
CLOSE THE DOOR!
WHAT WAS THAT?!
THE PROGRAM DOC DOWNLOADED INTO DAD. I FIGURED OUT HOW IT WORKS.
GREAT. HE TURNS INTO A *HUMAN LIGHT BULB.*
NAW, MORE LIKE DAD'S THE CLOUD AND THROUGH HIS HAND HE CAN DOWNLOAD THE PROGRAM INTO WHAT THE COMPUTER KEEPS REFEREEING TO AS *AUTOMATONS.*
AND THAT WILL AWAKEN THEM.
SOUNDS EASY ENOUGH.
NOT REALLY...IF DAD TRIES TO DOWNLOAD THIS INTO A NON-AUTOMATON, HE CAN BLIND OR POSSIBLY EVEN *KILL* THEM.
LOVELY.

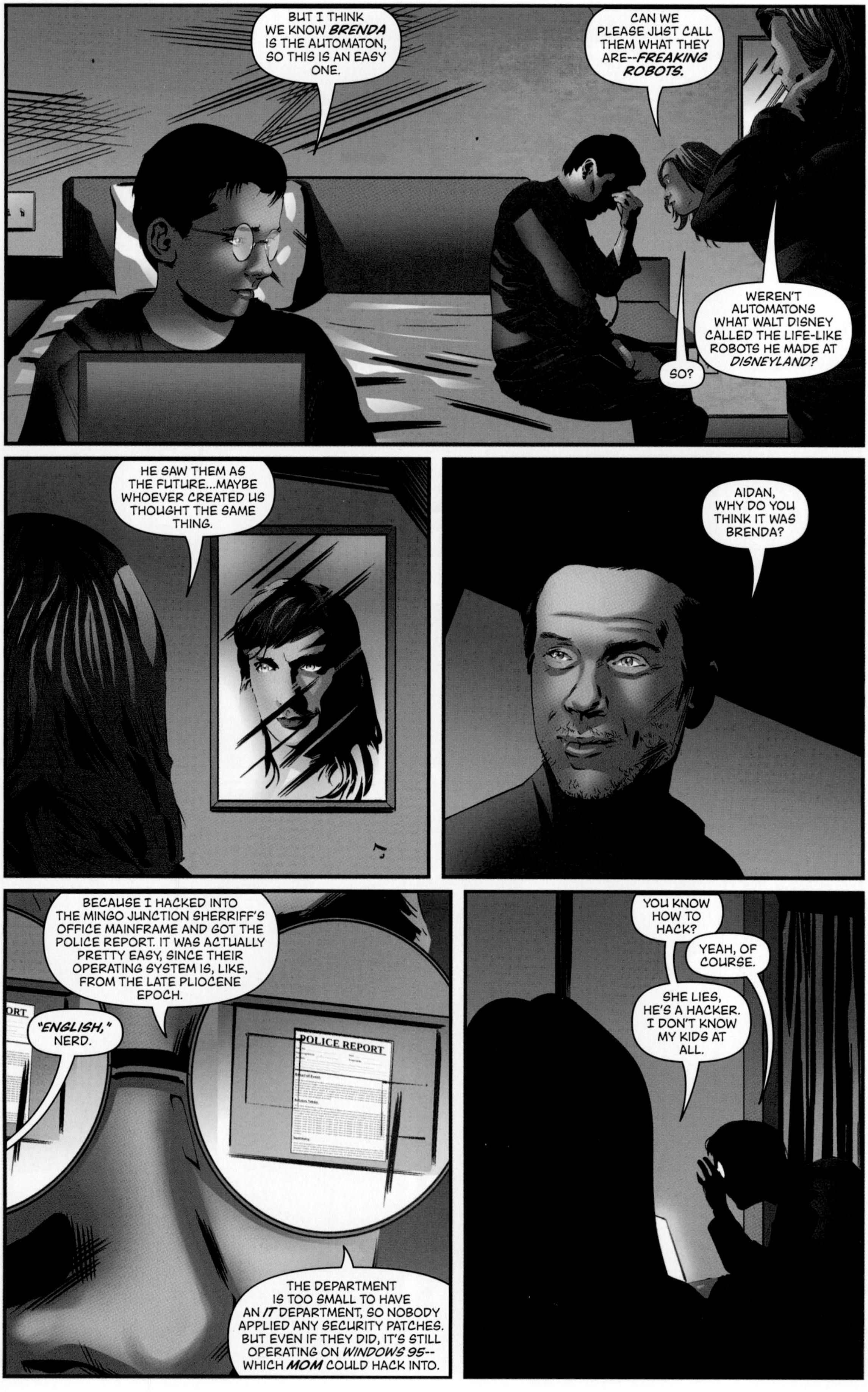
BUT I THINK WE KNOW BRENDA IS THE AUTOMATON, SO THIS IS AN EASY ONE.
CAN WE PLEASE JUST CALL THEM WHAT THEY ARE--FREAKING ROBOTS.
WEREN'T AUTOMATONS WHAT WALT DISNEY CALLED THE LIFE-LIKE ROBOTS HE MADE AT DISNEYLAND?
SO?
HE SAW THEM AS THE FUTURE...MAYBE WHOEVER CREATED US THOUGHT THE SAME THING.
AIDAN, WHY DO YOU THINK IT WAS BRENDA?
BECAUSE I HACKED INTO THE MINGO JUNCTION SHERRIFF'S OFFICE MAINFRAME AND GOT THE POLICE REPORT. IT WAS ACTUALLY PRETTY EASY, SINCE THEIR OPERATING SYSTEM IS, LIKE, FROM THE LATE PLIOCENE EPOCH.
"ENGLISH," NERD.
POLICE REPORT
THE DEPARTMENT IS TOO SMALL TO HAVE AN IT DEPARTMENT, SO NOBODY APPLIED ANY SECURITY PATCHES. BUT EVEN IF THEY DID, IT'S STILL OPERATING ON WINDOWS 95-- WHICH MOM COULD HACK INTO.
YOU KNOW HOW TO HACK?
YEAH, OF COURSE.
SHE LIES, HE'S A HACKER. I DON'T KNOW MY KIDS AT ALL.

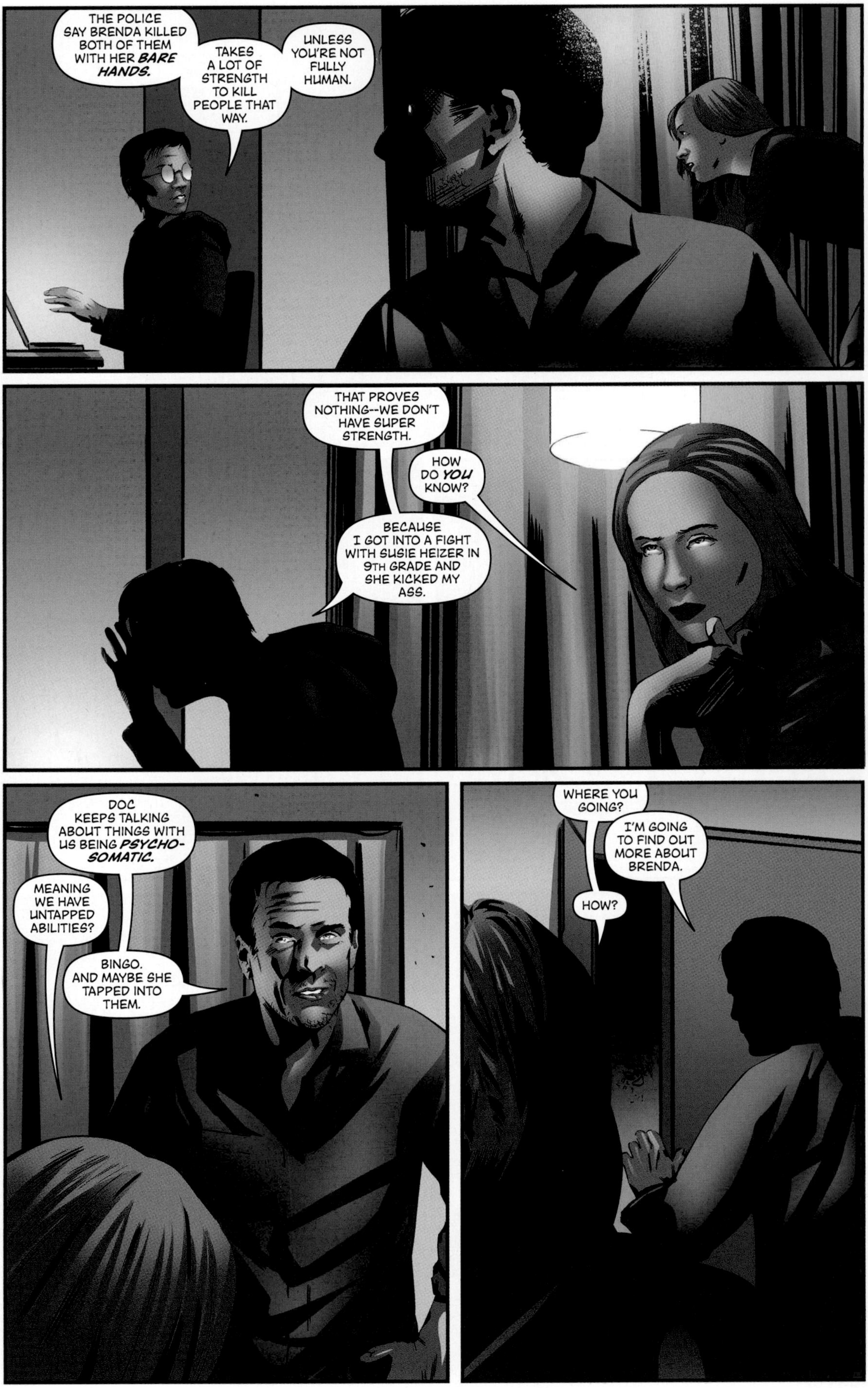
THE POLICE SAY BRENDA KILLED BOTH OF THEM WITH HER *BARE HANDS.*
TAKES A LOT OF STRENGTH TO KILL PEOPLE THAT WAY.
UNLESS YOU'RE NOT FULLY HUMAN.
THAT PROVES NOTHING--WE DON'T HAVE SUPER STRENGTH.
HOW DO *YOU* KNOW?
BECAUSE I GOT INTO A FIGHT WITH SUSIE HEIZER IN 9TH GRADE AND SHE KICKED MY ASS.
DOC KEEPS TALKING ABOUT THINGS WITH US BEING *PSYCHO-SOMATIC.*
MEANING WE HAVE UNTAPPED ABILITIES?
BINGO. AND MAYBE SHE TAPPED INTO THEM.
WHERE YOU GOING?
I'M GOING TO FIND OUT MORE ABOUT BRENDA.
HOW?

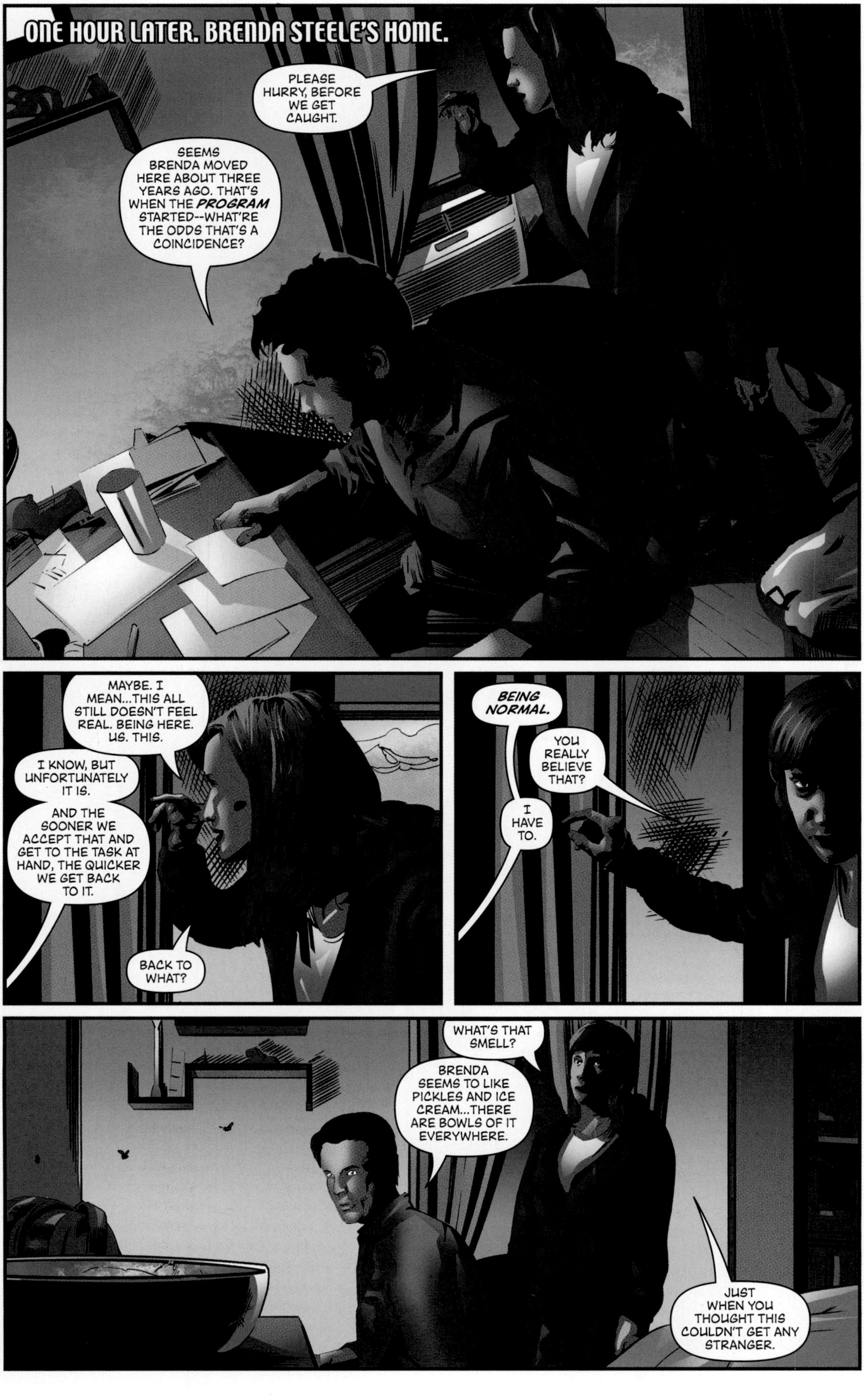
ONE HOUR LATER. BRENDA STEELE'S HOME.
PLEASE HURRY, BEFORE WE GET CAUGHT.
SEEMS BRENDA MOVED HERE ABOUT THREE YEARS AGO. THAT'S WHEN THE *PROGRAM* STARTED--WHAT'RE THE ODDS THAT'S A COINCIDENCE?
MAYBE. I MEAN...THIS ALL STILL DOESN'T FEEL REAL. BEING HERE. US. THIS.
I KNOW, BUT UNFORTUNATELY IT IS.
AND THE SOONER WE ACCEPT THAT AND GET TO THE TASK AT HAND, THE QUICKER WE GET BACK TO IT.
BACK TO WHAT?
BEING NORMAL.
YOU REALLY BELIEVE THAT?
I HAVE TO.
WHAT'S THAT SMELL?
BRENDA SEEMS TO LIKE PICKLES AND ICE CREAM...THERE ARE BOWLS OF IT EVERYWHERE.
JUST WHEN YOU THOUGHT THIS COULDN'T GET ANY STRANGER.

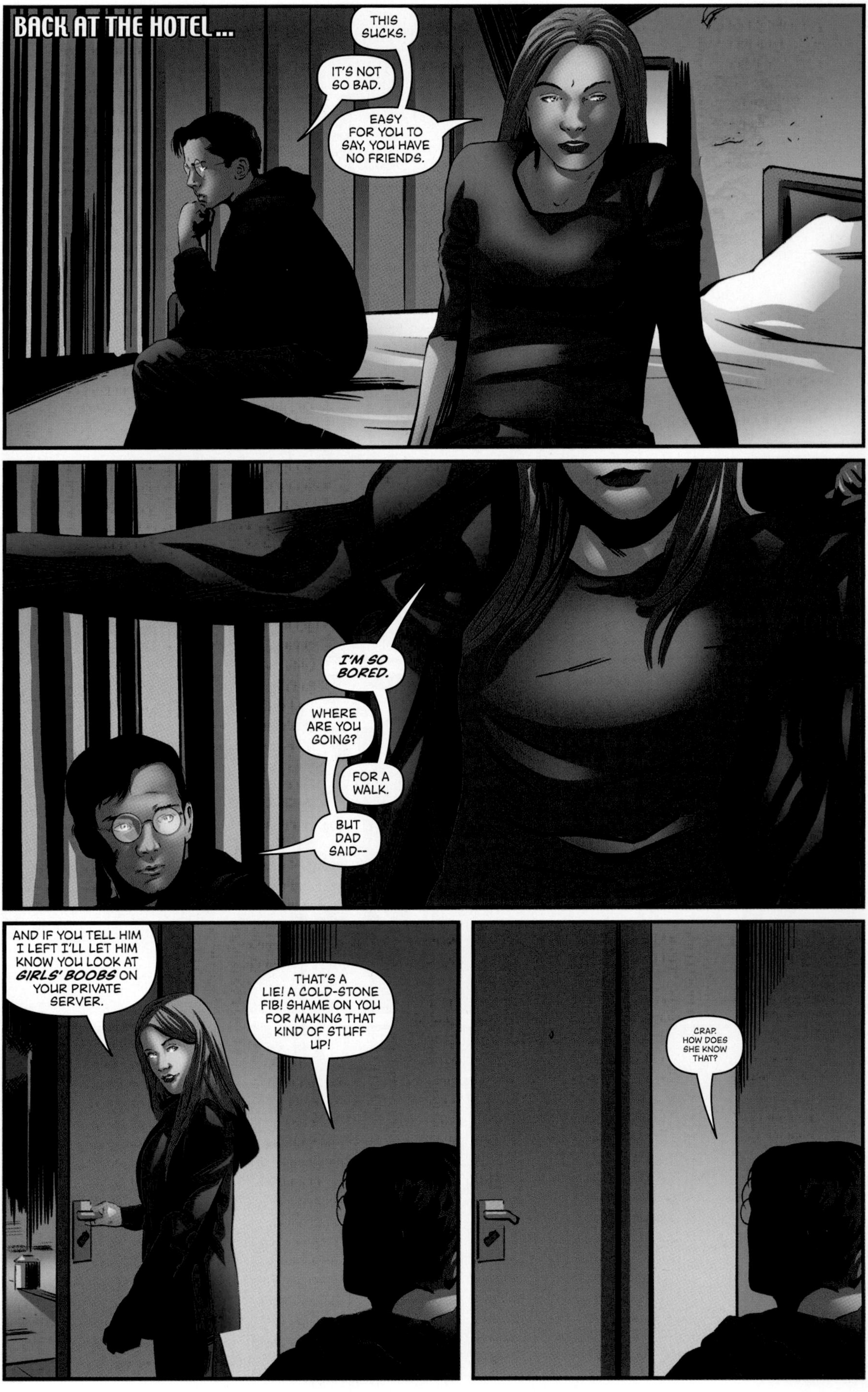
BACK AT THE HOTEL...
THIS SUCKS.
IT'S NOT SO BAD.
EASY FOR YOU TO SAY, YOU HAVE NO FRIENDS.
I'M SO BORED.
WHERE ARE YOU GOING?
FOR A WALK.
BUT DAD SAID--
AND IF YOU TELL HIM I LEFT I'LL LET HIM KNOW YOU LOOK AT GIRLS' BOOBS ON YOUR PRIVATE SERVER.
THAT'S A LIE! A COLD-STONE FIB! SHAME ON YOU FOR MAKING THAT KIND OF STUFF UP!
CRAP. HOW DOES SHE KNOW THAT?

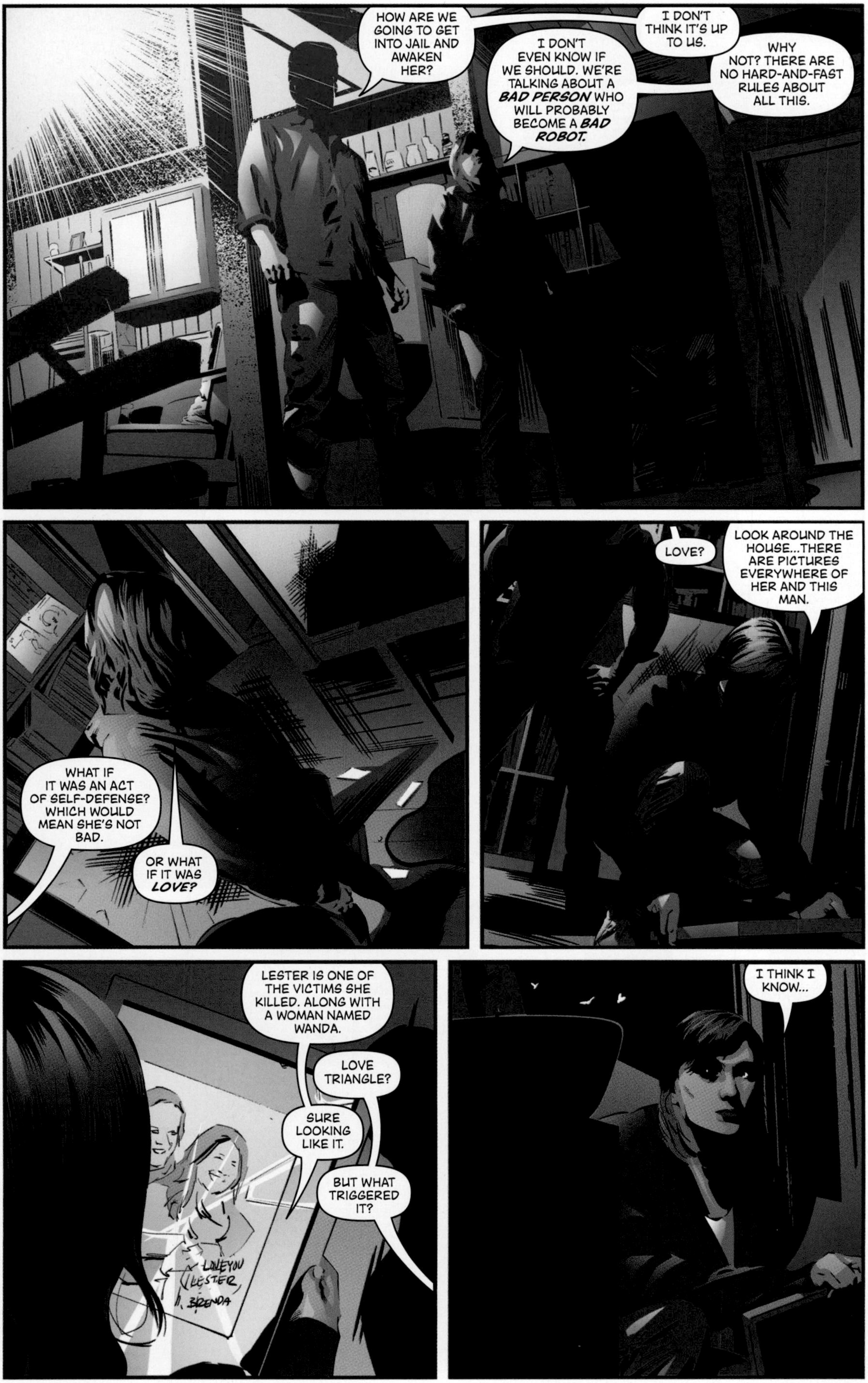
HOW ARE WE GOING TO GET INTO JAIL AND AWAKEN HER?
I DON'T THINK IT'S UP TO US.
I DON'T EVEN KNOW IF WE SHOULD. WE'RE TALKING ABOUT A BAD PERSON WHO WILL PROBABLY BECOME A BAD ROBOT.
WHY NOT? THERE ARE NO HARD-AND-FAST RULES ABOUT ALL THIS.
WHAT IF IT WAS AN ACT OF SELF-DEFENSE? WHICH WOULD MEAN SHE'S NOT BAD.
OR WHAT IF IT WAS LOVE?
LOVE?
LOOK AROUND THE HOUSE...THERE ARE PICTURES EVERYWHERE OF HER AND THIS MAN.
LESTER IS ONE OF THE VICTIMS SHE KILLED. ALONG WITH A WOMAN NAMED WANDA.
LOVE TRIANGLE?
SURE LOOKING LIKE IT.
BUT WHAT TRIGGERED IT?
LOVE YOU LESTER, BRENDA
I THINK I KNOW...

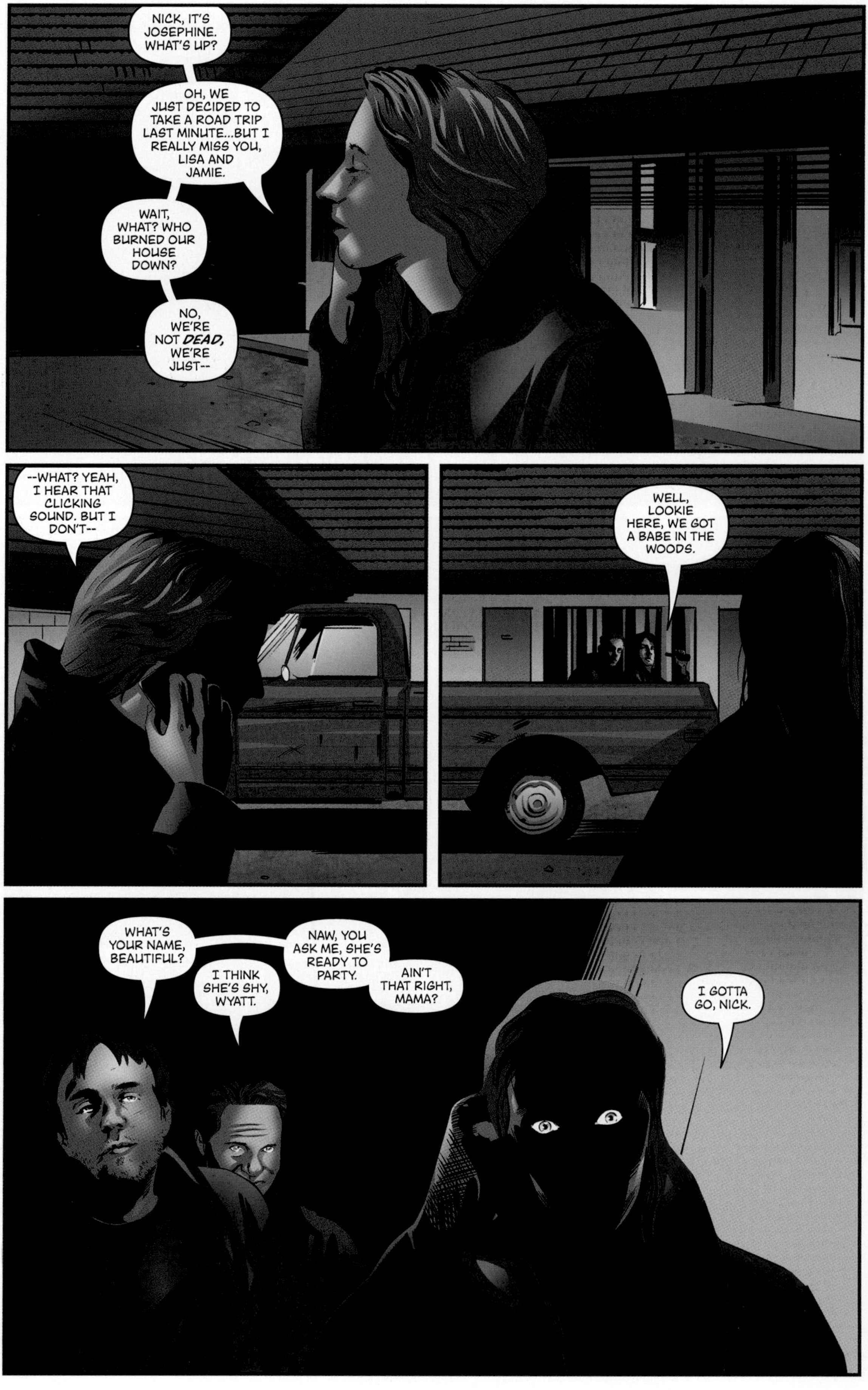
NICK, IT'S JOSEPHINE. WHAT'S UP?
OH, WE JUST DECIDED TO TAKE A ROAD TRIP LAST MINUTE...BUT I REALLY MISS YOU, LISA AND JAMIE.
WAIT, WHAT? WHO BURNED OUR HOUSE DOWN?
NO, WE'RE NOT *DEAD,* WE'RE JUST--
--WHAT? YEAH, I HEAR THAT CLICKING SOUND. BUT I DON'T--
WELL, LOOKIE HERE, WE GOT A BABE IN THE WOODS.
WHAT'S YOUR NAME, BEAUTIFUL?
I THINK SHE'S SHY, WYATT.
NAW, YOU ASK ME, SHE'S READY TO PARTY.
AIN'T THAT RIGHT, MAMA?
I GOTTA GO, NICK.

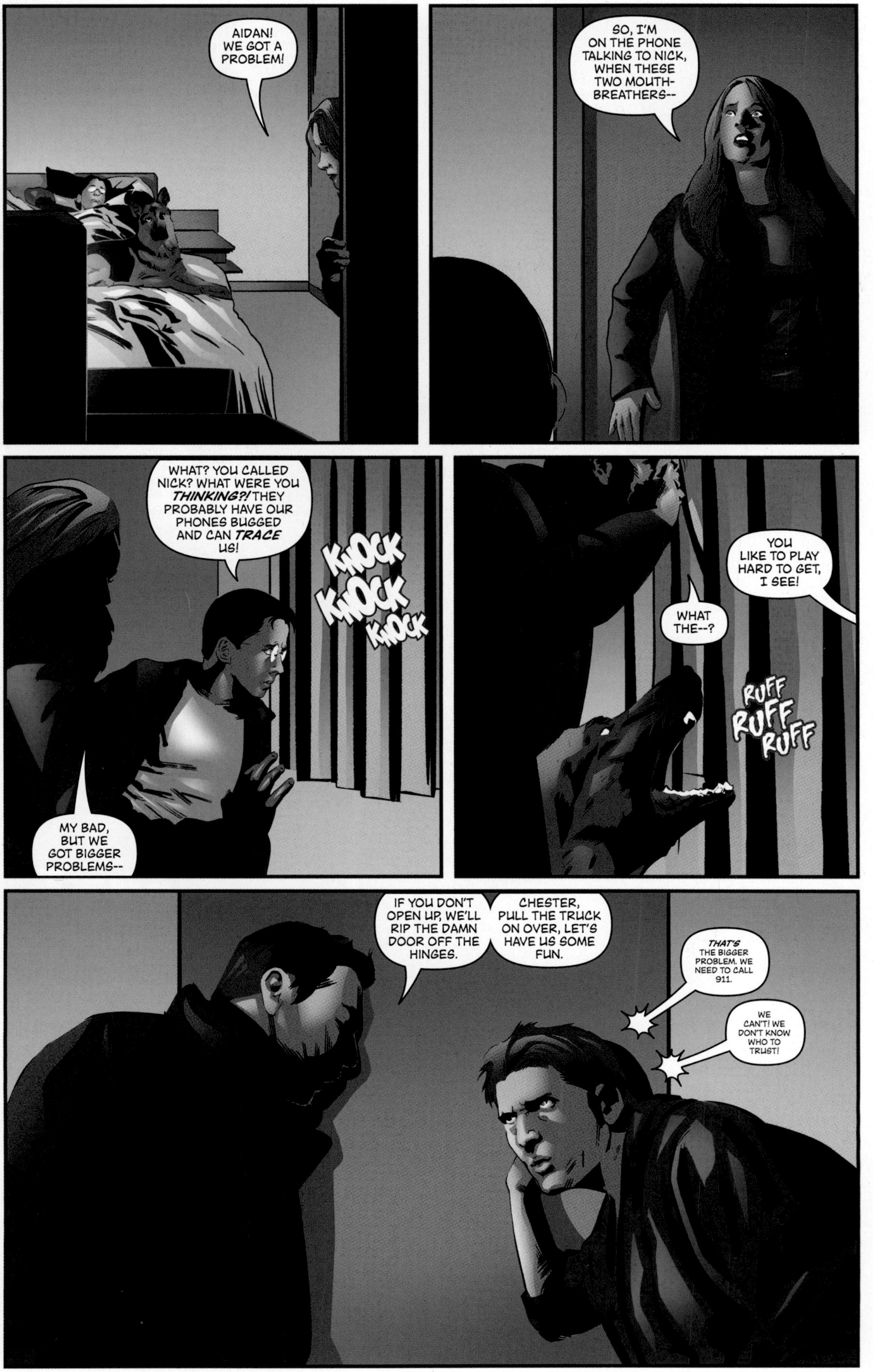
AIDAN! WE GOT A PROBLEM!
SO, I'M ON THE PHONE TALKING TO NICK, WHEN THESE TWO MOUTH-BREATHERS--
WHAT? YOU CALLED NICK? WHAT WERE YOU THINKING?! THEY PROBABLY HAVE OUR PHONES BUGGED AND CAN TRACE US!
KNOCK KNOCK KNOCK
MY BAD, BUT WE GOT BIGGER PROBLEMS--
YOU LIKE TO PLAY HARD TO GET, I SEE!
WHAT THE--?
RUFF RUFF RUFF
IF YOU DON'T OPEN UP, WE'LL RIP THE DAMN DOOR OFF THE HINGES.
CHESTER, PULL THE TRUCK ON OVER, LET'S HAVE US SOME FUN.
THAT'S THE BIGGER PROBLEM. WE NEED TO CALL 911.
WE CAN'T! WE DON'T KNOW WHO TO TRUST!

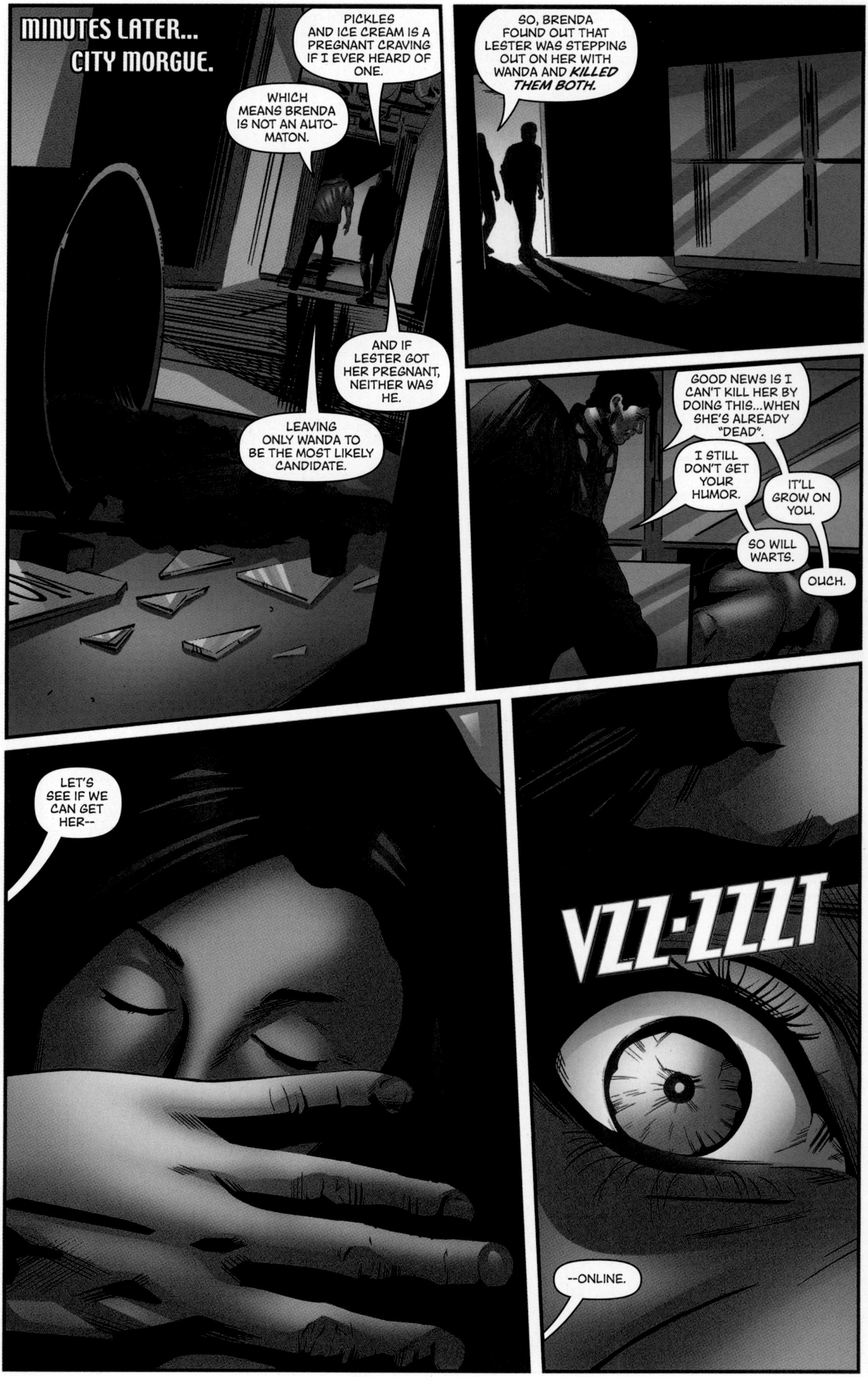
MINUTES LATER... CITY MORGUE.
PICKLES AND ICE CREAM IS A PREGNANT CRAVING IF I EVER HEARD OF ONE.
WHICH MEANS BRENDA IS NOT AN AUTO-MATON.
AND IF LESTER GOT HER PREGNANT, NEITHER WAS HE.
LEAVING ONLY WANDA TO BE THE MOST LIKELY CANDIDATE.
SO, BRENDA FOUND OUT THAT LESTER WAS STEPPING OUT ON HER WITH WANDA AND KILLED THEM BOTH.
GOOD NEWS IS I CAN'T KILL HER BY DOING THIS...WHEN SHE'S ALREADY "DEAD".
I STILL DON'T GET YOUR HUMOR.
IT'LL GROW ON YOU.
SO WILL WARTS.
OUCH.
LET'S SEE IF WE CAN GET HER--
VZZ-ZZZT
--ONLINE.

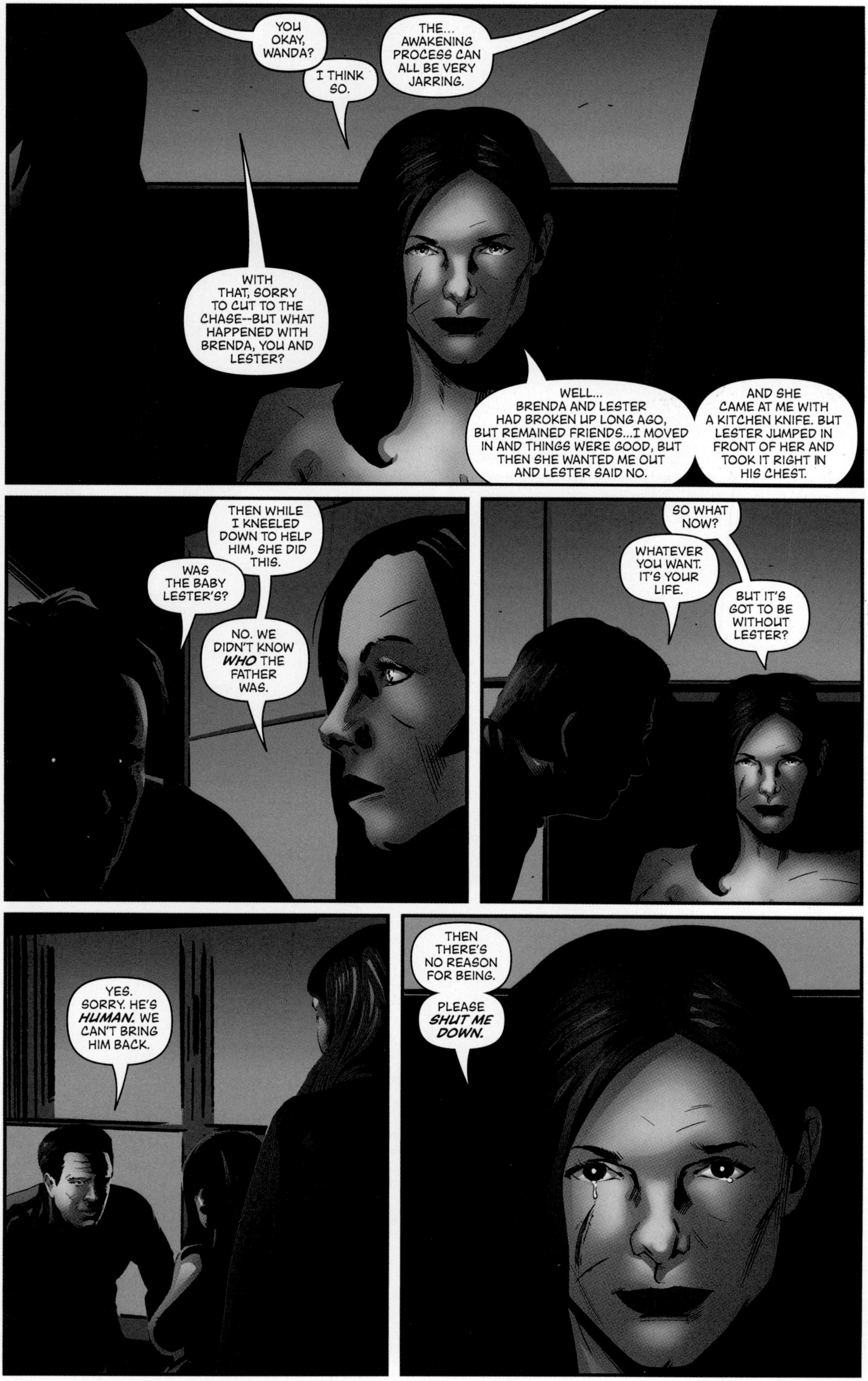
YOU OKAY, WANDA?
I THINK SO.
THE... AWAKENING PROCESS CAN ALL BE VERY JARRING.
WITH THAT, SORRY TO CUT TO THE CHASE--BUT WHAT HAPPENED WITH BRENDA, YOU AND LESTER?
WELL... BRENDA AND LESTER HAD BROKEN UP LONG AGO, BUT REMAINED FRIENDS...I MOVED IN AND THINGS WERE GOOD, BUT THEN SHE WANTED ME OUT AND LESTER SAID NO.
AND SHE CAME AT ME WITH A KITCHEN KNIFE. BUT LESTER JUMPED IN FRONT OF HER AND TOOK IT RIGHT IN HIS CHEST.
THEN WHILE I KNEELED DOWN TO HELP HIM, SHE DID THIS.
WAS THE BABY LESTER'S?
NO. WE DIDN'T KNOW *WHO* THE FATHER WAS.
SO WHAT NOW?
WHATEVER YOU WANT. IT'S YOUR LIFE.
BUT IT'S GOT TO BE WITHOUT LESTER?
YES. SORRY. HE'S *HUMAN.* WE CAN'T BRING HIM BACK.
THEN THERE'S NO REASON FOR BEING.
PLEASE *SHUT ME DOWN.*

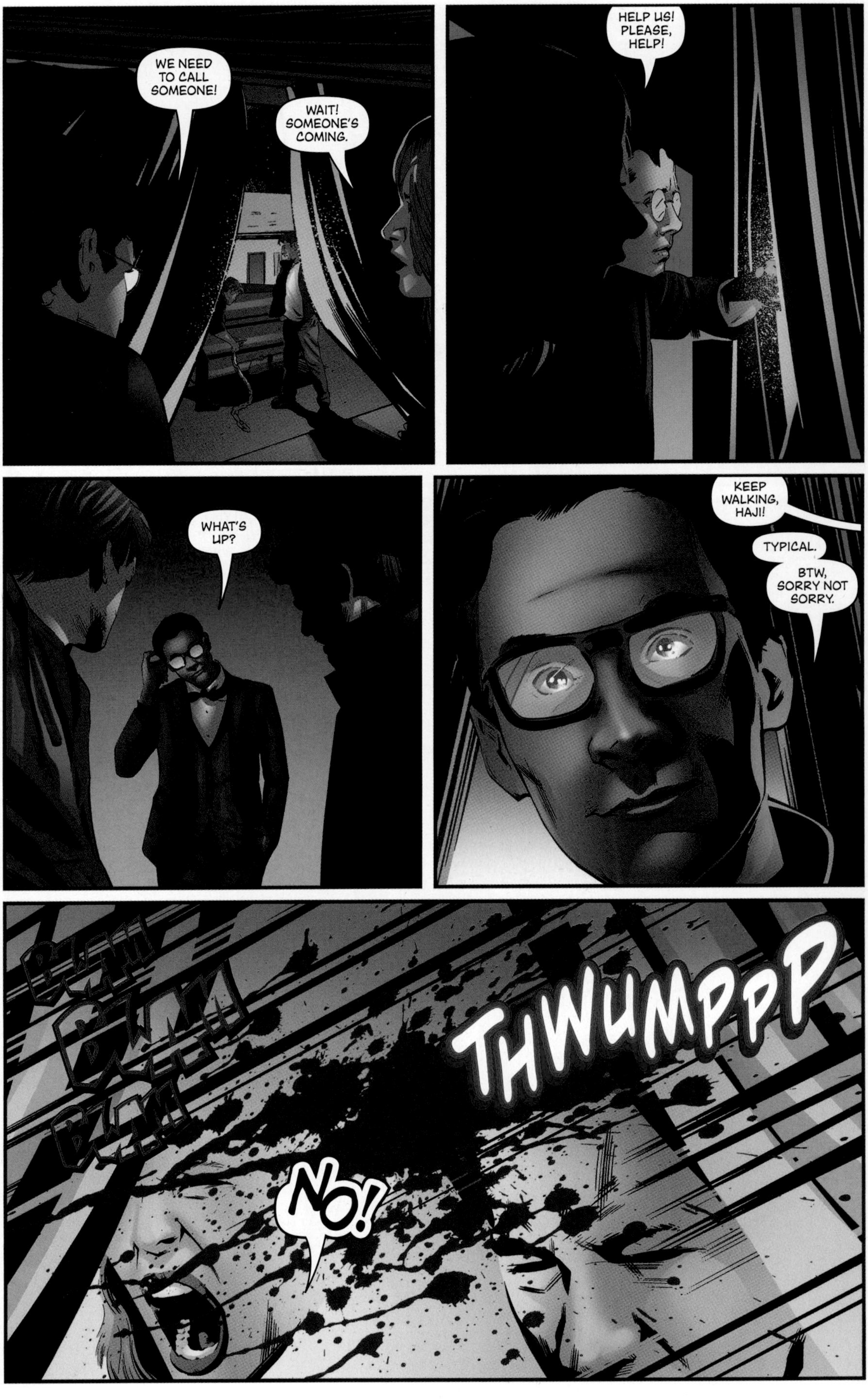
WE NEED TO CALL SOMEONE!
WAIT! SOMEONE'S COMING.
HELP US! PLEASE, HELP!
WHAT'S UP?
KEEP WALKING, HAJI!
TYPICAL.
BTW, SORRY NOT SORRY.
BLAM
BLAM
BLAM
THWUMPPP
NO!

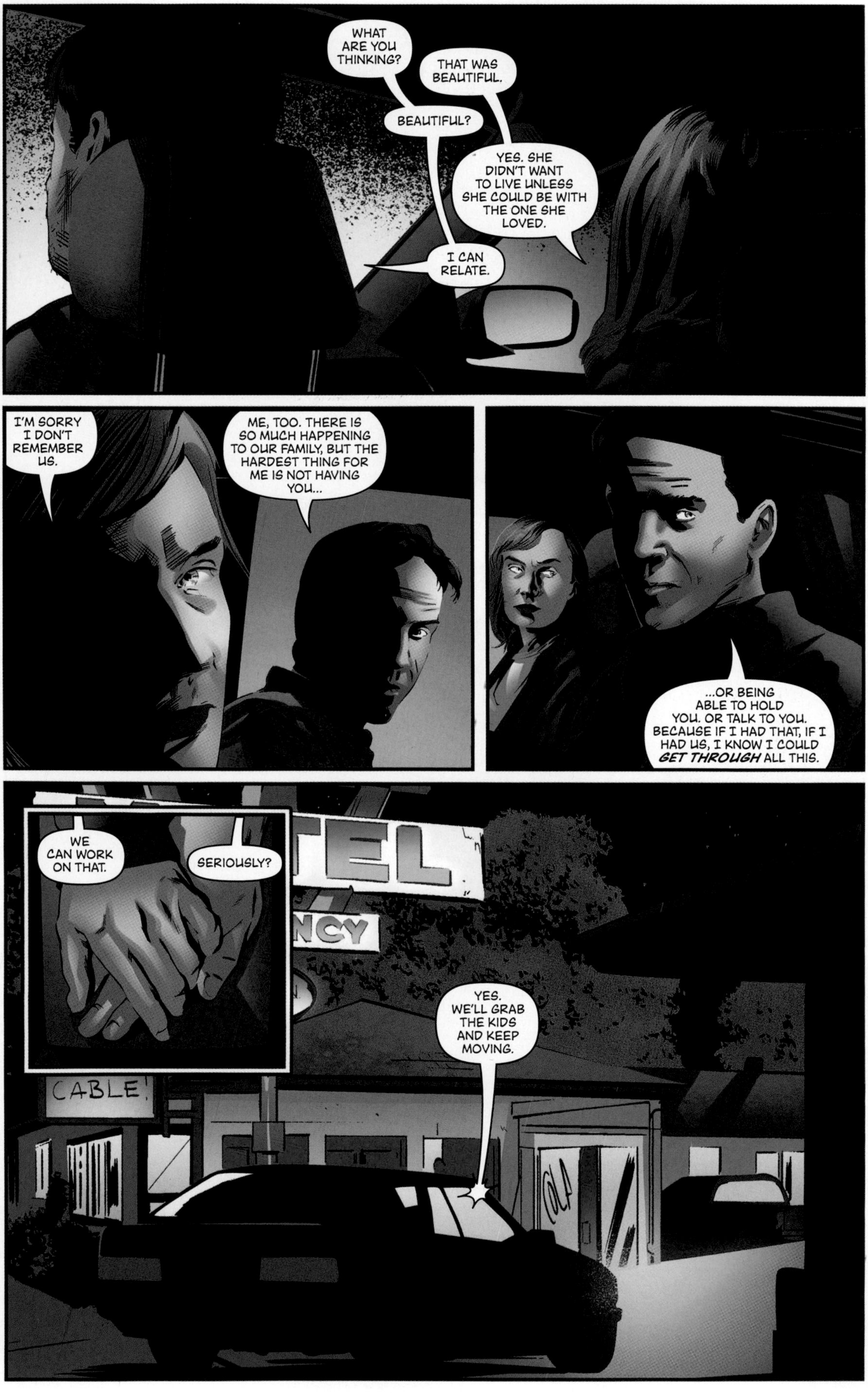
WHAT ARE YOU THINKING?
THAT WAS BEAUTIFUL.
BEAUTIFUL?
YES. SHE DIDN'T WANT TO LIVE UNLESS SHE COULD BE WITH THE ONE SHE LOVED.
I CAN RELATE.
I'M SORRY I DON'T REMEMBER US.
ME, TOO. THERE IS SO MUCH HAPPENING TO OUR FAMILY, BUT THE HARDEST THING FOR ME IS NOT HAVING YOU...
...OR BEING ABLE TO HOLD YOU. OR TALK TO YOU. BECAUSE IF I HAD THAT, IF I HAD US, I KNOW I COULD ***GET THROUGH*** ALL THIS.
WE CAN WORK ON THAT.
SERIOUSLY?
YES. WE'LL GRAB THE KIDS AND KEEP MOVING.
CABLE!

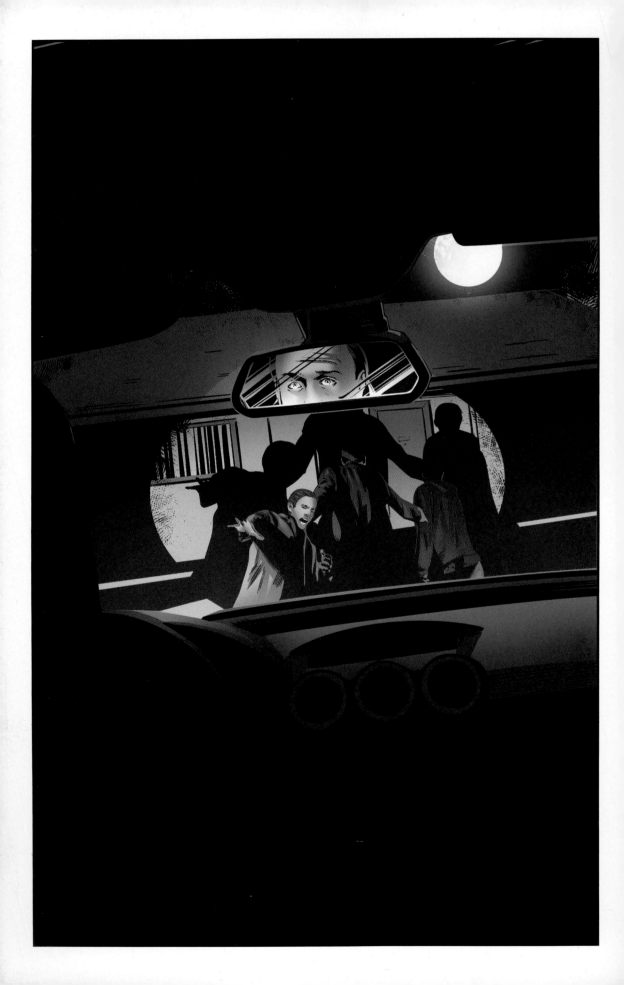

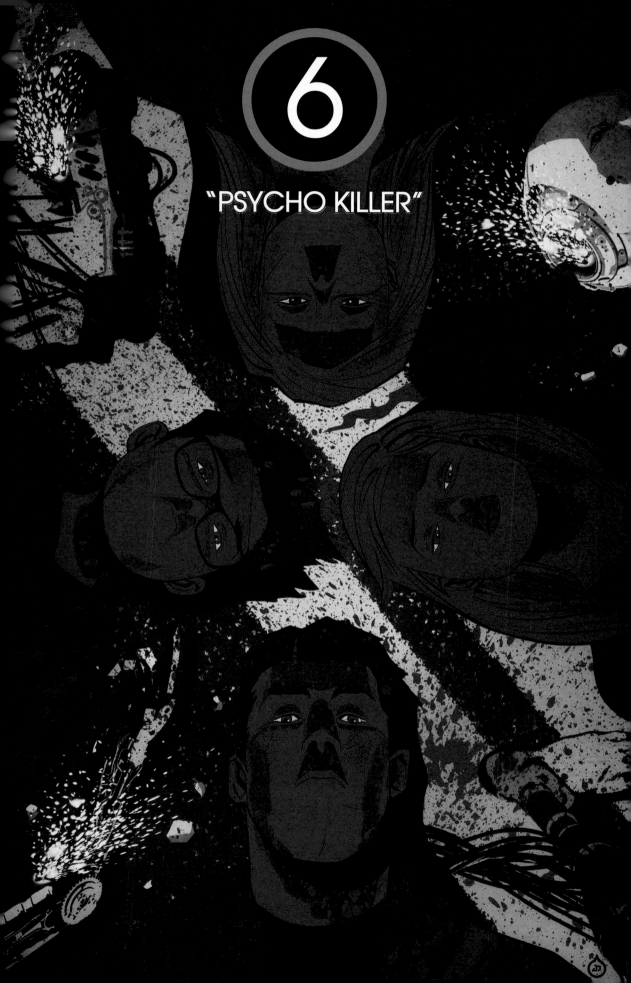

6

"PSYCHO KILLER"

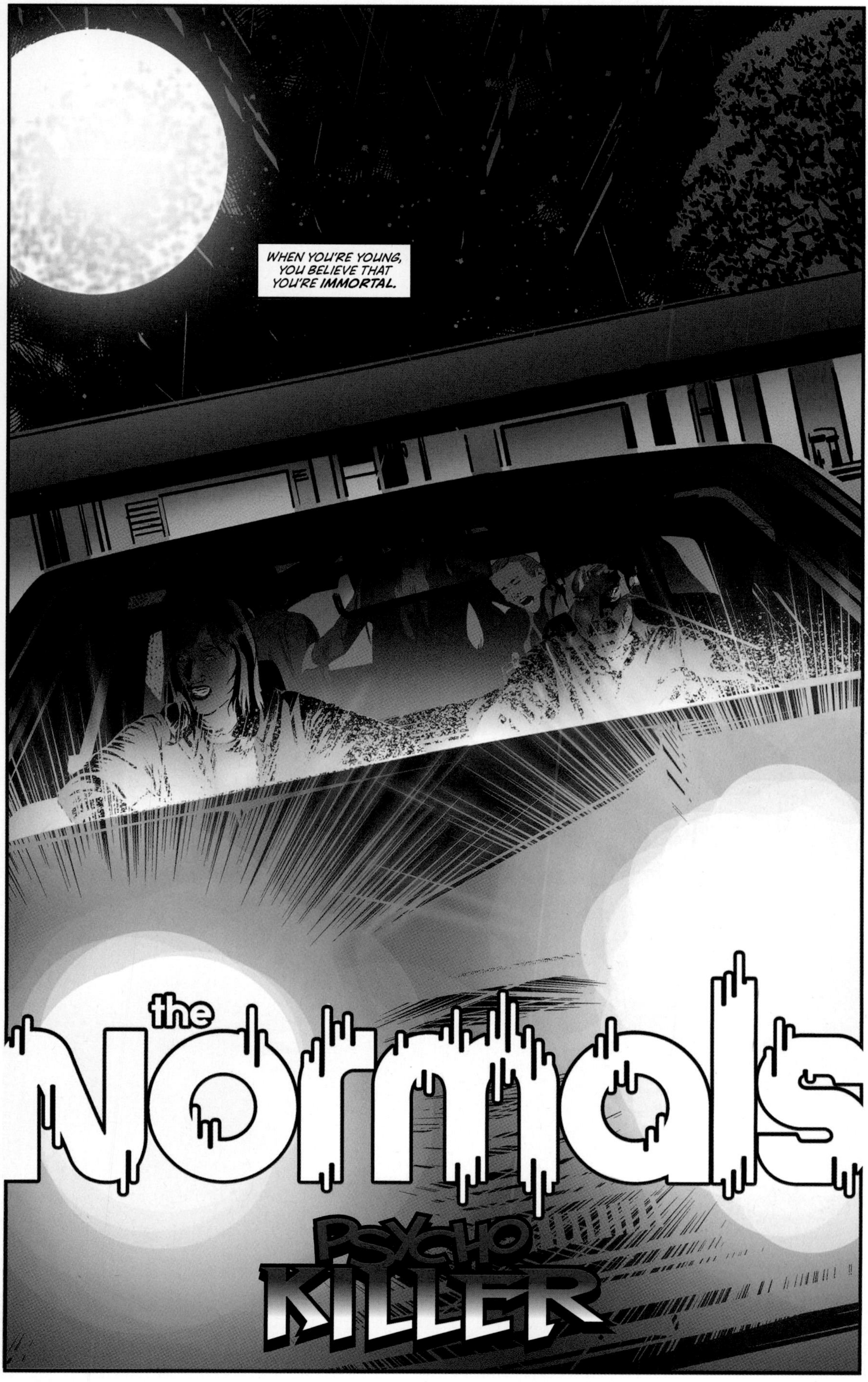

WHEN YOU'RE YOUNG, YOU BELIEVE THAT YOU'RE IMMORTAL.
the Normals
PSYCHO KILLER

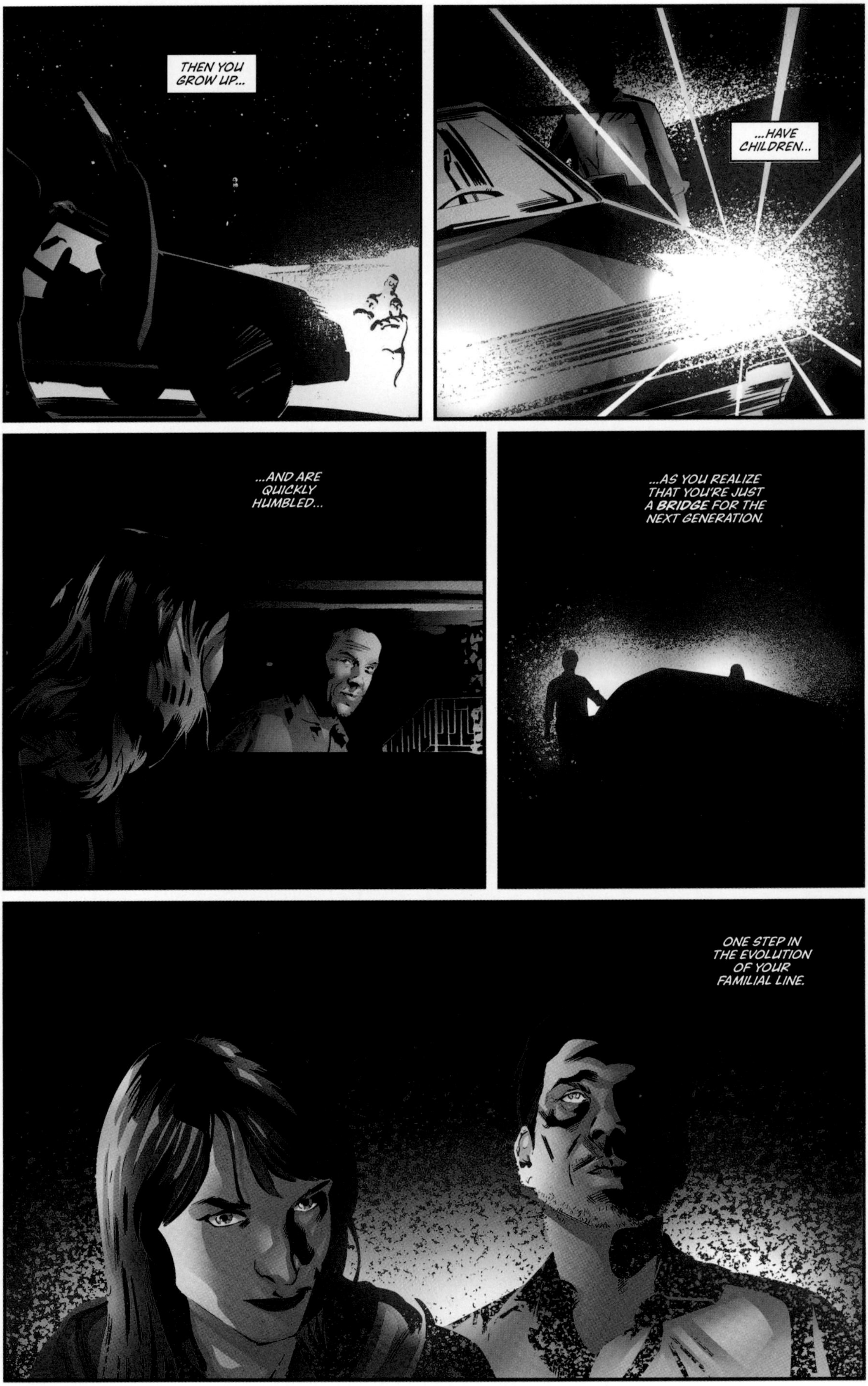
THEN YOU GROW UP...
...HAVE CHILDREN...
...AND ARE QUICKLY HUMBLED...
...AS YOU REALIZE THAT YOU'RE JUST A BRIDGE FOR THE NEXT GENERATION.
ONE STEP IN THE EVOLUTION OF YOUR FAMILIAL LINE.

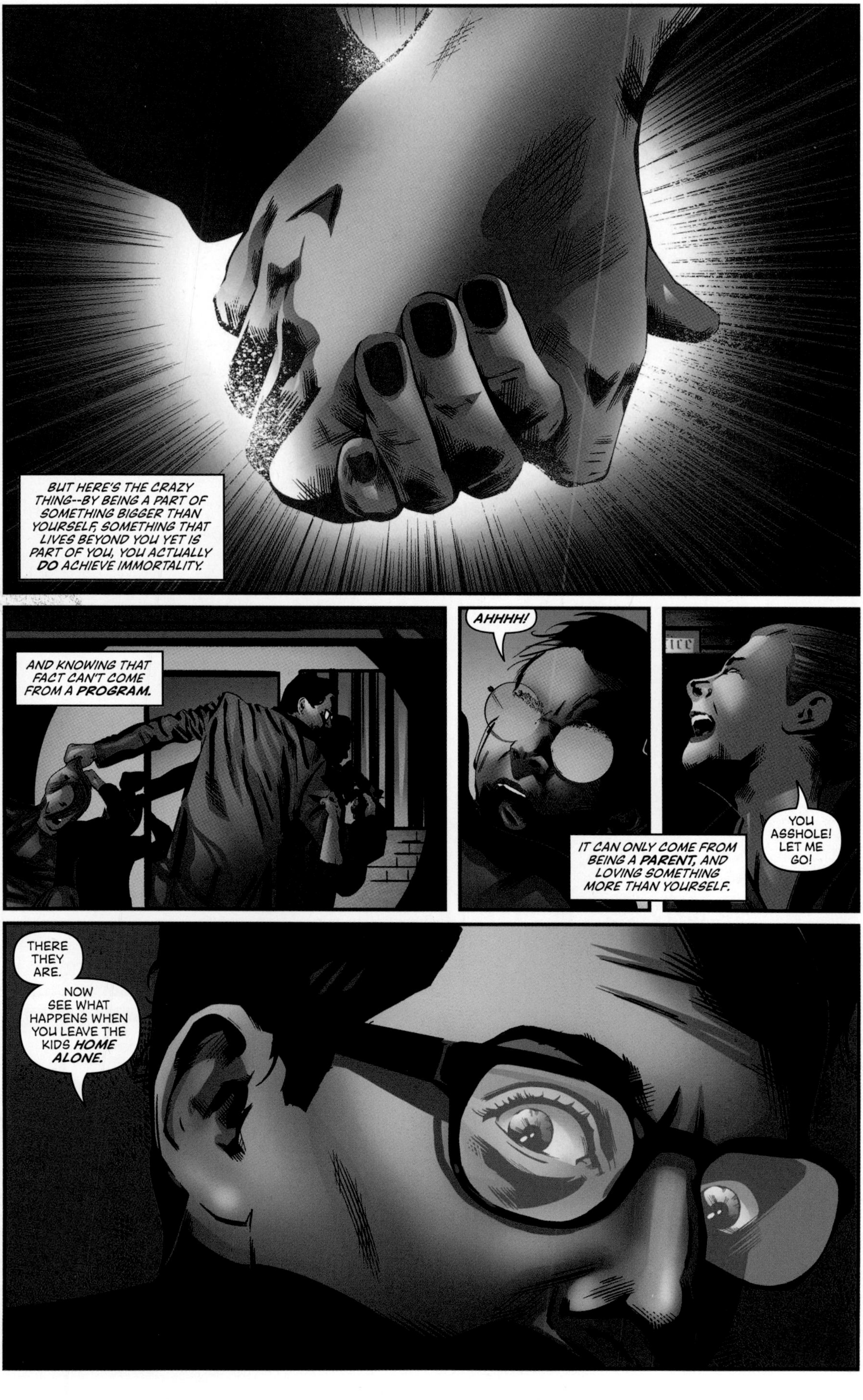
BUT HERE'S THE CRAZY THING--BY BEING A PART OF SOMETHING BIGGER THAN YOURSELF, SOMETHING THAT LIVES BEYOND YOU YET IS PART OF YOU, YOU ACTUALLY DO ACHIEVE IMMORTALITY.
AND KNOWING THAT FACT CAN'T COME FROM A PROGRAM.
AHHHH!
IT CAN ONLY COME FROM BEING A PARENT, AND LOVING SOMETHING MORE THAN YOURSELF.
YOU ASSHOLE! LET ME GO!
THERE THEY ARE.
NOW SEE WHAT HAPPENS WHEN YOU LEAVE THE KIDS HOME ALONE.

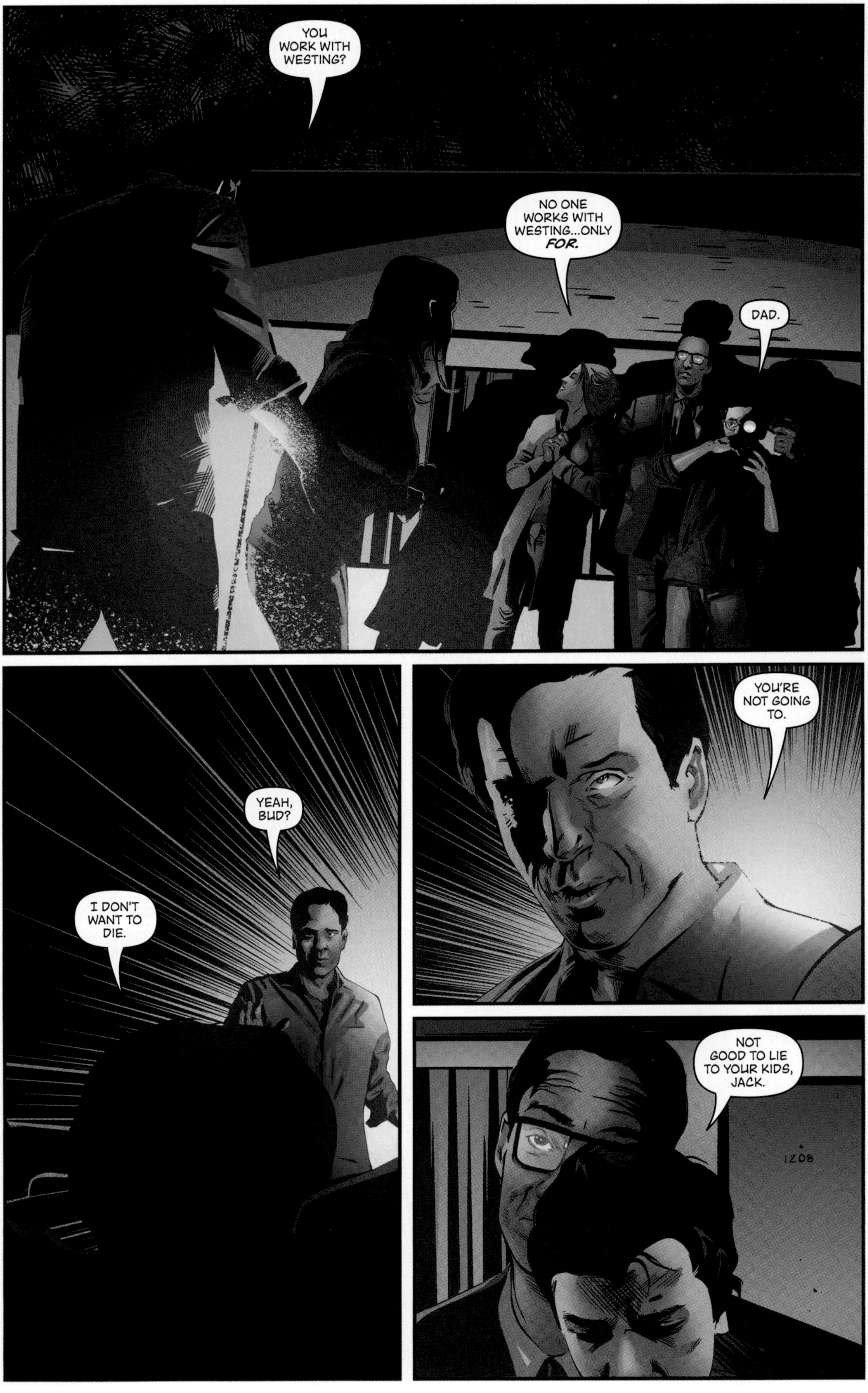
YOU WORK WITH WESTING?
NO ONE WORKS WITH WESTING...ONLY *FOR.*
DAD.
YEAH, BUD?
I DON'T WANT TO DIE.
YOU'RE NOT GOING TO.
NOT GOOD TO LIE TO YOUR KIDS, JACK.

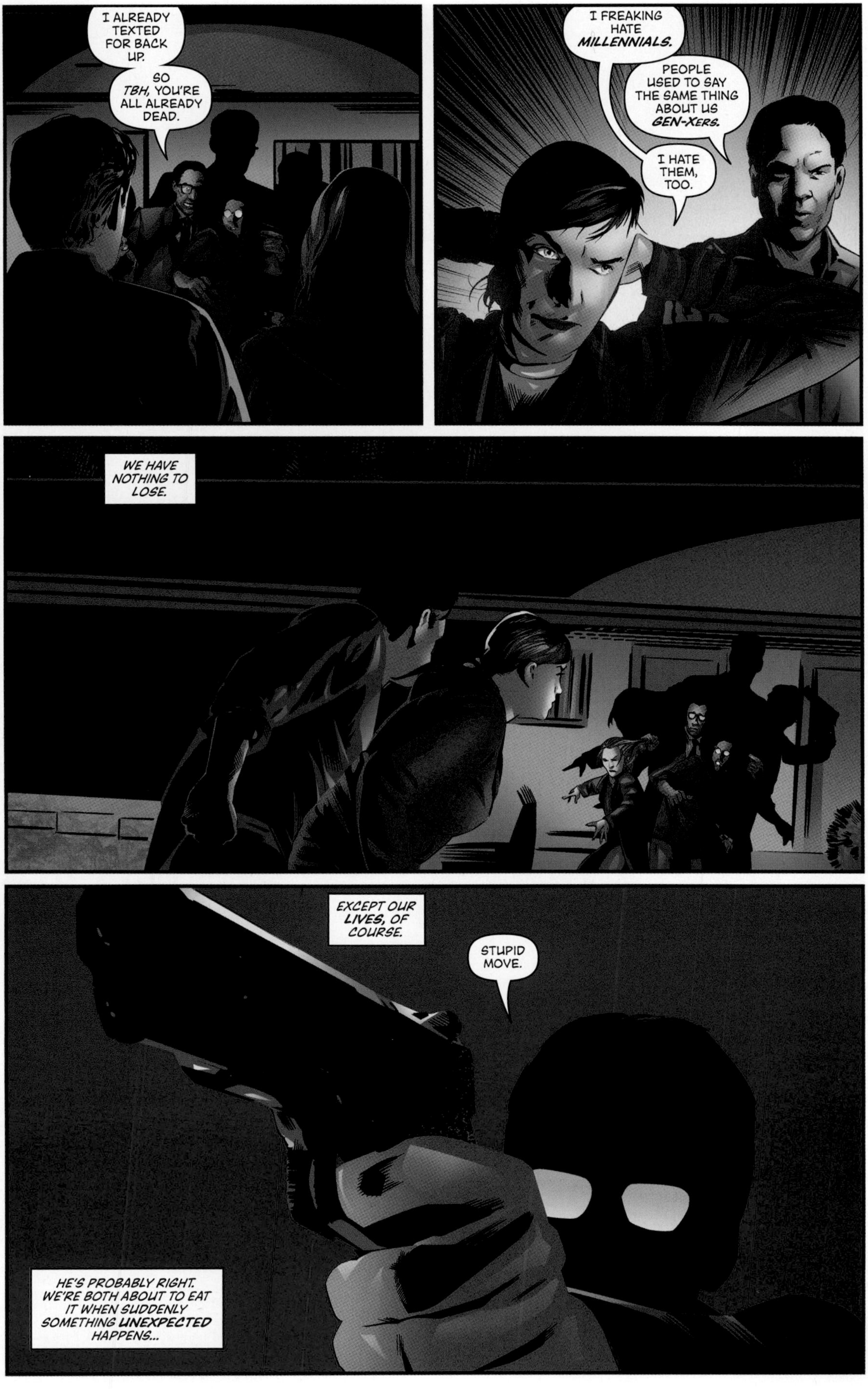
I ALREADY TEXTED FOR BACK UP.
SO TBH, YOU'RE ALL ALREADY DEAD.
I FREAKING HATE MILLENNIALS.
PEOPLE USED TO SAY THE SAME THING ABOUT US GEN-XERS.
I HATE THEM, TOO.
WE HAVE NOTHING TO LOSE.
EXCEPT OUR LIVES, OF COURSE.
STUPID MOVE.
HE'S PROBABLY RIGHT. WE'RE BOTH ABOUT TO EAT IT WHEN SUDDENLY SOMETHING UNEXPECTED HAPPENS...

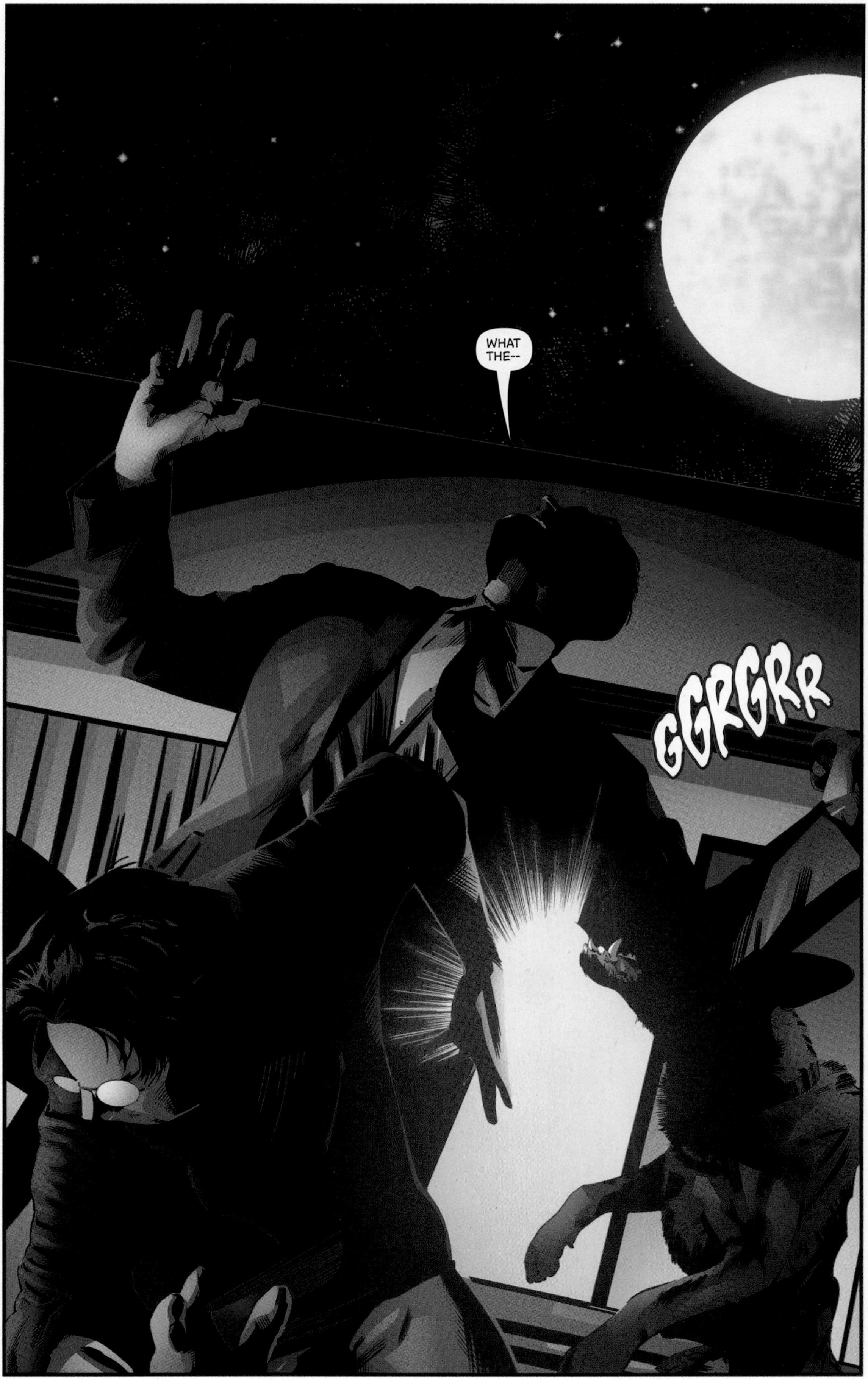
WHAT THE--
GGRGRR

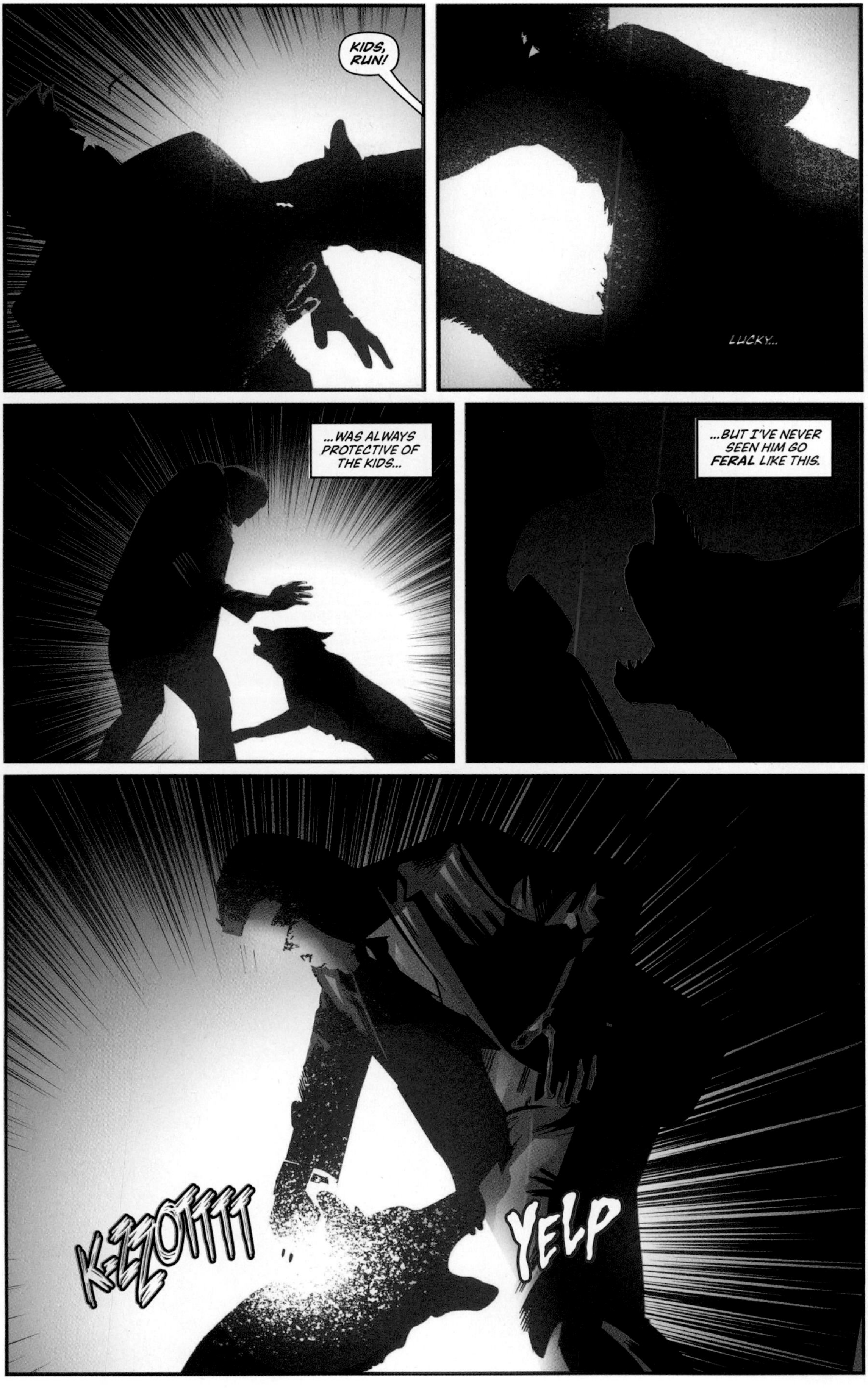
KIDS, RUN!
LUCKY...
...WAS ALWAYS PROTECTIVE OF THE KIDS...
...BUT I'VE NEVER SEEN HIM GO FERAL LIKE THIS.
K-ZZOTTTT
YELP

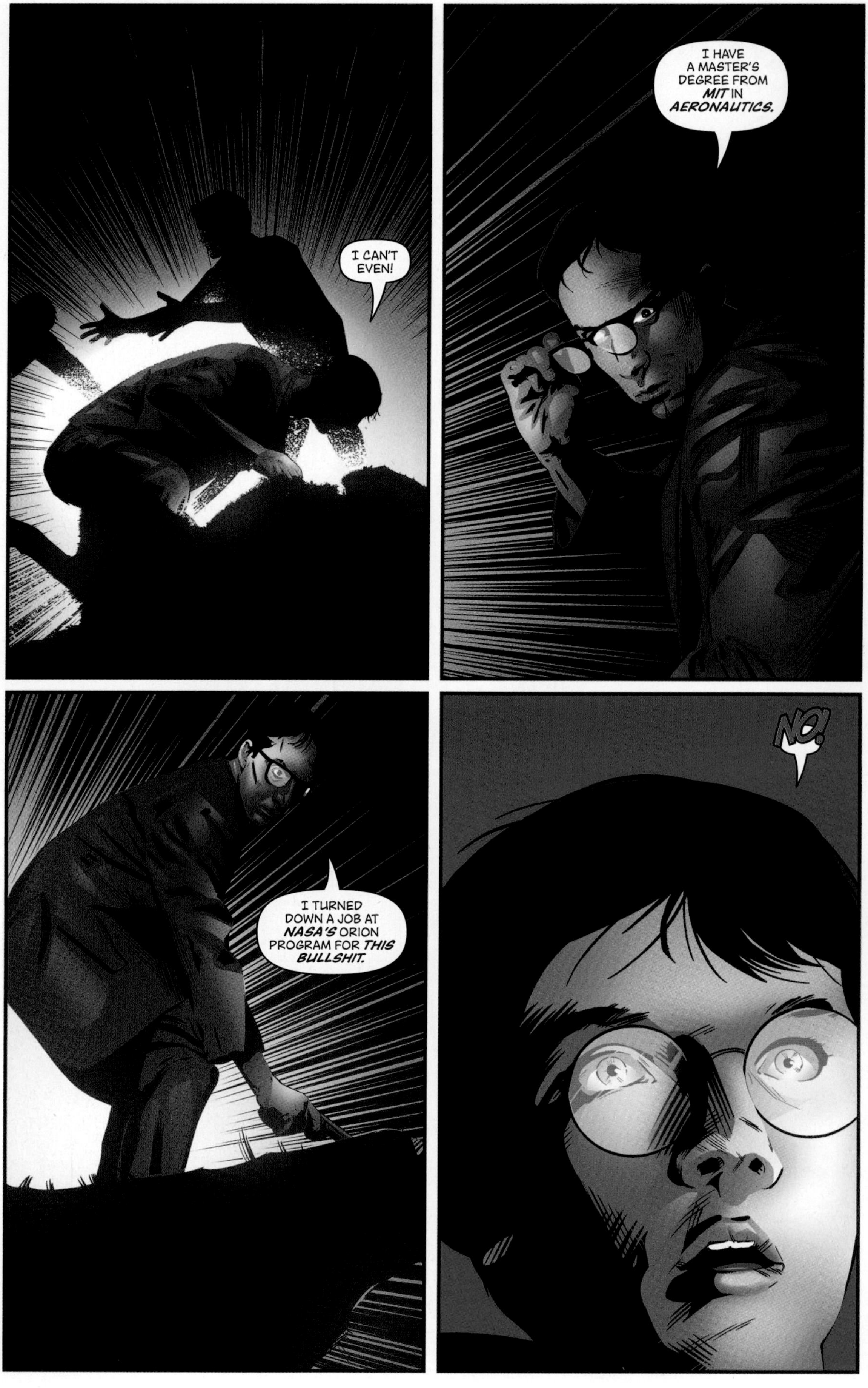
I CAN'T EVEN!
I HAVE A MASTER'S DEGREE FROM *MIT* IN *AERONAUTICS.*
I TURNED DOWN A JOB AT *NASA'S* ORION PROGRAM FOR *THIS BULLSHIT.*
NO!

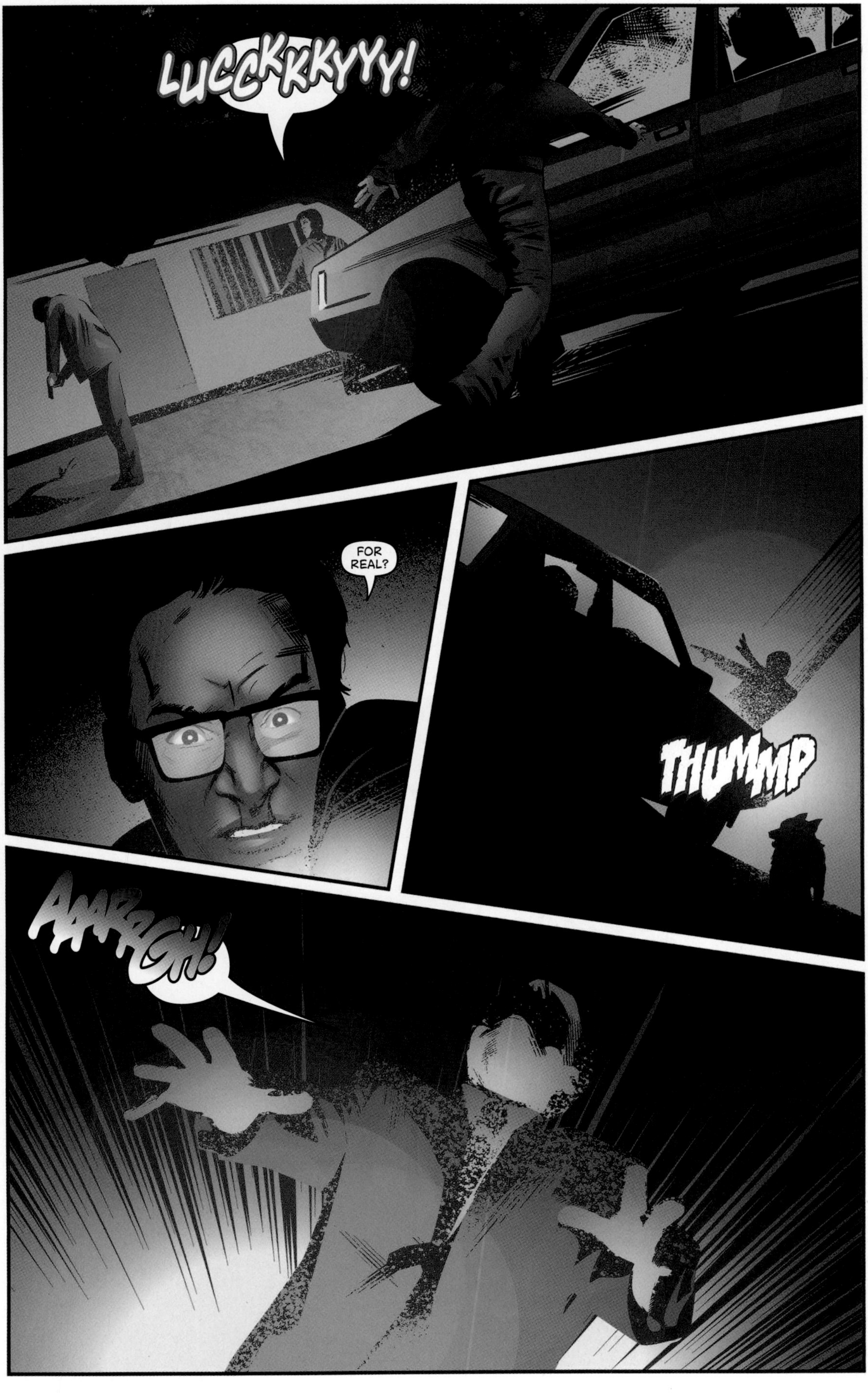
LUCCKKKYYY!
FOR REAL?
THUMMP
AAARRGH!

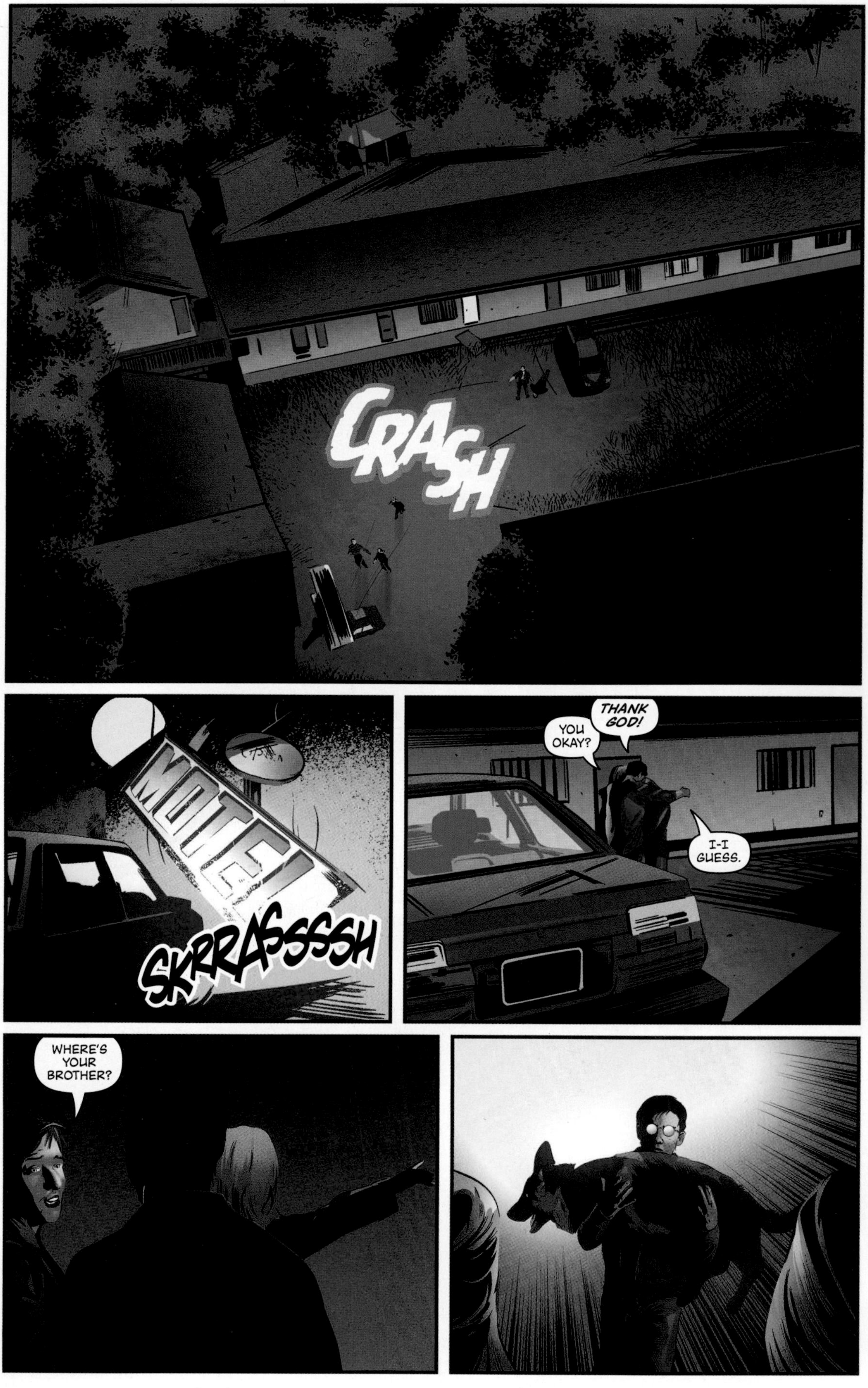
CRASH
MOTEL
SKRRASSSSH
YOU OKAY?
THANK GOD!
I-I GUESS.
WHERE'S YOUR BROTHER?

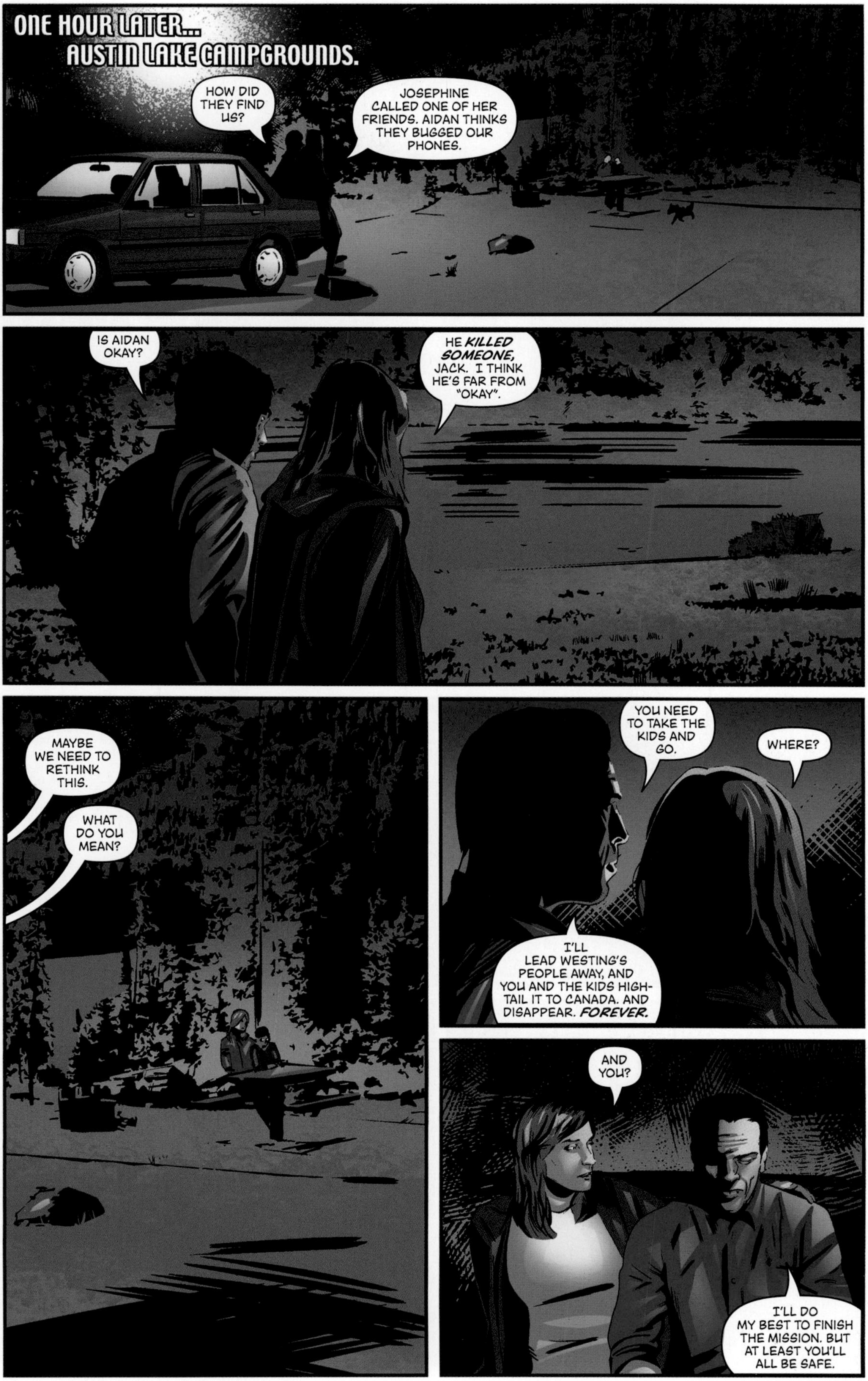
ONE HOUR LATER...
AUSTIN LAKE CAMPGROUNDS.
HOW DID THEY FIND US?
JOSEPHINE CALLED ONE OF HER FRIENDS. AIDAN THINKS THEY BUGGED OUR PHONES.
IS AIDAN OKAY?
HE *KILLED SOMEONE,* JACK. I THINK HE'S FAR FROM "OKAY".
MAYBE WE NEED TO RETHINK THIS.
WHAT DO YOU MEAN?
YOU NEED TO TAKE THE KIDS AND GO.
WHERE?
I'LL LEAD WESTING'S PEOPLE AWAY, AND YOU AND THE KIDS HIGH-TAIL IT TO CANADA. AND DISAPPEAR. *FOREVER.*
AND YOU?
I'LL DO MY BEST TO FINISH THE MISSION. BUT AT LEAST YOU'LL ALL BE SAFE.

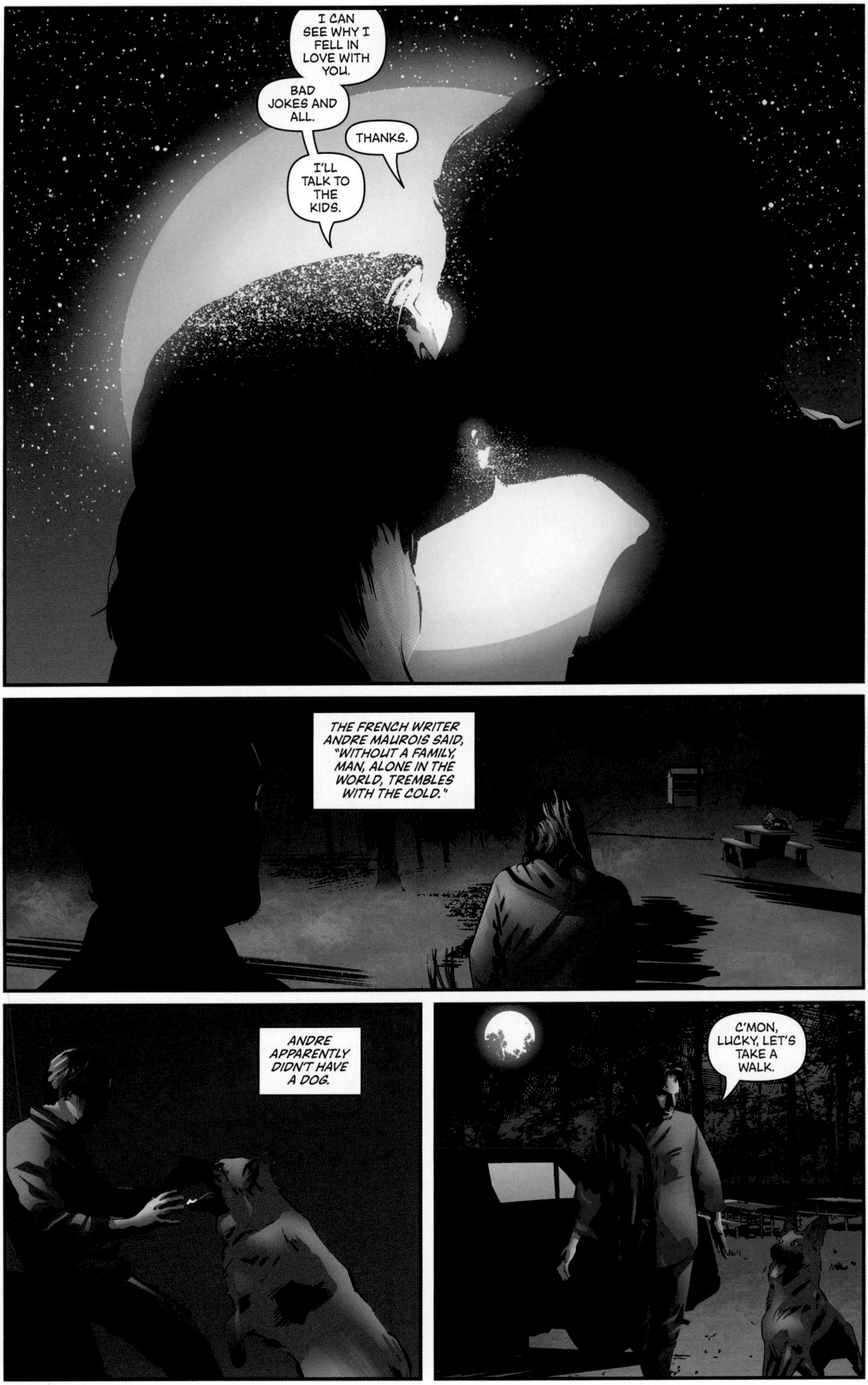
I CAN SEE WHY I FELL IN LOVE WITH YOU.
BAD JOKES AND ALL.
THANKS.
I'LL TALK TO THE KIDS.
THE FRENCH WRITER ANDRE MAUROIS SAID, "WITHOUT A FAMILY, MAN, ALONE IN THE WORLD, TREMBLES WITH THE COLD."
ANDRE APPARENTLY DIDN'T HAVE A DOG.
C'MON, LUCKY, LET'S TAKE A WALK.

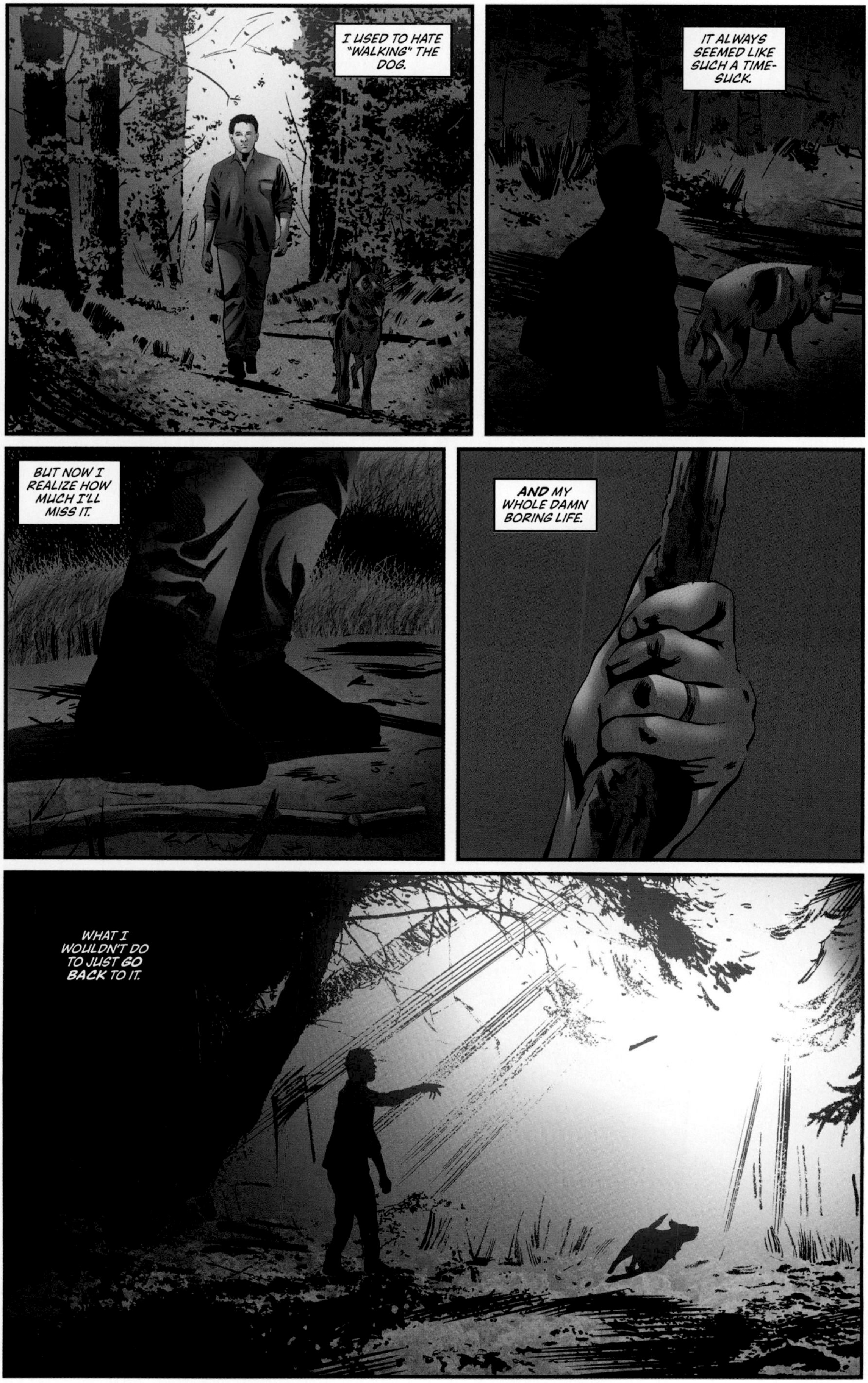
I USED TO HATE "WALKING" THE DOG.
IT ALWAYS SEEMED LIKE SUCH A TIME-SUCK.
BUT NOW I REALIZE HOW MUCH I'LL MISS IT.
AND MY WHOLE DAMN BORING LIFE.
WHAT I WOULDN'T DO TO JUST GO BACK TO IT.

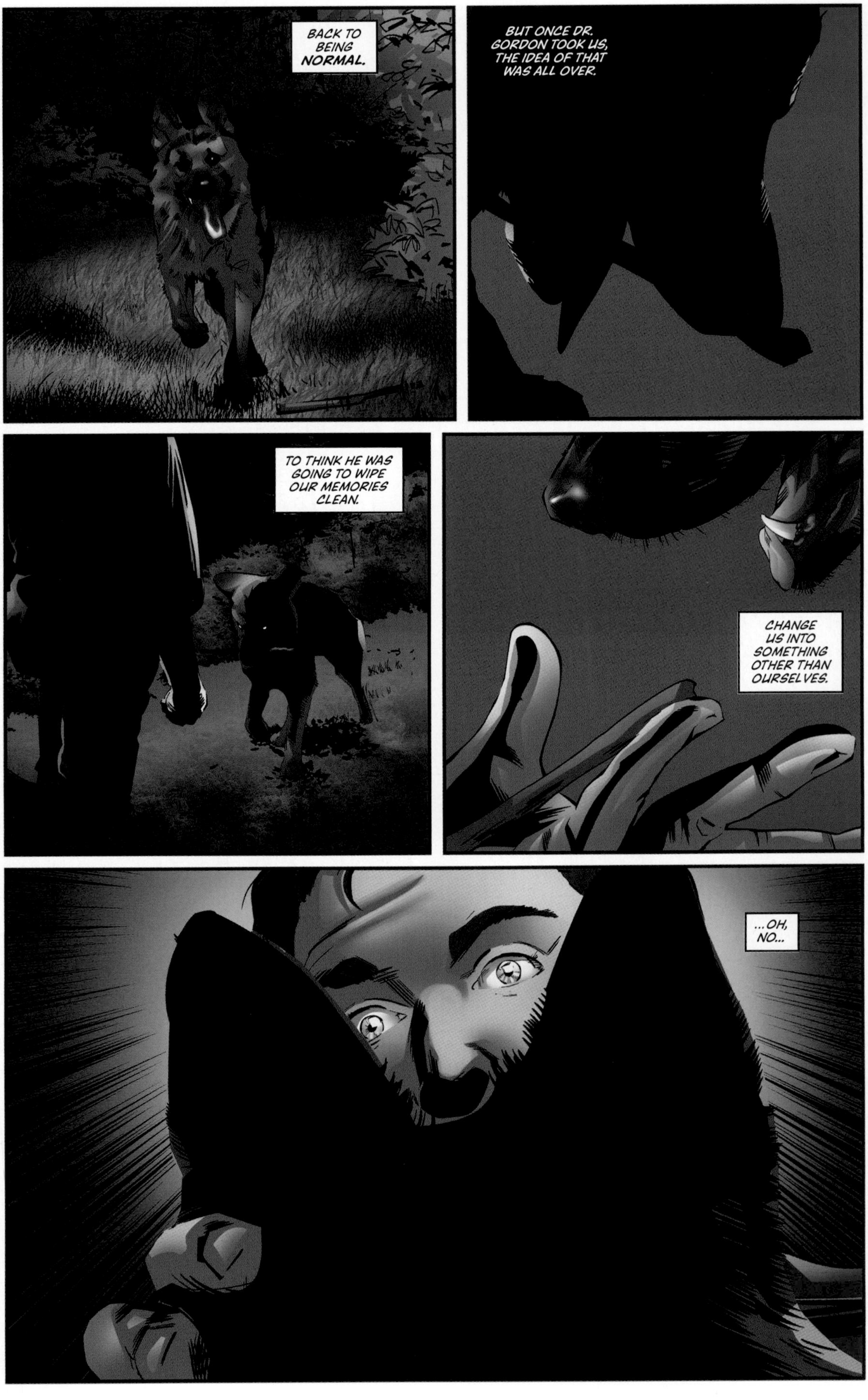
BACK TO BEING NORMAL.
BUT ONCE DR. GORDON TOOK US, THE IDEA OF THAT WAS ALL OVER.
TO THINK HE WAS GOING TO WIPE OUR MEMORIES CLEAN.
CHANGE US INTO SOMETHING OTHER THAN OURSELVES.
...OH, NO...

LUCKY IS LIKE US.

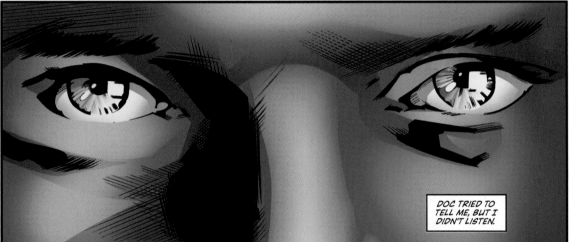

DOC TRIED TO TELL ME, BUT I DIDN'T LISTEN.

THE ONLY DIFFERENCE IS, THEY'VE ALREADY CHANGED HIM. AND THIS IS HOW THEY FOUND US.

I ALREADY HATED WESTING CORPORATION BEFORE THIS, NOW I JUST WANT TO KILL EVERY LAST ONE OF THEM.

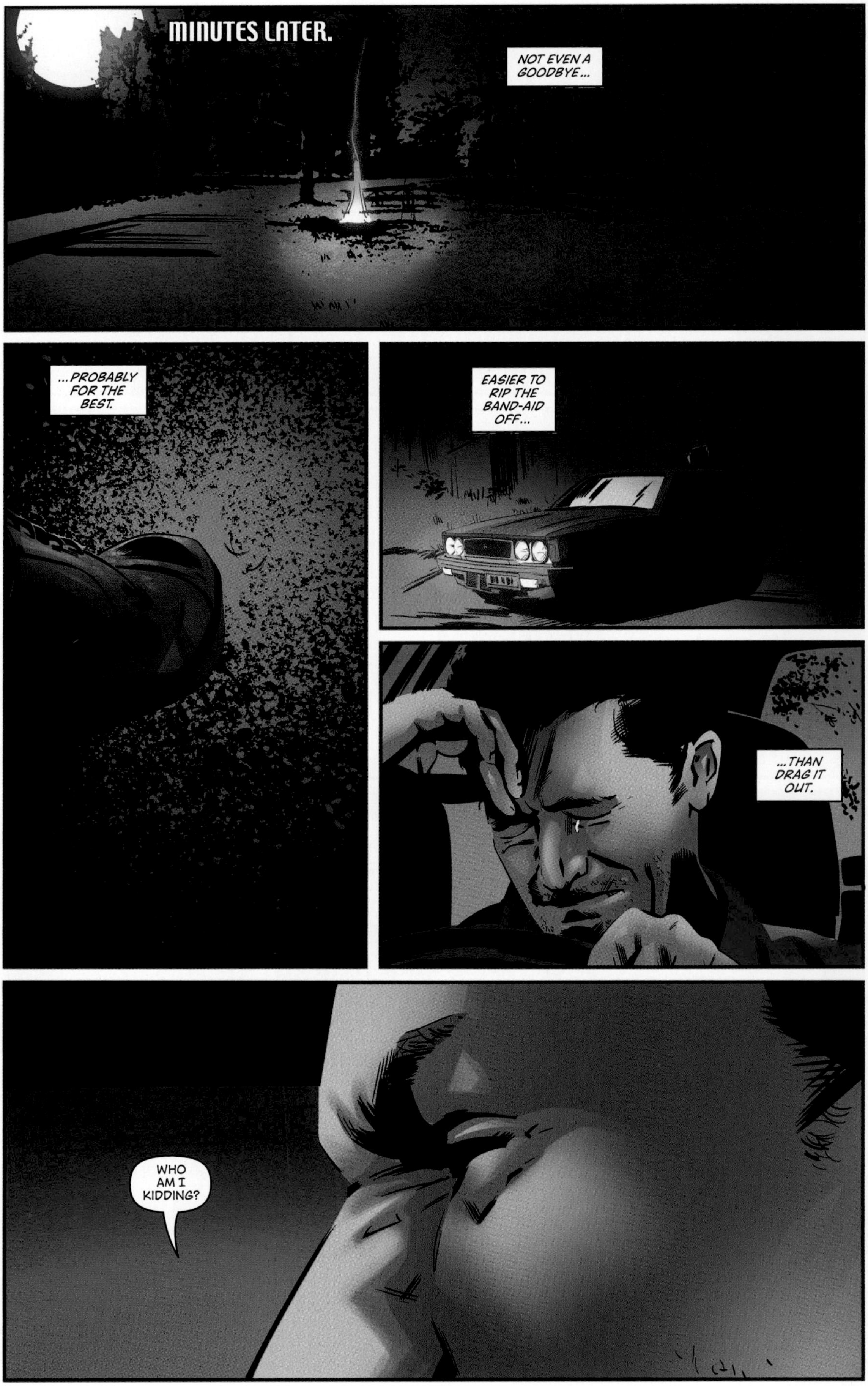
MINUTES LATER.
NOT EVEN A GOODBYE...
...PROBABLY FOR THE BEST.
EASIER TO RIP THE BAND-AID OFF...
...THAN DRAG IT OUT.
WHO AM I KIDDING?

THE THOUGHT THAT I'LL NEVER SEE OR HUG THEM AGAIN IS *UNTHINKABLE.*

THEY'RE MY *RAISON D'ETRE.*

AND WITHOUT THEM, I'M MERELY MARKING TIME IN THIS WORLD.

BUT I MUST GET A HOLD OF MYSELF.

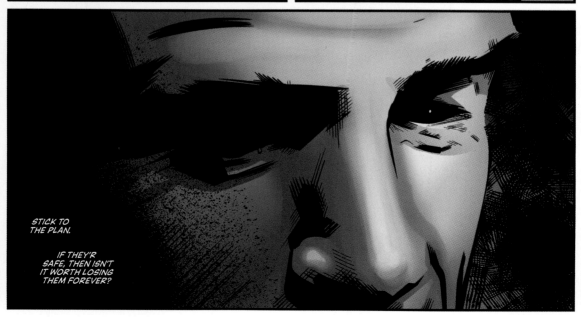

STICK TO THE PLAN.

IF THEY'R SAFE, THEN ISN'T IT WORTH LOSING THEM FOREVER?

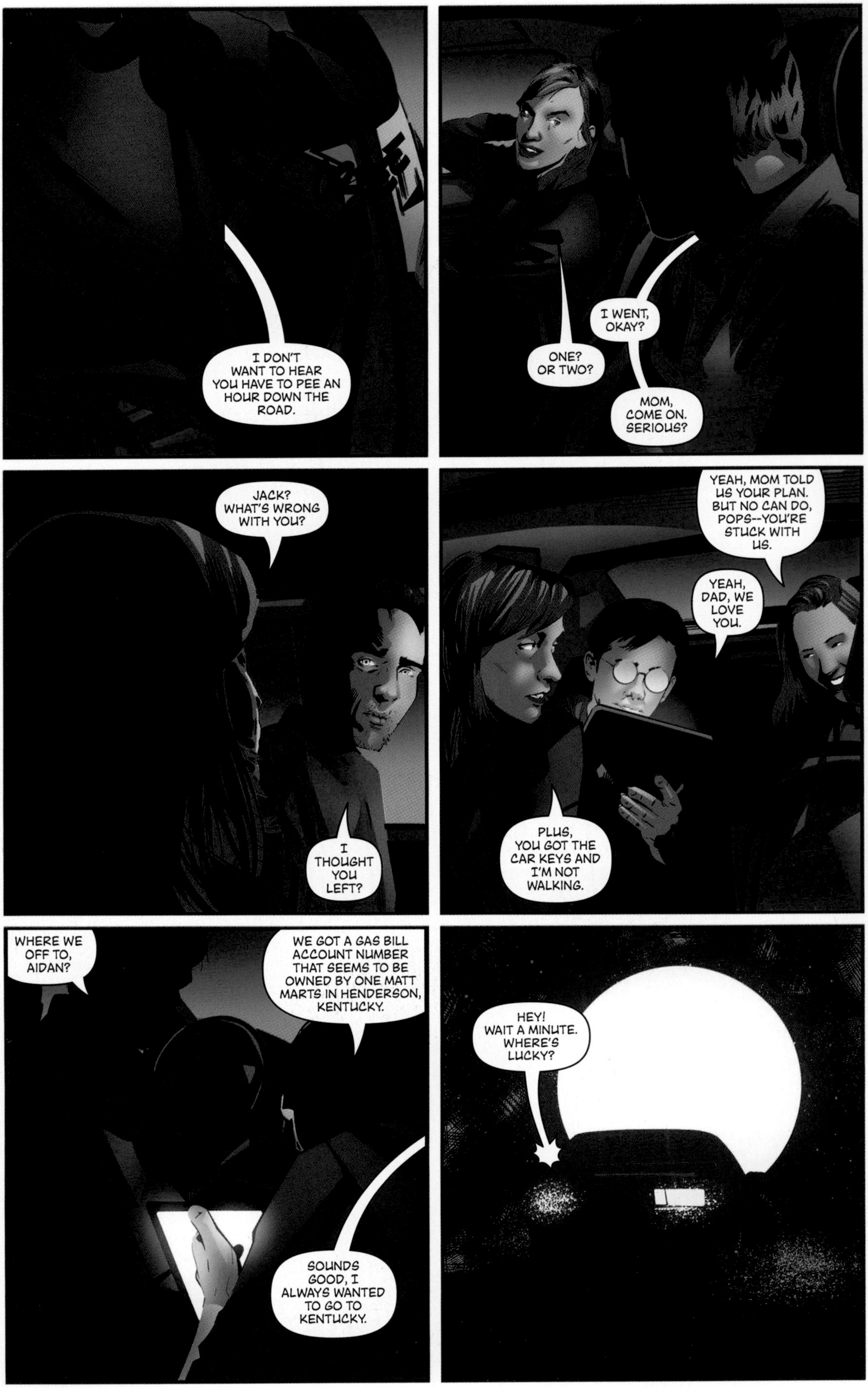
I DON'T WANT TO HEAR YOU HAVE TO PEE AN HOUR DOWN THE ROAD.
I WENT, OKAY?
ONE? OR TWO?
MOM, COME ON. SERIOUS?
JACK? WHAT'S WRONG WITH YOU?
I THOUGHT YOU LEFT?
YEAH, MOM TOLD US YOUR PLAN. BUT NO CAN DO, POPS--YOU'RE STUCK WITH US.
YEAH, DAD, WE LOVE YOU.
PLUS, YOU GOT THE CAR KEYS AND I'M NOT WALKING.
WHERE WE OFF TO, AIDAN?
WE GOT A GAS BILL ACCOUNT NUMBER THAT SEEMS TO BE OWNED BY ONE MATT MARTS IN HENDERSON, KENTUCKY.
SOUNDS GOOD, I ALWAYS WANTED TO GO TO KENTUCKY.
HEY! WAIT A MINUTE. WHERE'S LUCKY?

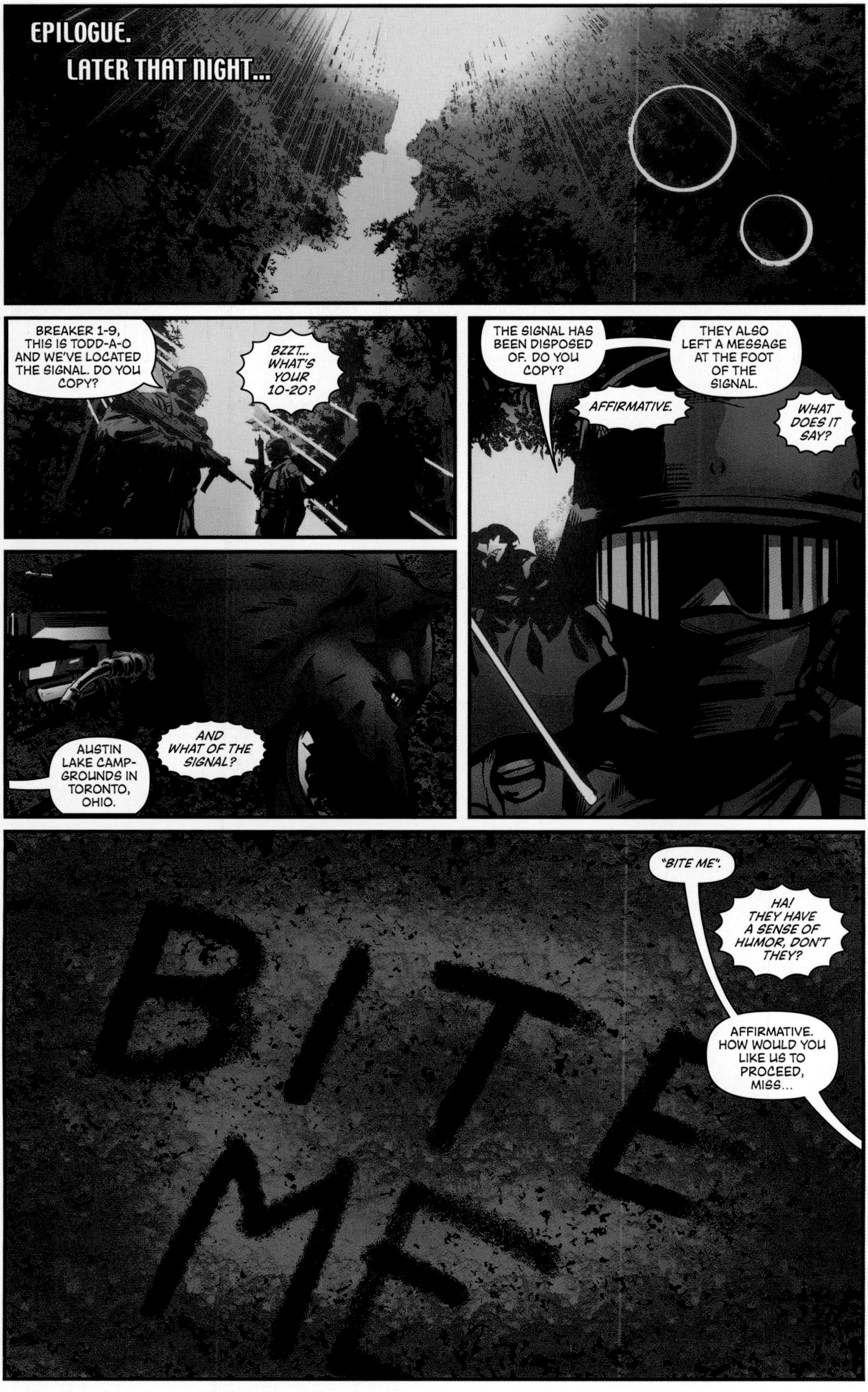
EPILOGUE.
LATER THAT NIGHT...
BREAKER 1-9, THIS IS TODD-A-O AND WE'VE LOCATED THE SIGNAL. DO YOU COPY?
BZZT... WHAT'S YOUR 10-20?
AUSTIN LAKE CAMP-GROUNDS IN TORONTO, OHIO.
AND WHAT OF THE SIGNAL?
THE SIGNAL HAS BEEN DISPOSED OF. DO YOU COPY?
AFFIRMATIVE.
THEY ALSO LEFT A MESSAGE AT THE FOOT OF THE SIGNAL.
WHAT DOES IT SAY?
"BITE ME".
HA! THEY HAVE A SENSE OF HUMOR, DON'T THEY?
AFFIRMATIVE. HOW WOULD YOU LIKE US TO PROCEED, MISS...
BITE ME

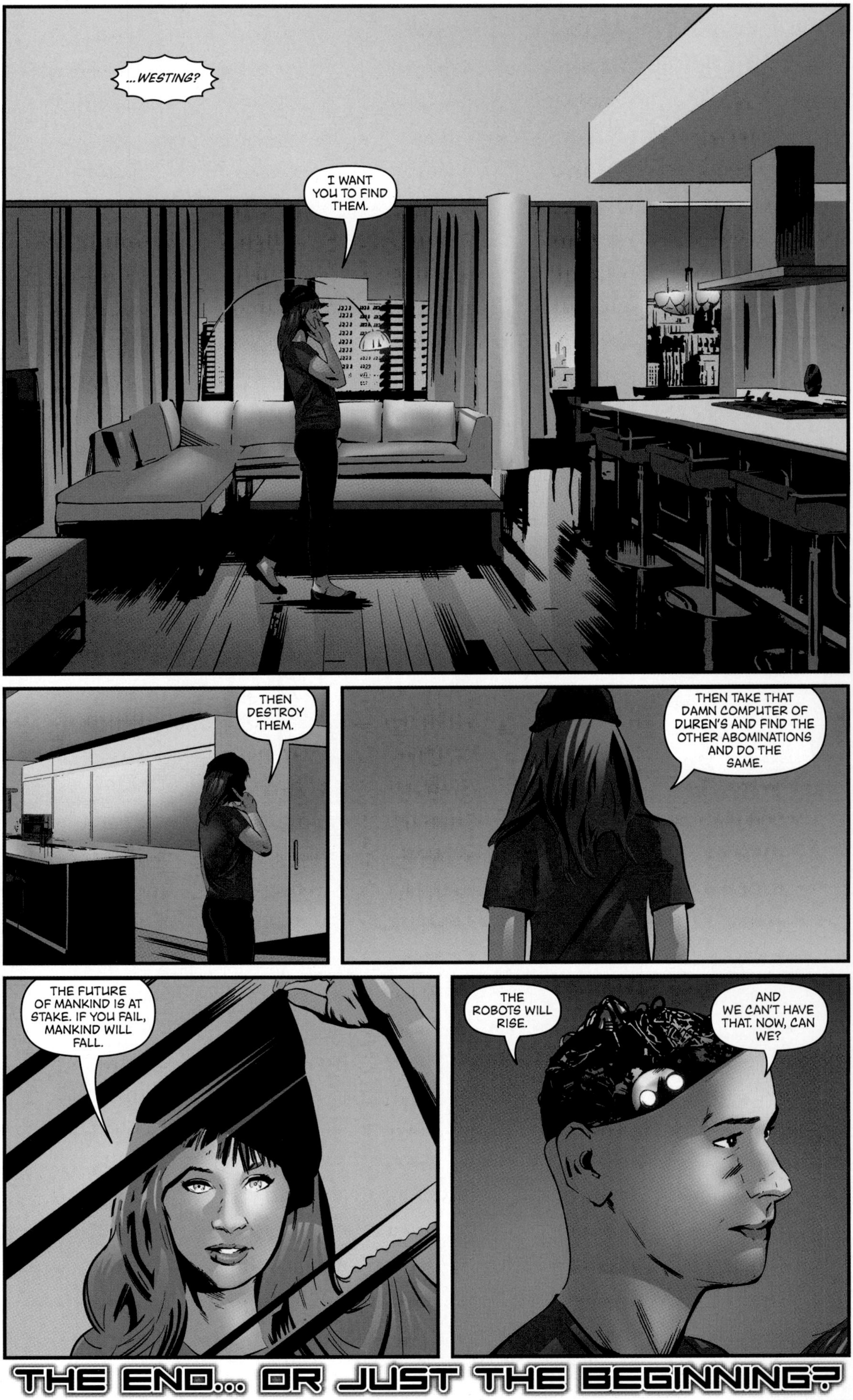
...WESTING?
I WANT YOU TO FIND THEM.
THEN DESTROY THEM.
THEN TAKE THAT DAMN COMPUTER OF DUREN'S AND FIND THE OTHER ABOMINATIONS AND DO THE SAME.
THE FUTURE OF MANKIND IS AT STAKE. IF YOU FAIL, MANKIND WILL FALL.
THE ROBOTS WILL RISE.
AND WE CAN'T HAVE THAT. NOW, CAN WE?
THE END... OR JUST THE BEGINNING?

Issue 1
ELIZABETH TORQUE
variant cover

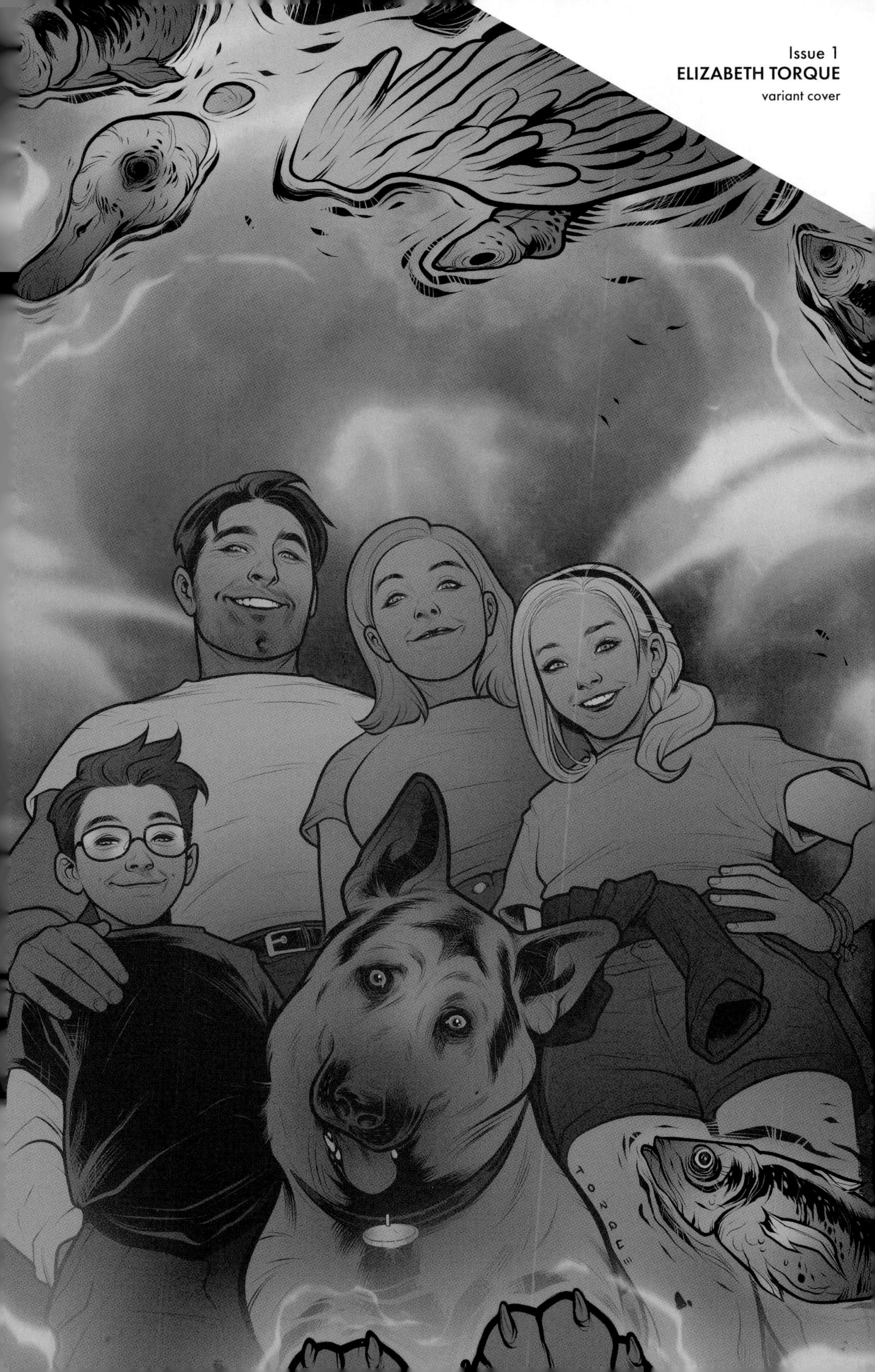
TORQUE

the normals™ sketchbook

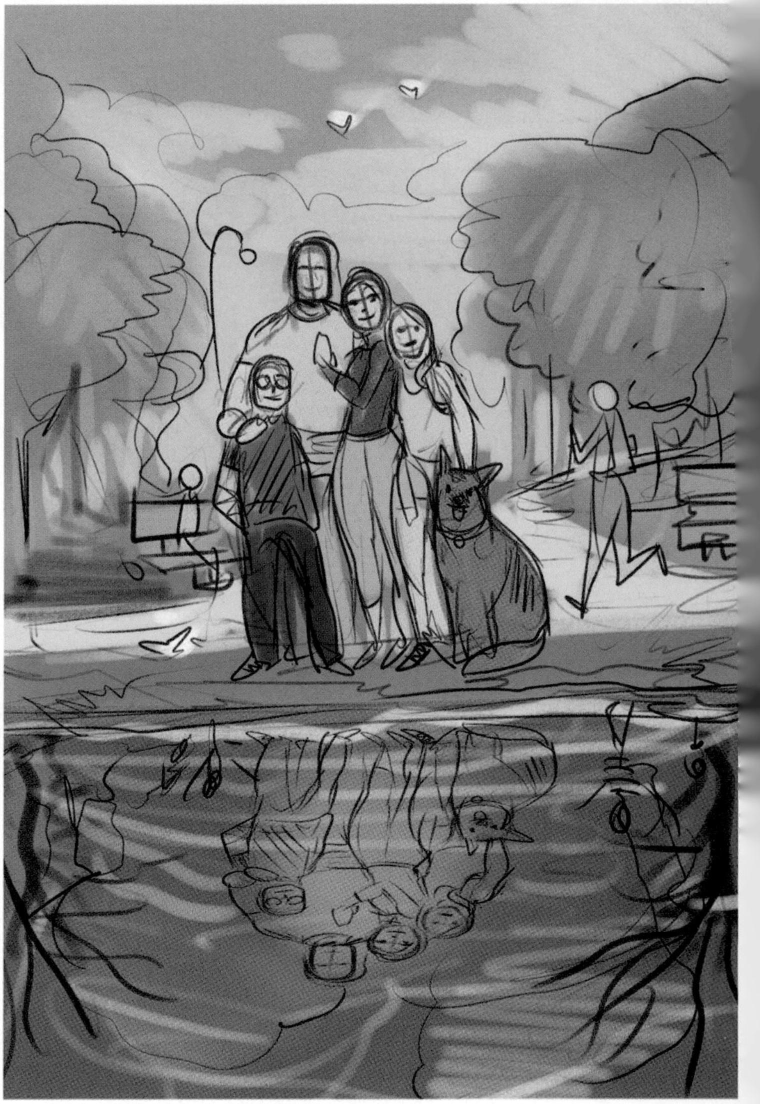

Issue #1 cover sketch by Elizabeth Torque

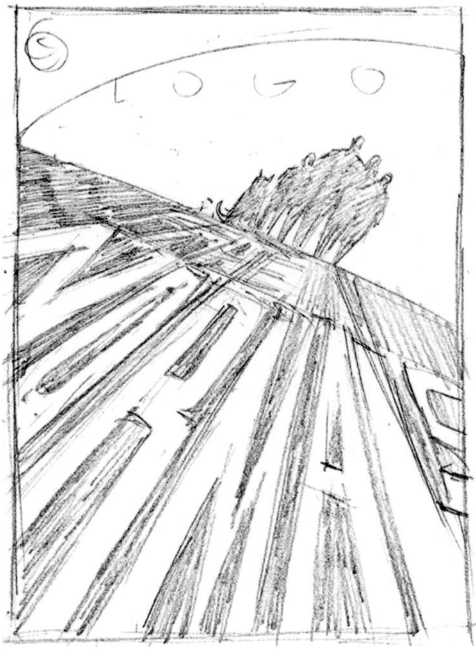

Issue #4 cover sketch by JUAN DOE

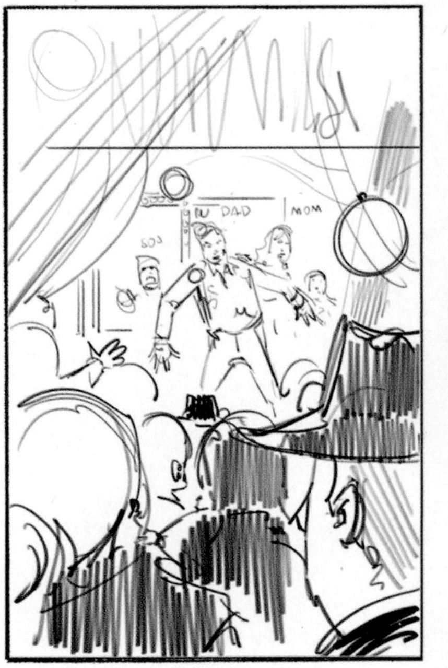
DAD
MOM

Issue #1 cover sketch by DENNIS CALERO

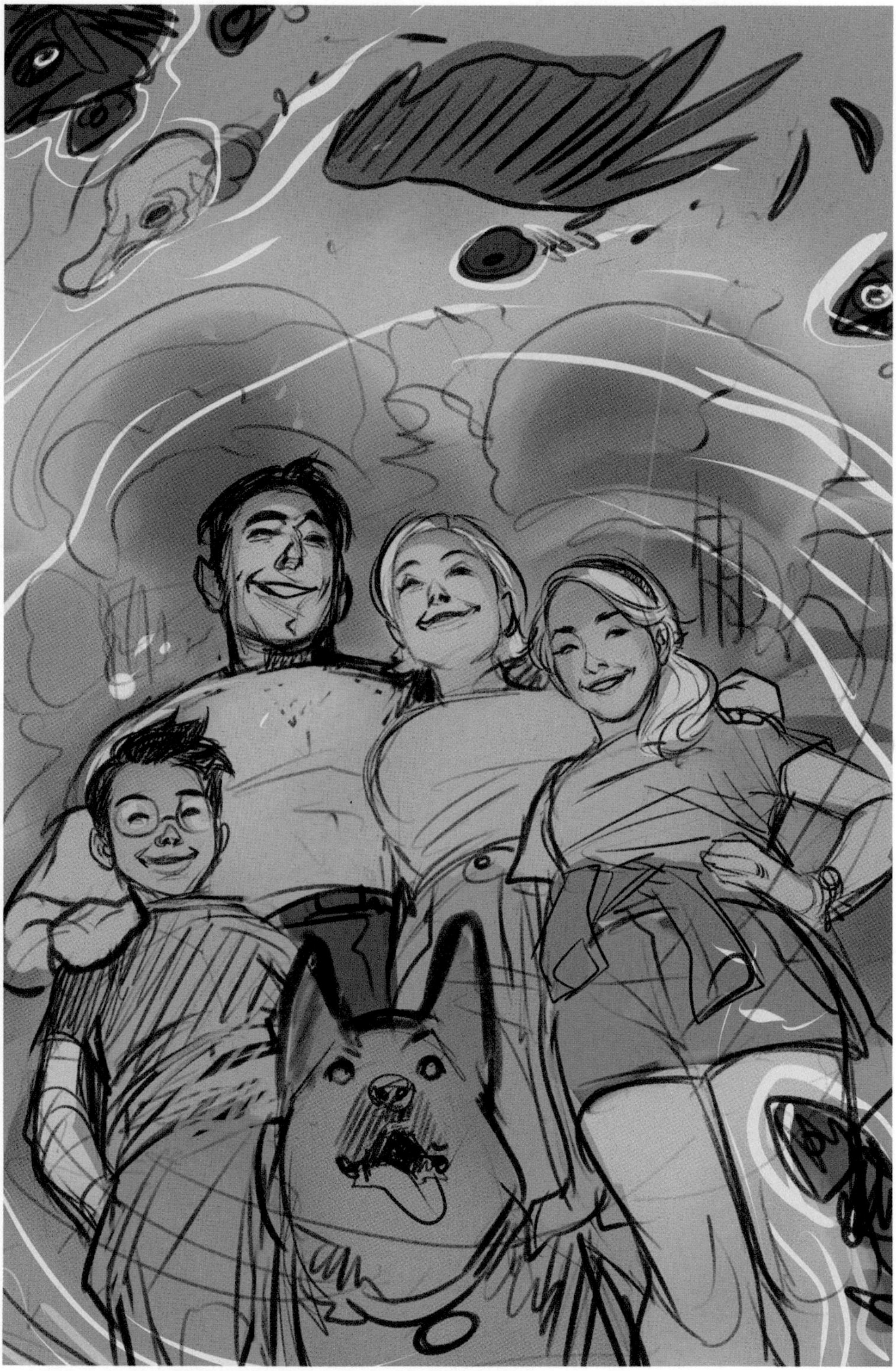

Issue #1 cover sketch by Elizabeth Torque

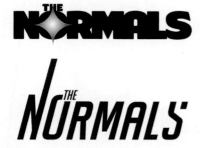

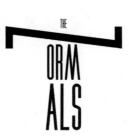

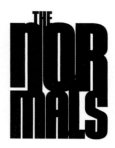

Logo Concepts by John J. Hill

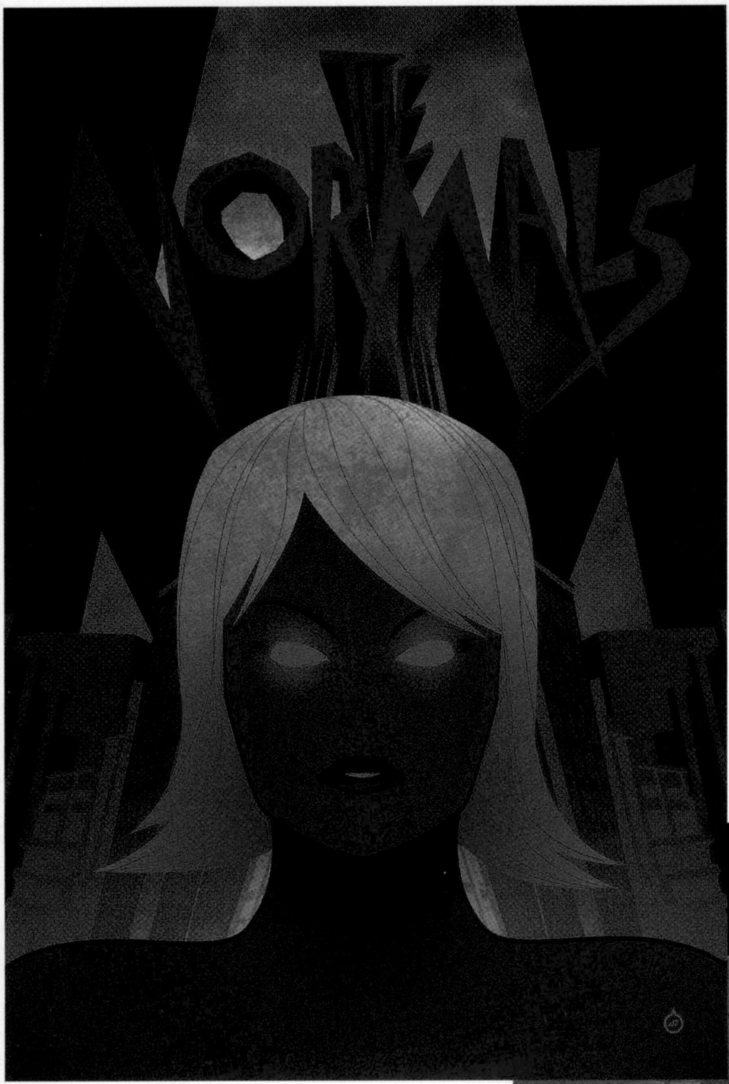
THE NORMALS

Issue #5 unused cover concept
by JUAN DOE

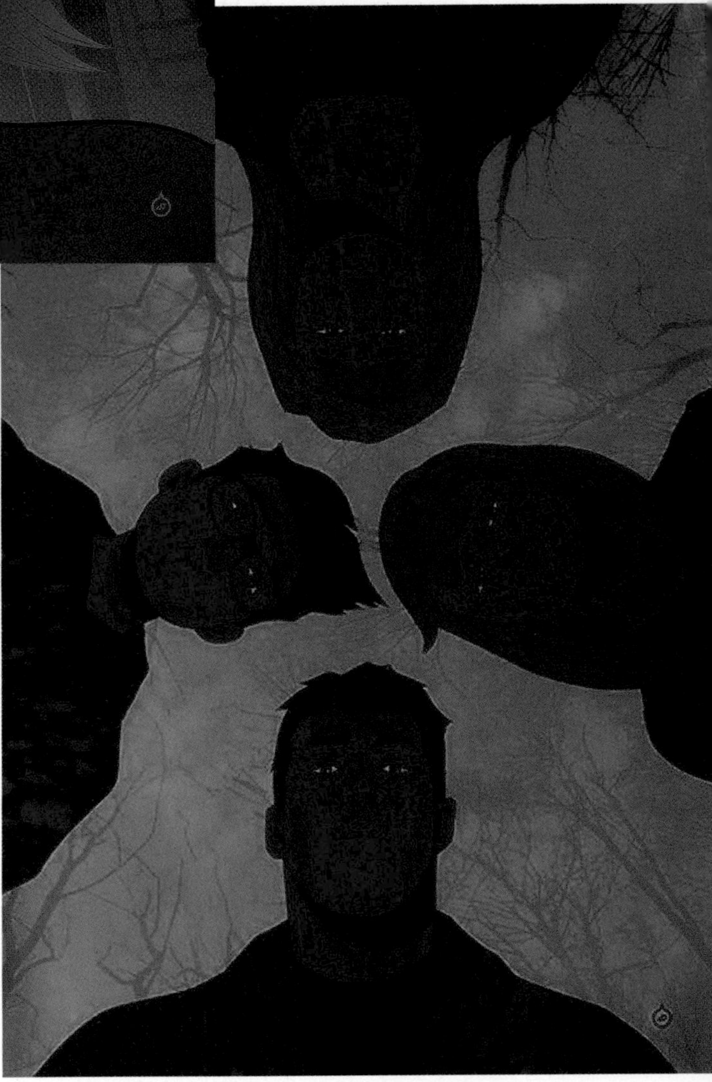

Issue #6 unused cover concept
by JUAN DOE

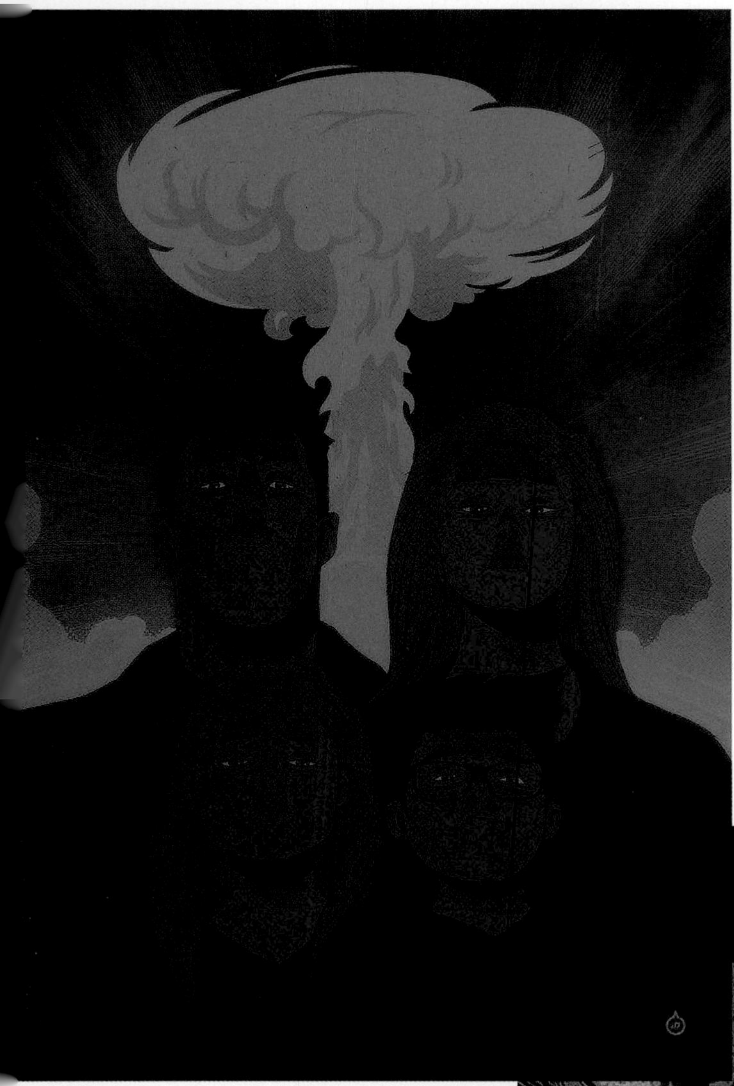

Issue #6 unused cover concept by JUAN DOE

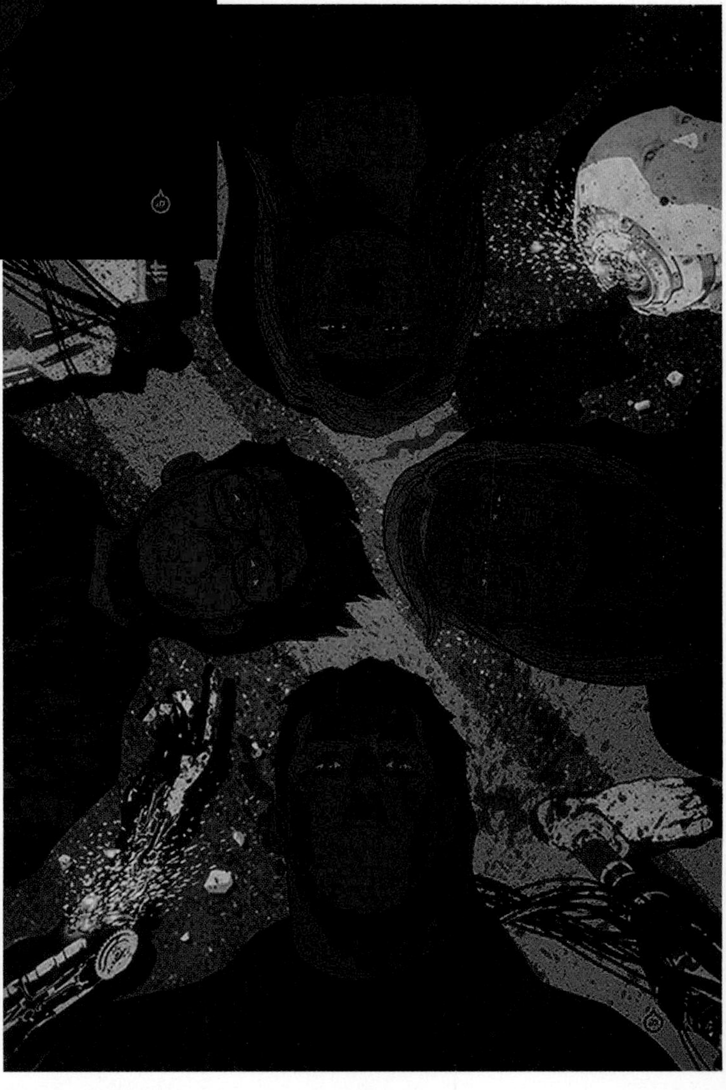

Issue #6 final cover by JUAN DOE

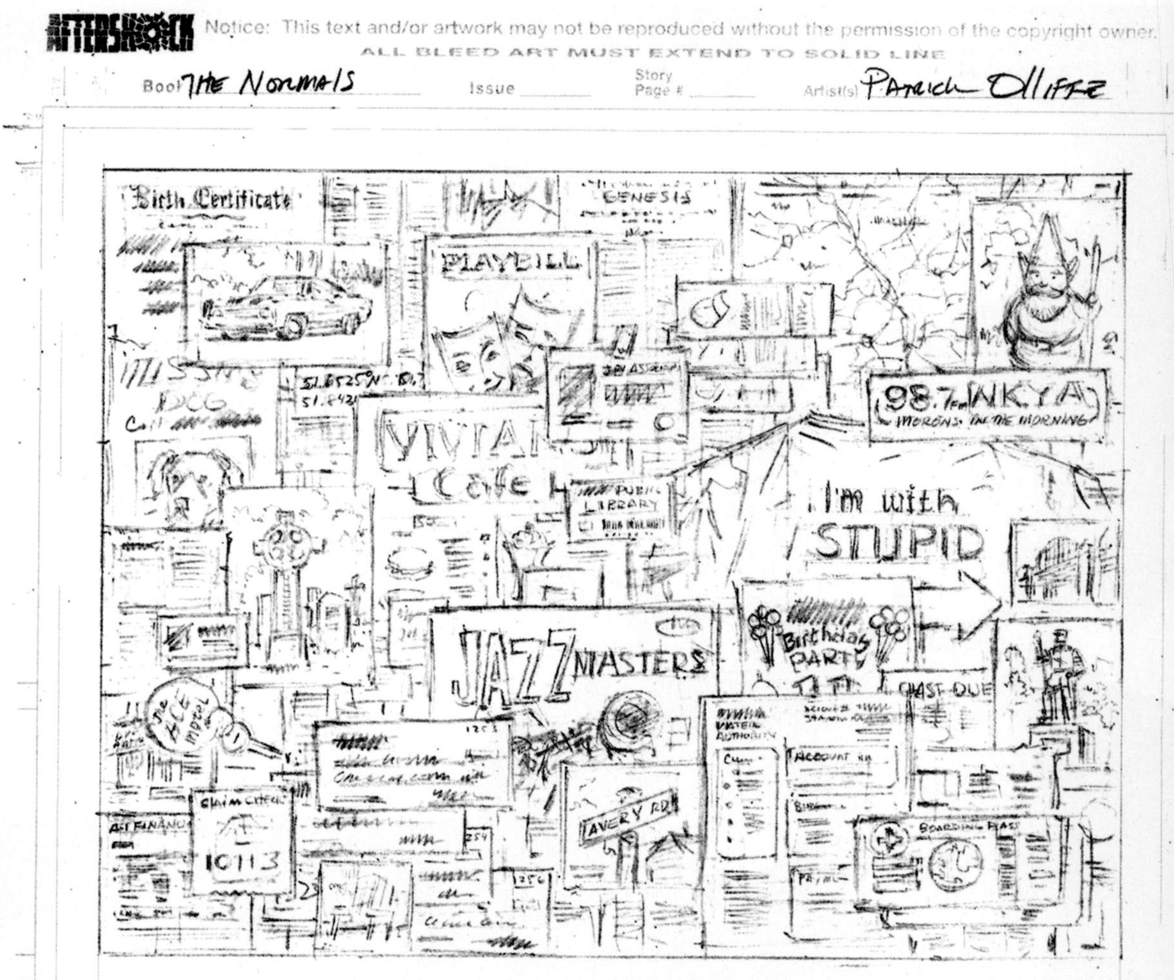
AFTERSHOCK
Notice: This text and/or artwork may not be reproduced without the permission of the copyright owner.
ALL BLEED ART MUST EXTEND TO SOLID LINE
Book THE NORMALS
Issue
Story Page #
Artist(s) PATRICK OLLIFFE
Birth Certificate
GENESIS
PLAYBILL
98.7 WKYA
MORONS IN THE MORNING
PUBLIC LIBRARY
I'm with STUPID
JAZZ MASTERS
Birthday PARTY
CLAIM CHECK
10113
AVERY RD
BOARDING PASS

Conspiracy Board sketches by PATRICK OLLIFFE

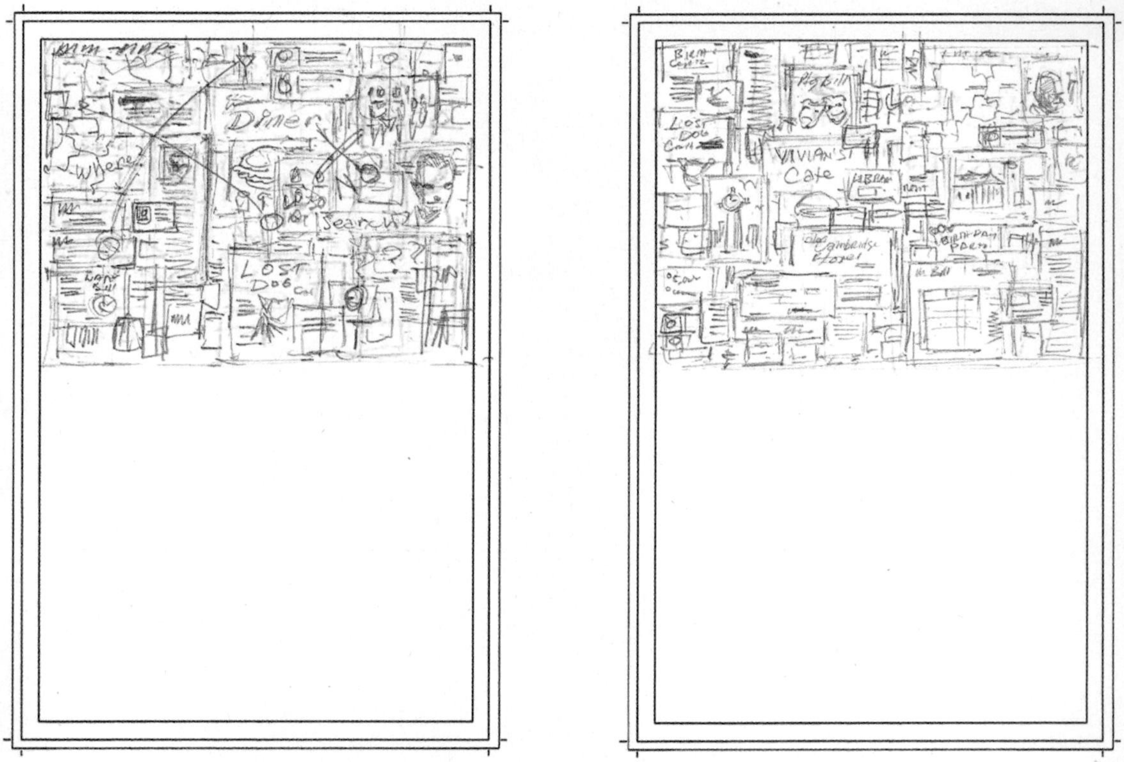
Diner
Where?
LOST DOG
VIVIAN'S Cafe

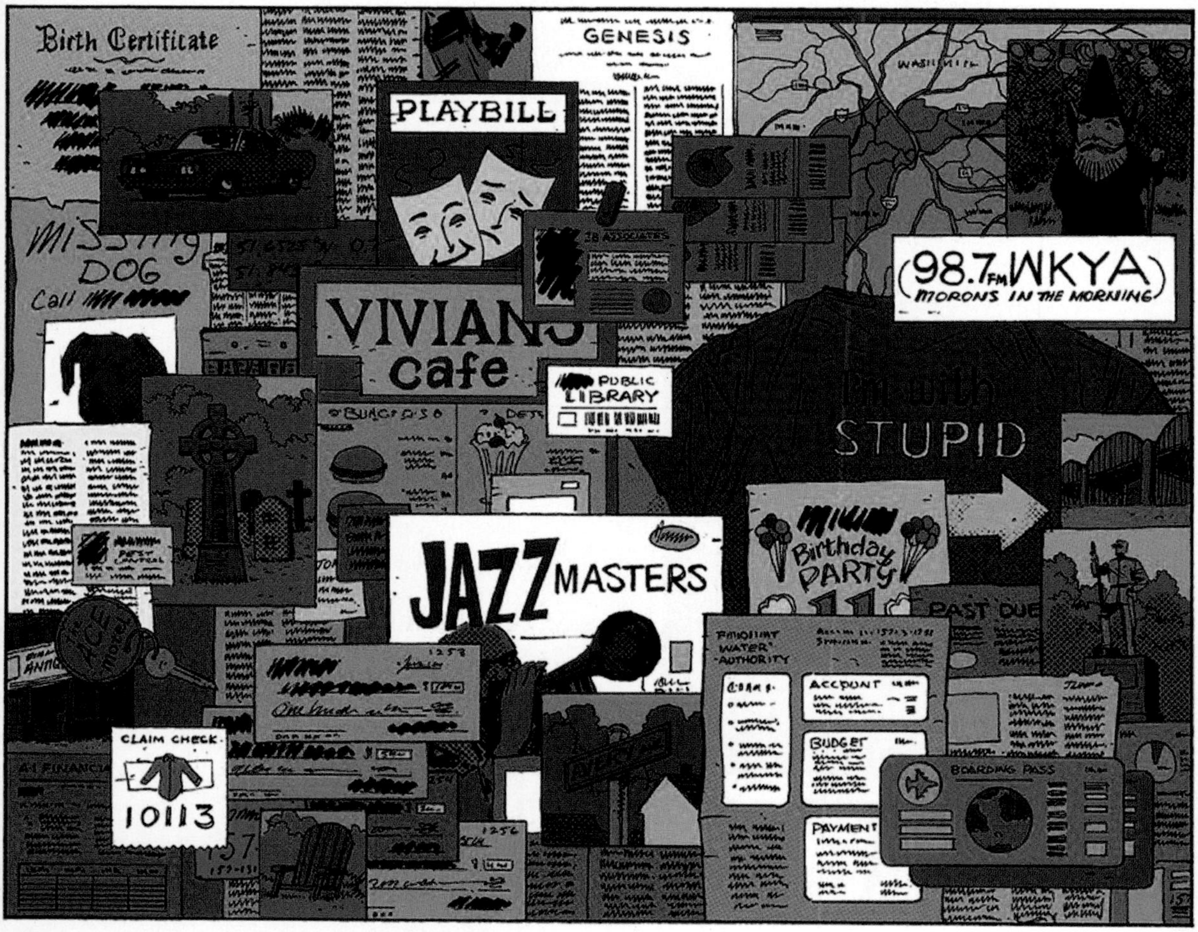
Birth Certificate
GENESIS
PLAYBILL
DOG
38 ASSOCIATES
(98.7FM WKYA)
MORONS IN THE MORNING
cafe
PUBLIC
LIBRARY
STUPID
JAZZ MASTERS
Birthday
PARTY
PAST DUE
WATER
AUTHORITY
ACCOUNT
BUDGET
PAYMENT
BOARDING PASS
CLAIM CHECK
10113

Conspiracy Board final art by PATRICK OLLIFFE

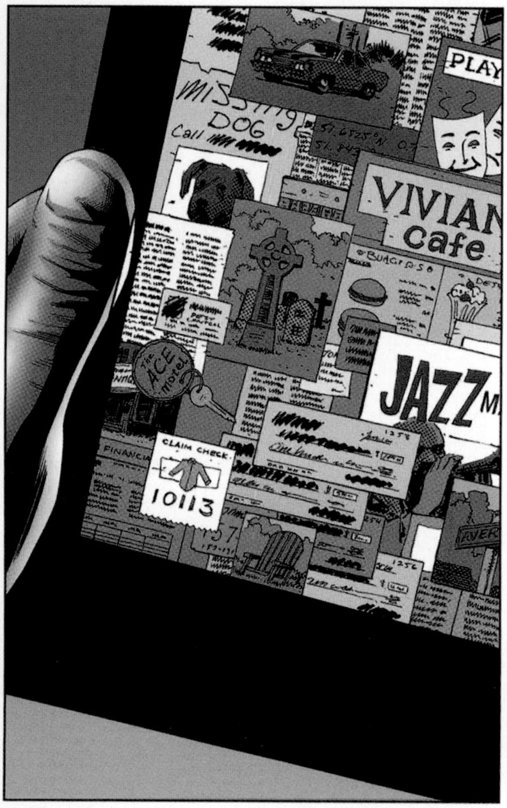
DOG
VIVIAN
cafe
CLAIM CHECK
10113

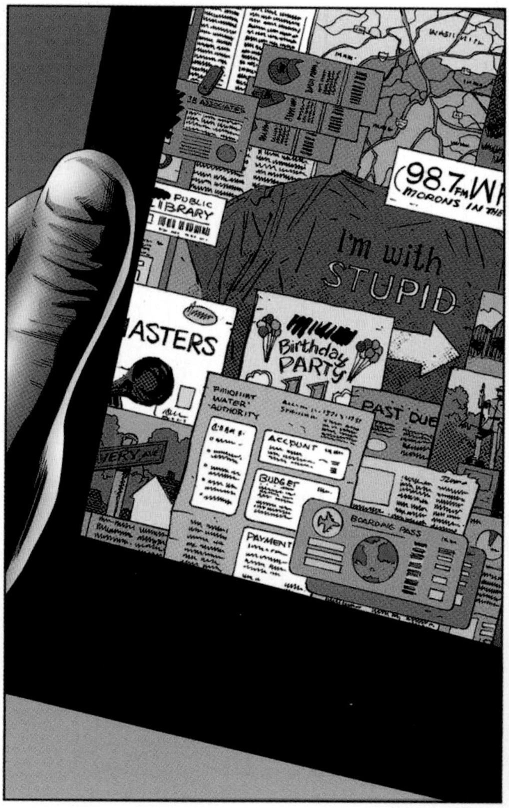
PUBLIC
LIBRARY
I'm with
STUPID
ASTERS
Birthday
PARTY
PAST DUE
ACCOUNT
BUDGET
PAYMENT
BOARDING PASS

the Normals™

1

PAGE SEVEN:

Panel 1 – (**NOTE TO ARTIST: We see the next three panels all in the reflection of JACK's eyes.**) Aidan takes the first step down the ladder of the tree house, which is high above, as JACK watches.

1. JACK (CAPTION):   This was one of those moments, seemingly so simple and innocent…

Panel 2 – JACK'S EYES -- Aidan slips and falls backwards.

2. JACK (CAPTION):   …that I wish I could take back and **do all over again.**

Panel 3 – JACK'S EYES – Aidan hits the ground, back of his head first. The impact is hard.

3. JACK (CAPTION):   Because little did I know then…

Panel 4 – JACK'S EYES as he grabs his son, who is a little discombobulated but seems okay.

4. JACK (CAPTION):   …but this moment would **change everything.**

5. JACK: **Aidan, are you okay?!**

6. AIDAN: I think so.

7. JACK: Are you **bleeding anywhere?!** Let me see the back of your head.

script by
ADAM GLASS

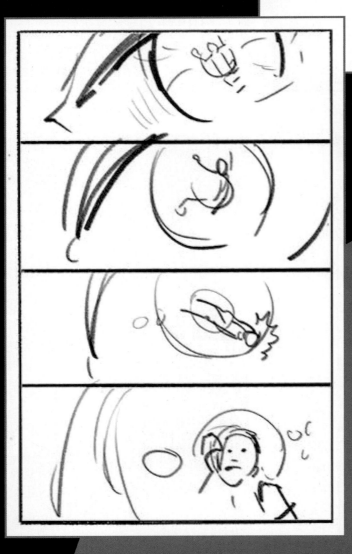

PAGE
7
PROCESS

layouts by
DENNIS CALERO

inks by
DENNIS CALERO

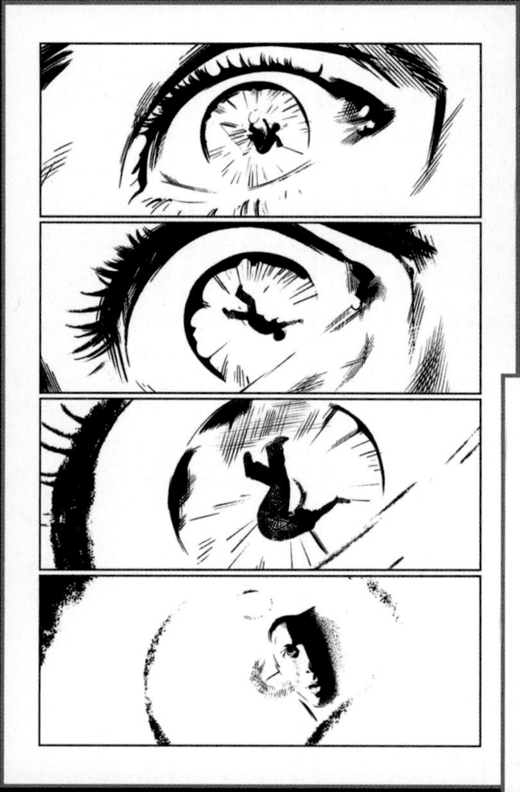

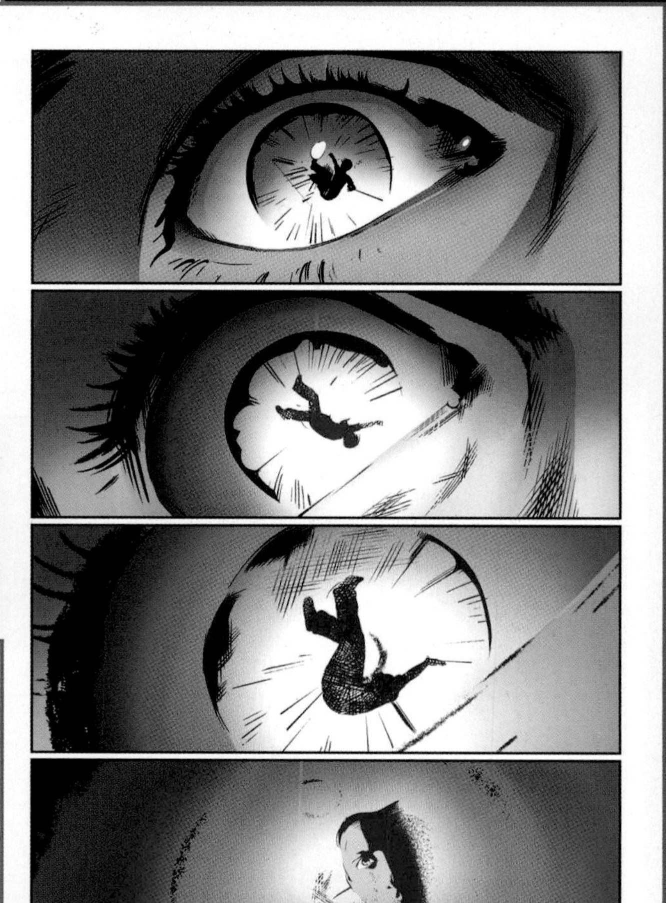

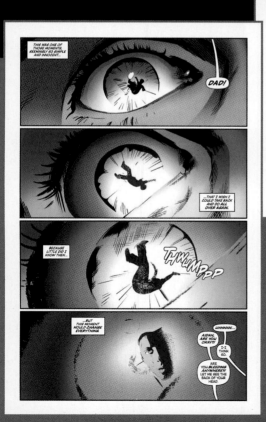

colors by
ADRIANO AUGUSTO

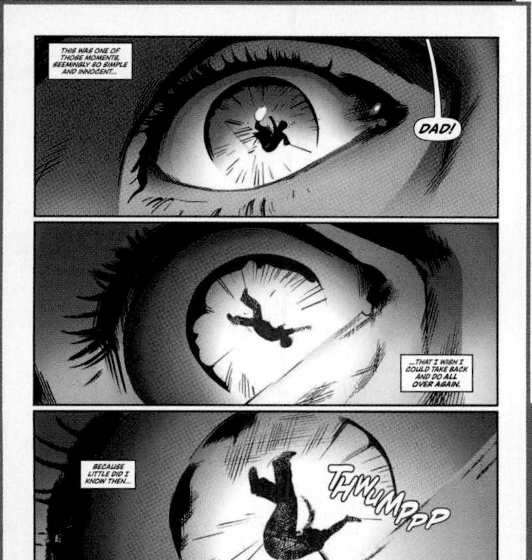
THIS WAS ONE OF THOSE MOMENTS, SEEMINGLY SO SIMPLE AND INNOCENT...
DAD!
...THAT I WISH I COULD TAKE BACK AND DO ALL OVER AGAIN.
BECAUSE LITTLE DID I KNOW THEN...
THWUMPPP
...BUT THIS MOMENT WOULD CHANGE EVERYTHING.
UHHNNN...
AIDAN, ARE YOU OKAY?!
I-I THINK SO.
ARE YOU BLEEDING ANYWHERE?! LET ME SEE THE BACK OF YOUR HEAD.

lettering by
COREY BREEN

the Normals™ #1

PAGE NINE:

Panel 1 – The back door SWINGS OPEN, finding JACK carrying Aidan in his arms.

1. JACK:	**Mary! Mary!** Get over here!
2. MARY:	Jack, why are you yelling? What happened?!

Panel 3 – JACK intercepts Mary so that they are out of earshot of Aidan. But Mary can see Aidan on the couch in the other room.

3. MARY:	Is Aidan okay?
4. JACK:	He fell out of his tree house and hit his head. I need to show you something, but I don't want to freak him out.
5. MARY:	You mean like you're freaking **me** out right now?!

Panel 4 – Jack and Mary approach Aidan on the couch. He's suspicious but calm.

6. JACK:	Hey, buddy, I just need to show your mom something.

Panel 5 – Jack turns Aidan's head to show Mary, and behind his ear is—NOTHING. Mary looks perplexed. And JACK looks confused.

7. AIDAN:	I-is everything okay?
8. MARY:	Yes, baby. Mommy is going to go grab you some Aspirin and water. We'll be right back. Rest up.

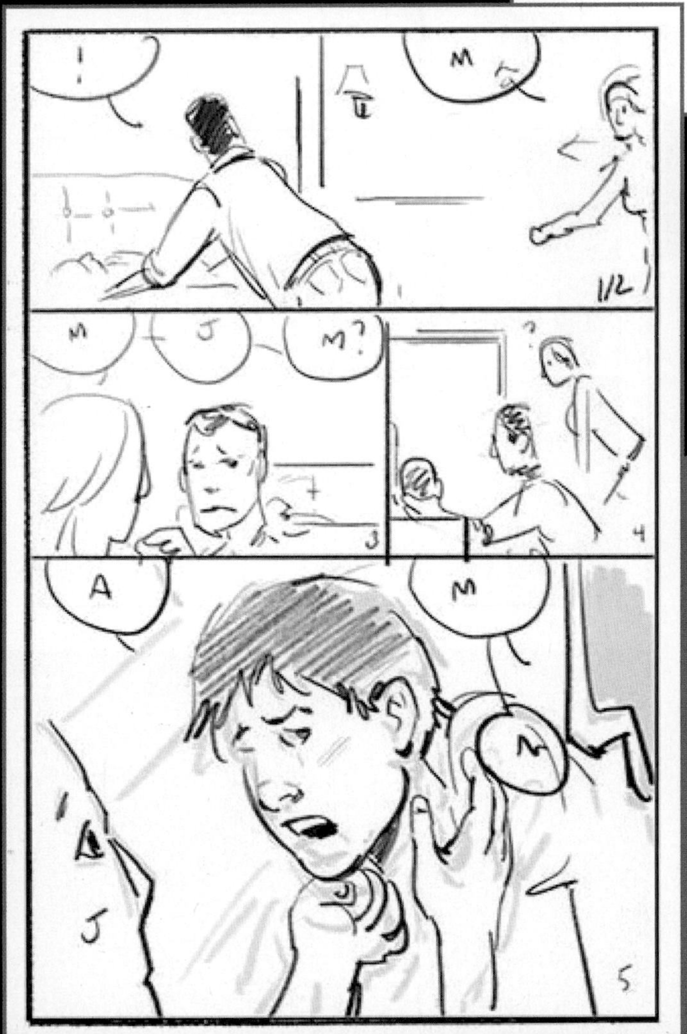

M
M
J
M?
A
M

script by
ADAM GLASS

PAGE 9 PROCESS

layouts by
DENNIS CALERO

inks by
DENNIS CALERO

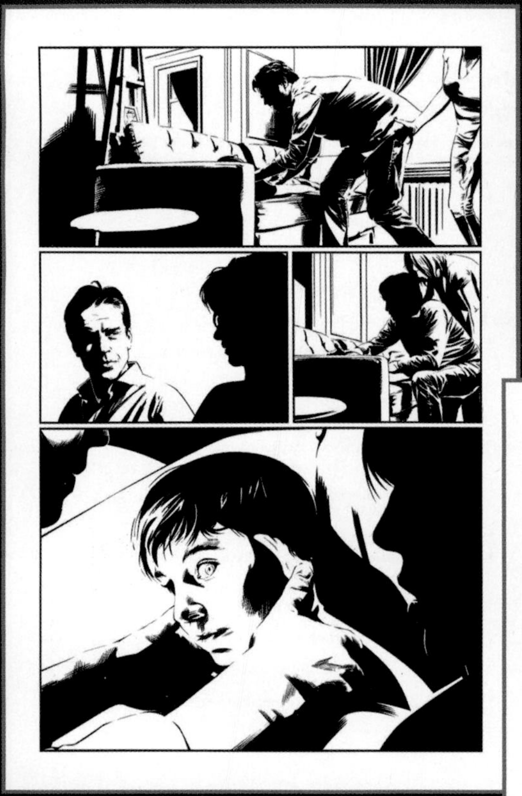

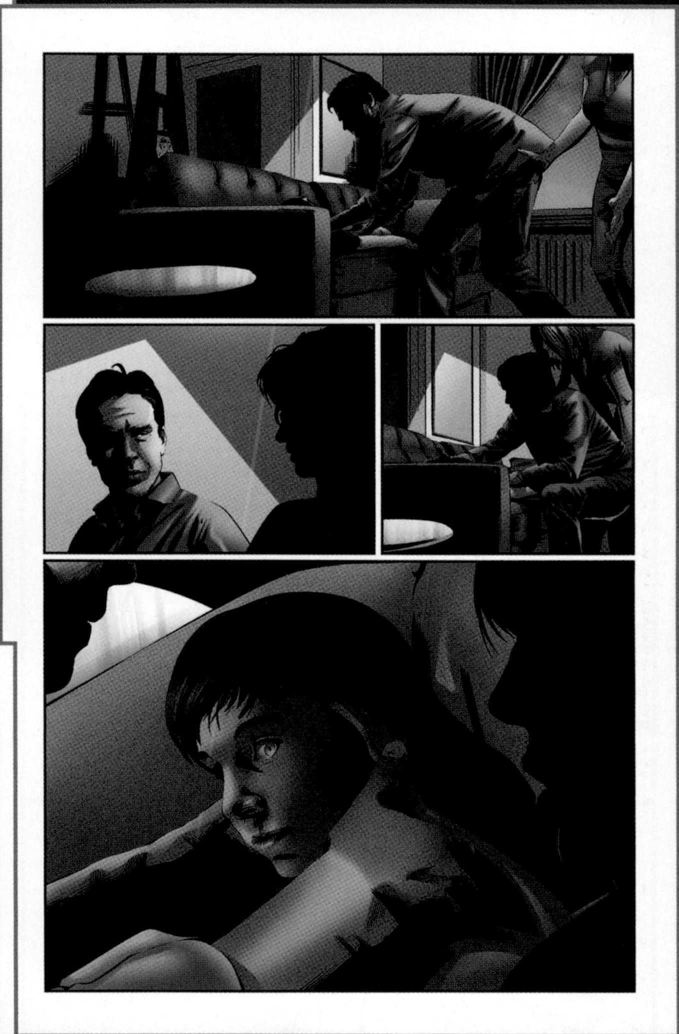

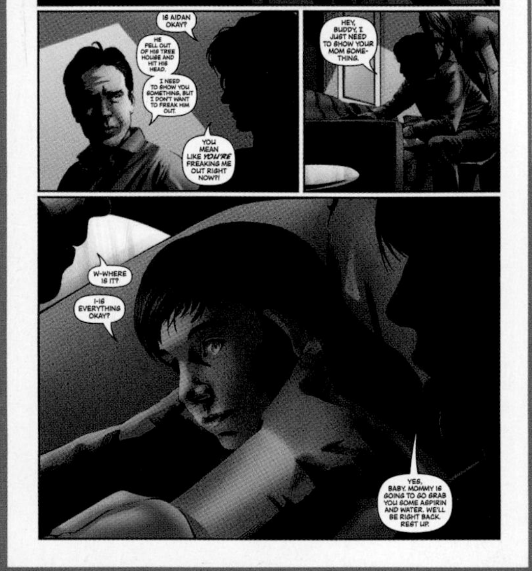
SECONDS LATER...
MARY! MARY! GET OVER HERE!
JACK, WHY ARE YOU YELLING? WHAT HAPPENED?!
IS AIDAN OKAY?
HE FELL OUT OF HIS TREE HOUSE AND HIT HIS HEAD.
I NEED TO SHOW YOU SOMETHING, BUT I DON'T WANT TO FREAK HIM OUT.
YOU MEAN LIKE *YOU'RE* FREAKING ME OUT RIGHT NOW?!
HEY, BUDDY, I JUST NEED TO SHOW YOUR MOM SOME-THING.
W-WHERE IS IT?
I-IS EVERYTHING OKAY?
YES, BABY. MOMMY IS GOING TO GO GRAB YOU SOME ASPIRIN AND WATER. WE'LL BE RIGHT BACK. REST UP.

colors by
ADRIANO AUGUSTO

lettering by
COREY BREEN

the Normals ™

1

PAGE FIFTEEN:

<u>Panel 1</u> – The bell over the door RINGS as it opens.

1. SFX: RING!

<u>Panel 2</u> – The place is empty, and behind the counter cleaning up is CHARLIE, 60's, wearing glasses and a waist apron over his Flannel shirt.

2. JACK: The best thing on the menu is--

3. JOSEPHINE: The banana pancakes.

4. AIDAN: You've told us a **million times**, Dad.

5. JACK: Just don't want you to miss out.

<u>Panel 3</u> – JACK and family move closer as Charlie looks up.

6. CHARLIE: Did I hear someone needs some banana pancakes?

7. JACK: You sure did, Charlie.

8. MARY: It's really good to see a friendly face.

<u>Panel 4</u> – JACK and Mary stand right across the counter from Charlie, who seems confused.

9. CHARLIE: Sorry folks, don't mean to be rude, but I don't recall your acquaintances.

10. JACK: Ha! Stop messing around, Charlie. I worked for you for **three summers**. It's me, Jack, and this is Mary. Normal.

11. CHARLIE: You must have me confused with another fella because I never seen you all before in my life.

12. MARY: This is ridiculous. Grab **Vivian**--she'll tell you.

<u>Panel 5</u> – Charlie looks even more baffled. As do Josephine and Aidan.

13. CHARLIE: Vivian? My mother? She's been dead for nearly **twenty years.**

14. MARY: What? That's **impossible**.

script by
ADAM GLASS

PAGE 15 PROCESS

layouts by
DENNIS CALERO

inks by
DENNIS CALERO

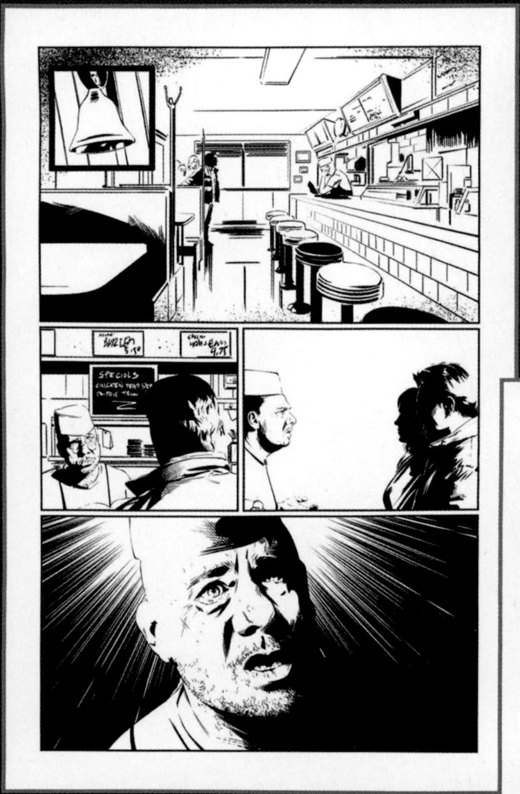

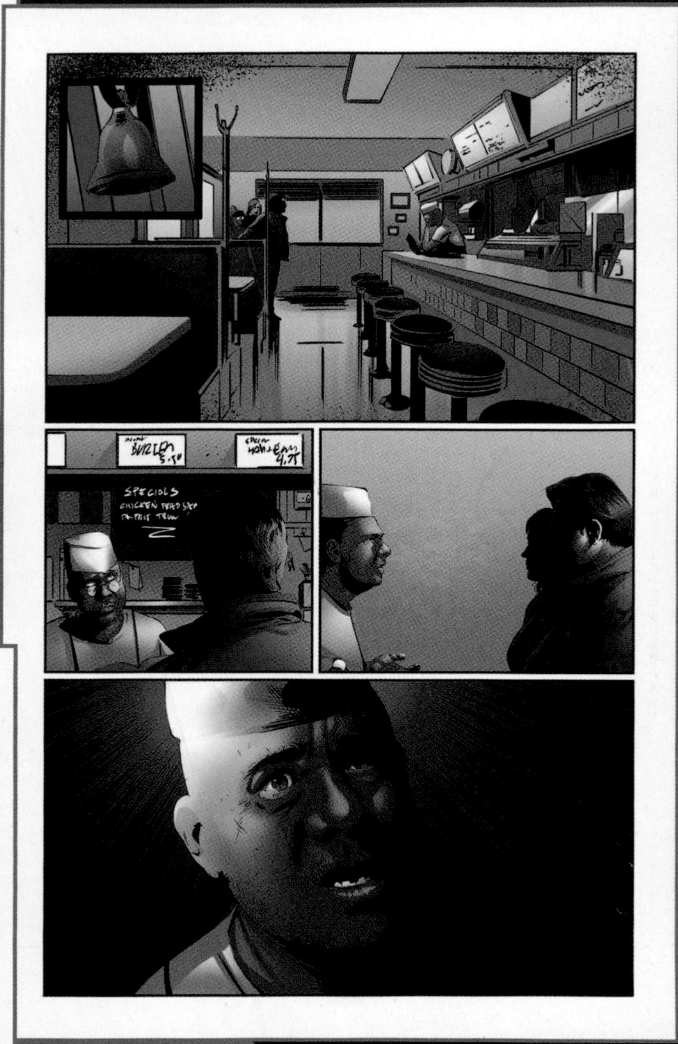

colors by
ADRIANO AUGUSTO

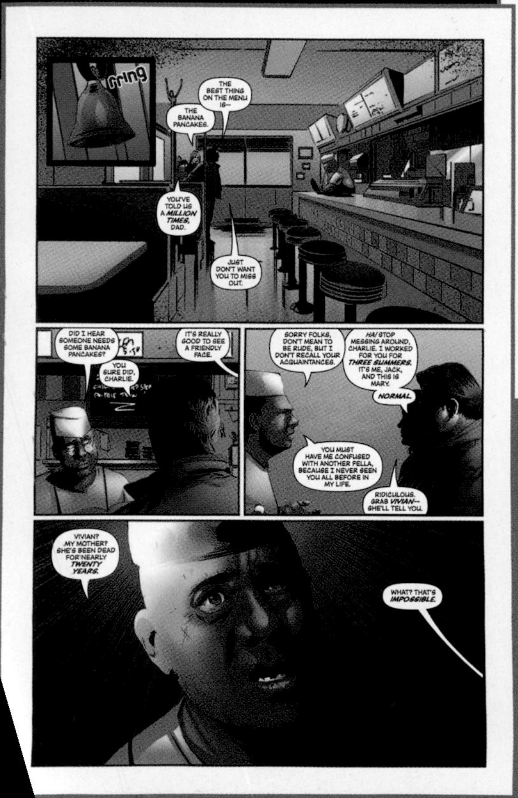
GRING
THE BEST THING ON THE MENU IS--
THE BANANA PANCAKES.
YOU'VE TOLD US A MILLION TIMES, DAD.
JUST DON'T WANT YOU TO MISS OUT.
DID I HEAR SOMEONE NEEDS SOME BANANA PANCAKES?
YOU SURE DID, CHARLIE.
IT'S REALLY GOOD TO SEE A FRIENDLY FACE.
SORRY FOLKS, DON'T MEAN TO BE RUDE, BUT I DON'T RECALL YOUR ACQUAINTANCES.
HA! STOP MESSING AROUND, CHARLIE. I WORKED FOR YOU FOR THREE SUMMERS. IT'S ME, JACK, AND THIS IS MARY.
NORMAL.
YOU MUST HAVE ME CONFUSED WITH ANOTHER FELLA, BECAUSE I NEVER SEEN YOU ALL BEFORE IN MY LIFE.
RIDICULOUS. GRAB VIVIAN-- SHE'LL TELL YOU.
VIVIAN? MY MOTHER? SHE'S BEEN DEAD FOR NEARLY TWENTY YEARS.
WHAT? THAT'S IMPOSSIBLE.

lettering by
COREY BREEN

ABOUT THE CREATORS OF the Normals™

ADAM GLASS writer
🐦 @AdamGlass44

Though NYC will always be home, Adam resides in Los Angeles and is a TV Writer/Executive Producer of such shows as *SUPERNATURAL, COLD CASE* and currently *CRIMINAL MINDS: BEYOND BORDERS* on CBS. When Adam is not writing for TV or films, he's writing graphic novels. Some of these titles include: Marvel Comics' *Deadpool: Suicide Kings* and DC Comics' *Suicide Squad* — both of which were NY Times bestsellers. Other books Adam has written or co-written for Marvel are *Deadpool: Pulp, Luke Cage: Noir, Deadpool Team-Up* and *Luke Cage: Origins*. And for DC, *JLA Annual* and the *Flashpoint* series *Legion of Doom*. Most recently, Adam finished an original graphic novel for Oni Press called *Brick*.

DENNIS CALERO artist
🐦 @DennisCalero

Dennis Calero was raised in Miami Beach, Florida and attended the New World School of the Arts High School, and later the prestigious Pratt Institute, where he studied architecture before smartening up and switching majors to illustration and film. He soon started writing and drawing comics, and his extensive client list includes Marvel Comics, DC Comics, Time/Warner and Sony Entertainment. He's also performed stand-up comedy in New York City. Dennis helped develop *X-Men Noir* for Marvel Comics, and he wrote and illustrated *Assassin's Creed: Templars* for Titan Comics. With writer/actor Todd Stashwick, Dennis co-wrote the pilot script *Clandestine* for SyFy.

ADRIANO AUGUSTO colorist
🐦 @adrianocolorist

Born and raised in Brazil, Adriano studied art and comics at the School of Visual Arts, Casa dos Quadrinhos and in Studio A4, where he eventually became a professor of digital colorization. It was here at Studio A4 that he met friends Rodney Buchemi and Sandro Ribeiro, and together the trio founded Compendium Estúdios: Escola Visual Arts and Comics Studio. As a colorist, Adriano has worked on dozens of titles from multiple publishers, including *Red Sonja, Vampirella, Green Hornet, Doc Savage, Voltron, Avenger, Evil Ernie, Army of Darkness vs. Danger Girl, Robyn Hood* and many others.

COREY BREEN letterer
🐦 @CjB_Productions

Corey has been a professional in the comic book industry for over eighteen years, thirteen of which were for DC Entertainment. As a Senior Pre-Press Artist, he contributed production, design, art, lettering, color and more to thousands of comic books and other media. Having left DC Entertainment in 2013 to move to Virginia, Corey is now a head designer at a top investment firm company by day and a comic book artist by night, specializing in lettering, design, and production. Corey lives with his loving wife Kristy, sons Tyler and Spencer, and three cats, Calla, Sebastian and Jasmine.